# LESSONS FROM THE
# VIRTUAL CLASSROOM

## Other Books by Rena M. Palloff and Keith Pratt

The Excellent Online Instructor: Strategies for Professional Development

Assessing the Online Learner: Resources and Strategies for Faculty

Building Online Learning Communities: Effective Strategies for the Virtual Classroom, Second Edition

Collaborating Online: Learning Together in Community

The Virtual Student: A Profile and Guide to Working with Online Learners

# LESSONS FROM THE VIRTUAL CLASSROOM

## The Realities of Online Teaching

SECOND EDITION

Rena M. Palloff
Keith Pratt

**JB JOSSEY-BASS™**

A Wiley Brand

Published by Jossey-Bass
A Wiley Imprint
One Montgomery Street, Suite 1200, San Francisco, CA 94104-4594—www.josseybass.com

Jossey-Bass books and products are available through most bookstores. To contact Jossey-Bass directly call our Customer Care Department within the U.S. at 800-956-7739, outside the U.S. at 317-572-3986, or fax 317-572-4002.

Wiley publishes in a variety of print and electronic formats and by print-on-demand. Some material included with standard print versions of this book may not be included in e-books or in print-on-demand. If this book refers to media such as a CD or DVD that is not included in the version you purchased, you may download this material at http://booksupport.wiley.com. For more information about Wiley products, visit www.wiley.com.

**Library of Congress Cataloging-in-Publication Data**
Palloff, Rena M., date
  Lessons from the virtual classroom : the realities of online teaching /
Rena M. Paloff, Keith Pratt. –
Second edition.
      pages cm—(The Jossey-Bass higher and adult education series)
  Rev. ed. of : Lessons from the cyberspace classroom, 2001.
  Includes bibliographical references and index.
    ISBN 978-1-118-12373-7 (pbk.); ISBN 978-1-118-22475-5 (ebk);
ISBN 978-1-118-23822-6 (ebk); ISBN 978-1-118-26282-5 (ebk)
    1. Web-based instruction.   2. Distance education.   I. Pratt, Keith, date
II. Palloff, Rena M., 1950-
Lessons from the cyberspace classroom.   III. Title.
  LB1044.87.P34 2013
  371.33'44678–dc23

                                                    2013005849

Printed in the United States of America
SECOND EDITION
*PB Printing* 10  9  8  7  6  5  4  3

# CONTENTS

---

## PART ONE: RETHINKING EDUCATION FOR AN ONLINE WORLD    1

**PART TWO: TEACHING AND LEARNING ONLINE   85**

# FIGURES, TABLE, AND EXHIBITS

## Figures

## Table

## Exhibits

# PREFACE TO THE SECOND EDITION: THE FACE OF ONLINE LEARNING TODAY

The thought of doing a second edition of this book at first seemed to be a daunting task. We asked our editors to seek out prerevision reviews of the original edition because we continued to receive good feedback about its usefulness, although we knew it was somewhat outdated. We worried about how we might stay true to the original work while updating it. We needn't have worried: as we read the book anew and looked at the reviews, it became clear to us that much of the content in the original was woefully out of date. Some of the issues remain current, such as administrative concerns and disparities in technology integration and use. But many new issues and concerns have emerged in the past ten years, some of which we might never have anticipated.

We opened the original *Lessons from the Cyberspace Classroom,* which has been retitled for this revised edition, with a discussion of how little technology changes had impacted online learning. We did not anticipate any major technological changes at the time that might change the face of this form of education. How wrong we were! For example, the use of mobile technology and social networking are just two technological changes that are significantly changing how education occurs online. These changes, as well as the ways in which online education has evolved and is conducted currently, are the substance of this new edition.

Change is coming fast and furious, and because of that, focusing on a predominant form of a course management system, for example, will date this work before it is even published. Therefore, although we present and discuss many technologies in this edition, our main concern continues to be best practices in the delivery of education online. That is the focus of our work in this edition, along with the questions and issues that continue to arise about this form of education. Consequently, we do not reference or present screen shots of course management systems as we did in the first edition. Who knows what the status of those will be even within the next three to five years?

## Online Learning in the Twenty-First Century

Some of the developments that we discussed in the original edition remain worthy of discussion. Updates to those, along with some newer concerns, form the complexion of online learning today. They raise concerns that we considered ten years ago but may have since evolved and therefore discuss in more detail in this edition.

### The Costs of Teaching Online

Smaller colleges and universities are entering the online learning market to increase their reach and resultant student base and because both students and faculty are demanding it. Ten years ago, we commented on the disparity between institutions with the budgets to support online learning and those without those resources. This is not as much of an issue today with the advent of open source course management systems, the use of blogs and wikis that are in the public domain, and the use of mobile technologies. These developments may in fact help to shrink what has been termed the digital divide. That said, however, the ability to train and support faculty and students, as well as maintain an increasingly technological environment, are very real costs that institutions with shrinking budgets and enrollments find difficult to maintain.

### Faculty Control over the Academic Process

It is rare today to find wholesale faculty objection to the development of online course offerings and programs. However, pockets of faculty resistance to teaching online still exist, and in many cases, faculty are still struggling with decisions about whether to teach online and what technologies to include should they make that decision. In many instances, faculty still have little to no influence over the course management systems in use in their institutions or the technology choices being made in general. Consequently, questions continue to be raised about the degree to which faculty should be involved in these decisions, which have serious implications for course design and delivery.

## Course Ownership

Do instructors own the courses they develop, or are these courses institutional property? We raised this question ten years ago, and it remains a question. Increasingly, institutions are moving in the direction of offering prewritten courses that instructors facilitate as a function of the scalability of online programs. However, some of the questions we raised about this issue earlier remain current: Should instructors who teach a course developed by someone else be permitted to alter that course to suit their own teaching styles and both eliminate and include material that they deem either unnecessary or more important? Instructors still need to know who "owns" courses and course material. In the face-to-face classroom, as instructors develop and deliver their own courses, this has not been an issue. In the online classroom, it is.

## Continuing Training Needs

Unfortunately, academic institutions assume that if they offer online courses and programs, teachers will know how to teach in that environment and, more important, students will know how to learn or engage with the material. Our experience in both teaching online courses and consulting with instructors, faculty developers, and administrators across the United States continues to show us that the opposite is true. Instructors in fact need training and assistance in making the transition to the online environment, but this is not happening with the frequency or quality that it should. Students also need to be taught how to learn online, although we rarely see orientation programs for online learners.

Teaching and learning through the use of technology requires more than mastery of a software program, although that continues to be the focus of instructor training. It takes an awareness of the impact that this form of learning has on the learning process itself. As more institutions and their instructors enter the online classroom and encounter both successes and difficulties in the process, they are coming face-to-face with the realities of online teaching and asking more, not fewer, questions about how to make this transition successfully. Furthermore, not all instructors enter online teaching at the same point, and rarely, if ever, is training customized to fit the experience level of those who need it. Consequently we offer concrete suggestions for course development and delivery. We also offer suggestions to instructors who are being asked to teach a class they did not create.

## Advances in Technology

Although we said that we do not intend to focus on technology in this book, we do need to discuss some of the changes that have occurred and how they are having an impact on online learning today. Mobile technology, such as cell phones and tablet computers, are literally changing the face of online learning. Open source course management systems are making it easier for instructors and their institutions to develop and deliver online offerings. Social networking technologies such as Facebook and Twitter are infiltrating online classes. The use of Web 2.0 technologies is moving us in the direction of learner-generated content and greater empowerment of learners. All of these are important developments that bear exploration.

## Advances in K–12 Online Learning

Although not a major focus of this book, online learning is most definitely making an impact in the K–12 sector. As a result, pressure increases on community colleges and higher education to increase and improve online offerings. Students are graduating from high school in search of online courses and are far more skilled in making use of online resources than students in the past. Many institutions are still not up to this challenge and need to understand how to prepare themselves for students who are demanding more in terms of the use of technology and online delivery.

## The Regulatory Environment

In recent years, higher education has come under the scrutiny of the U.S. Department of Education, resulting in regulations aimed at reducing time to degree completion and the amount of financial aid required to complete a degree. In addition, there has been concern about the relationship of a degree to graduates' ability to find employment. Online learning has come under additional fire with regard to state authorizations for conducting education, along with concerns about the quality of the courses and programs being offered online. Some of these regulations, such as the one regarding state authorization, have been deferred. However, administrators of online programs or in colleges and universities where online courses are being offered are looking at what it will take to meet that requirement once it goes into effect. If a school is located in California, for example, and admits students from every state in the union, will that school need authorization from every state in order to do so? These unanswered questions for administrators are of concern.

## Organization of the Contents

We have not significantly altered the organization of the book from the original edition. However, to assist readers with the ability to navigate the myriad issues we explore in it, each chapter begins with a brief discussion of the issues it addresses. We also present tips at the conclusion of each chapter and have organized them according to the audience they are to serve: instructors, faculty developers, or administrators.

The chapters in part 1 look at the issues involved in rethinking education in an increasingly online world. Chapter 1 reviews the issues that are of greatest concern today to all interested readers. Chapter 2, geared to instructors and faculty developers, explores the delivery of effective online teaching. Chapter 3 is aimed at administrators and addresses current issues in the development and delivery of online education. Chapter 4 focuses on technology and looks not only at the impact of technology but also at the various tools that are shaping online learning now.

The audience for part 2 of this book is primarily instructors, instructional designers, and faculty developers. However, administrators will also benefit from understanding the needs of these groups in transforming and moving classes online (chapter 5), being asked to teach a course developed and designed by another (chapter 6), the issues and concerns of virtual students (chapter 7), and the classroom dynamics that can and do emerge when teaching online (chapter 8). The closing chapter ties together all of the themes presented throughout this book. In so doing, it is meant to support all readers in looking backward at the lessons we have learned over the past ten years and how those may inform the next ten. Appendix A provides two faculty training examples to assist readers in putting the principles presented in this book into practice. The first is a general orientation for instructors who are moving into online teaching, and the second focuses on community building in online classes. Appendix B provides additional resources for instructors and those who support them in their online teaching work. Included are listings of communities of practice, online teaching certification programs, journals, and the like.

When we first presented this book in 2001, it was a logical follow-up to our first book, *Building Learning Communities in Cyberspace* (Palloff & Pratt, 1999). Since that time, we have revised that first book to look anew at the importance of building a learning community as part of the delivery of online instruction. We also provided a guidebook to the construction of an effective course for those entering the online arena for the first time. As we have continued to write, speak, and consult using the concepts from the first book as well as our others, and to teach online, we have been learning more about the realities of online teaching every day. This second edition should help take instructors, faculty developers, and administrators further into the process as we explore the issues that they face regularly. We have designed this book primarily for these professionals. It will also be helpful to those in the corporate sector who are being asked with increasing frequency to develop employee training programs that are delivered entirely online. Readers will gain greater understanding of the forces that continue to shape education in new and exciting ways. The book also provides readers with new tips, tools, and insights to equip them to enter and participate with greater confidence in this constantly changing environment.

*March 2013*

Rena M. Palloff
*Alameda, California*

Keith Pratt
*Delight, Arizona*

# THE AUTHORS

*Rena M. Palloff* is owner of Crossroads West, which works with institutions, organizations, and corporations interested in the development of online distance learning and training programs and conducting faculty development training and coaching. In addition, she has consulted extensively in health care, academic settings, and addiction treatment for well over twenty years. Palloff is faculty at Fielding Graduate University in the master's degree program in organizational management and development and in the School of Educational Leadership and Change, where she designed a master's degree in education program focusing on teaching online, integrating technology in the K–12 classroom, and the use of social media in education. She is adjunct faculty at Capella University as well, in the School of Social and Behavioral Sciences, teaching and mentoring in the professional doctorate in social work. She also conducts faculty development training for the University of the Rockies and mentors doctoral dissertations at Walden University.

Palloff received a bachelor's degree in sociology from the University of Wisconsin-Madison and a master's degree in social work from the University of Wisconsin-Milwaukee. She holds a master's degree in organizational development and a Ph.D. in human and organizational systems from Fielding Graduate University.

• • •

*Keith Pratt* began his government career as a computer systems technician with the U.S. Air Force. He served in various positions, including supervisor of computer systems maintenance, chief of the Logistics Support Branch, chief of the Telecommunications Branch, and superintendent of the Secure Telecommunications Branch. After leaving the air force, Pratt held positions as registrar and faculty (Charter College), director (Chapman College), and trainer and consultant (the Growth Company). As an adjunct faculty member at Wayland Baptist University and the University of Alaska, Pratt taught courses in communications, business, management, organizational theories, and computer technology. He was assistant professor in the international studies program and chair of the management information systems program, main campus and overseas, at Ottawa University in Ottawa, Kansas. He currently teaches online at Wayland Baptist University, Capella University, and Walden University.

Pratt graduated from Wayland Baptist University with a dual degree in business administration and computer systems technology. He has an M.S. in human resource management from Chapman University, an M.S. in organizational development, a Ph.D. in human and organizational systems from Fielding Graduate University, and an honorary doctorate of science from Moscow State University.

Since 1994 Palloff and Pratt have collaboratively conducted pioneering research and training in the emerging areas of online group facilitation, face-to-face and online community building, program planning and development of distance learning programs, and management and supervision of online academic programs. In conjunction with Fielding Graduate University, they developed the online teaching and learning academic certificate program designed to assist faculty in becoming effective online facilitators and course developers.

# ACKNOWLEDGMENTS

Many of our readers have told us over the years that they have used our book originally titled *Lessons from the Cyberspace Classroom* as a guide to starting their work in online teaching and learning and also as a training manual for other faculty. For a few years, you've been asking us to update it: we heard you and hope that this work helps you to continue yours. Thanks for the encouragement!

Once again, we thank the patient, supportive, and dedicated people at Jossey-Bass. Thanks in particular to Erin Null and Alison Knowles. Thanks also to those of you who have helped make the online presentations of our work possible. It has been a great experience to do the Online Teaching and Learning Conferences and the Wiley Learning Institute.

Thanks to George Engel for introducing us to the wonderful world of mobile technology and for your great contribution to the book in chapter 4. We're looking forward to continuing our work together!

We always thank Fielding Graduate University for supporting our work and for the other universities with which we're affiliated—Capella, Walden, University of the Rockies, and Wayland Baptist—for giving voice to our practice of online teaching. We also warmly acknowledge our students: without you, this book would not be here!

Thanks, of course, to our families. Your patience and love help us to do what we do and push us onward in the exploration of new ways to pursue our passion.

# LESSONS FROM THE
# VIRTUAL CLASSROOM

PART ONE

# RETHINKING EDUCATION FOR AN ONLINE WORLD

CHAPTER ONE

# ONLINE LEARNING IN THE TWENTY-FIRST CENTURY

Because of the changing nature of students today, economic pressures, and rapid implementation of distance learning courses and programs, definitions of what constitutes education and learning are changing too. Whereas years ago instructors viewed their students as blank slates whose minds could be filled with the information they were imparting, current constructivist theory holds that students create knowledge and meaning through their interaction with one another, the instructor, and their environment. A more collaborative approach to learning, such as that promoted by constructivist thought, can yield deeper levels of knowledge creation (Brooks & Brooks, 2000). The use of distance learning technologies and, more specifically, online learning, have both grown out of and contributed to the changes now occurring in the delivery of education.

The changes stemming from the delivery of online classes in academic institutions are being met with the support of educators but also with some discomfort. Although the level of discomfort may be decreasing for some, skepticism about the quality of online education persists (Allen, Seaman, Lederman, & Jaschik, 2012). To illustrate the changes occurring in the attitudes of educators about online learning, we revisit a sampling of the opinions expressed by instructors faced with teaching online that were published in the 1999 edition of *Academe:*

> Some students learn better in a course in which they can interact with the professor in person. Others, however, thrive in an online environment. Shy students, for example, tend to feel liberated online, as do many foreign students who are unsure of their spoken English. (Maloney, p. 21)

> Being there is irreplaceable . . . Education involves more than lectures and class discussions. Our students learn from us what scholars in our disciplines do. We show the discipline of the mind and evaluate whether our students are catching on . . . When students feel themselves identifying with us and our disciplines, they come to appreciate the struggle for knowledge; some may even choose to become part of the intellectual adventure. (Martin, p. 35)

> The reality is that technology is playing, and will continue to play, a critical role in teaching and learning. As a pedagogical tool, distance education probably leads to different educational outcomes from those achieved with traditional classroom-based instruction—some better, some worse . . . The real debate needs to focus on identifying which approaches work best for teaching students, period. (Merisotis, p. 51)

Although we continue to hear similar opinions expressed today, online learning has become ubiquitous. As a result, the level of resistance expressed in 1999 has begun to wane to some degree, and we see at least a willingness to try online teaching. A very recent study, conducted by the Babson Survey Research Group (Allen et al., 2012), indicates that instructors report being more pessimistic than optimistic about online learning. They are skeptical about the quality of learning outcomes from online courses and resist teaching online. Interestingly, 75 percent of the sample participating in the study teach full time and are not teaching online. The study indicated that part-time, non-tenure-track instructors are far more open to online teaching than their full-time, tenured colleagues. The authors of the study speculate that the amount of time involved with online teaching, which may or may not be fairly compensated, is part of the problem. And yet the number of students enrolling in online courses has increased dramatically: the number of students enrolled in online courses in 2010 was estimated at 6.1 million (Allen et al., 2012).

Research conducted at the University of Central Florida indicates that what was previously described as a continuum from fully face-to-face to fully online classes has significantly decreased and soon will no longer exist (Allen & Seaman, 2004, 2005; Young & Chamberlain, 2006). Most face-to-face classes now include some form of technology integration, sometimes termed "supplementation" or "Web facilitation," and it was predicted that by 2013, the vast majority of courses offered in higher education would be hybrid, meaning that they will be at least 40 percent online (Allen & Seaman, 2004). Based on our experience and observations, this prediction has come to pass. Consequently, the new continuum moves from technologically enhanced classes to fully online classes rather than from fully face-to-face classes to fully online classes.

The advent of mobile technology has served to increase technology use in traditional classes as well. Assignments now include the use of Twitter and texting, as well as the ability to access online course sites by using a cell phone or tablet, such as an iPad. Given the vast amount of technology available, instructors are now at least willing to experiment with its use. A social policy instructor told one of us recently that her concern about the lack of interest in her required class led her to conduct a focus group with her undergraduate students. She found that students wanted to see the use of some forms of technology, particularly wikis, as a way to engage them and allow them to explore the content collaboratively. Students are increasingly demanding the inclusion of technology into courses, and instructors need to respond.

Regardless of any residual discomfort, online education is here to stay. Ronald Phipps and Jamie Merisotis of the Institute for Higher Education Policy noted in their groundbreaking 1999 report on distance education, "Technology is having, and will continue to have, a profound impact on colleges and universities in America and around the globe. Distance learning, which was once a poor and often unwelcome stepchild within the academic community, is becoming increasingly more visible as a part of the higher education family" (p. 29).

An early survey of trends in online education (Kim & Bonk, 2006) concluded that as the demand for online learning increased, the most important skills for an online instructor would be how to moderate or facilitate learning and how to develop or plan for high-quality online courses. The demand for online courses in higher education has continued to increase; in addition, more K–12 instruction is going online, with students and teachers using a vast array of Internet resources, social networks, and new educational technologies. The Sloan Consortium Survey of Online Learning (Allen & Seaman, 2011) reveals that the number of higher education students enrolled in online courses has exceeded 6 million and shows no evidence of decline. The Sloan report concludes that the economic downturn in the United States has helped increase the demand for online courses and programs.

As a result, there is a demand for teachers and college-level instructors who have the necessary skills to integrate such technologies into the face-to-face classroom, as well as to facilitate fully online or partially online (blended or hybrid) classes (Lorenzo, 2011), and students of education are seeking to gain these skills. Traditional schools of education are currently not meeting this demand. Given these facts, what has been the impact of this phenomenon on education? How does learning online affect learning in general? How should decisions be made about such elements as course management systems, courses offered, faculty who will teach online, and course development? What are the ethical and legal implications of these decisions? How do we train faculty to understand and use online learning and online learning technologies effectively and about the new teaching approaches required for their effective delivery? How do we teach faculty to build interactivity and community through the use of technology into what might otherwise be a flat, text-based medium? We explore these questions and more in this book as we discuss the lessons learned from today's online classrooms.

In this chapter, we review the state of online learning today, including an initial discussion of current and emerging technology, which we continue in chapter 4. We also review some of the critical issues facing both instructors and administrators in online teaching and learning and look at some of the lessons for higher education that are emerging from the K–12 sector. We close this chapter with a discussion of the effectiveness of online teaching and learning.

## Online Learning Today

Not all online classes are created equal. A white paper posted on the website of Blackboard, a course management company, defines online education as "an approach to teaching and learning that utilizes Internet technologies to communicate and collaborate in an educational context. This includes technology that supplements traditional classroom training with web-based components and learning environments where the educational process is experienced online" (Blackboard, n.d., p. 1). We continue to agree with this definition, although it was written many years ago. The technologies that can be used are changing, and the definition indicates that there is more than one way to deliver online classes, something that is becoming increasingly true as new technologies are incorporated into online teaching. One form is not necessarily preferable to another, however, and the technology used depends to a great extent on the content of the course being taught and the experience of the instructor and students. A good way for instructors to begin is by using technology to enhance an on-campus class. As they gain experience in teaching online, moving from an enhanced approach to one in which a class is wholly delivered online becomes easier.

Enhancement to what is happening in the face-to-face classroom can be achieved through the use of an electronic textbook, which likely includes associated learning activities on a companion website and "lecture" material. Some instructors use an asynchronous discussion board located on a course site online or the addition of chat or synchronous discussions; they may even simply use e-mail. All of this technology will likely also be used in a class that is conducted completely or almost completely online, the difference being that there may be minimal or no scheduled face-to-face sessions associated with the class.

Emerging technologies are changing the face of online learning. The use of cell phones, smart phones, tablets, and iPods are allowing mobile access to parts or all of a student's online courses. What are known as Web 2.0 and now Web 3.0 technologies allow users to create content within or as an adjunct to online courses. As a result, students can create presentations, co-construct material using wikis (collaboratively created web pages), and keep blogs (Web logs or online journals) and interact with others who are blogging. Social networking technologies hold the possibility of delivering courses outside the institution's formal course management system. These exciting developments also carry with them issues and concerns that we address in this book.

One of the main issues continues to be adequate faculty training to construct and deliver high-quality courses. Few campuses currently offer the type of training that faculty need to succeed online. When instructors are simply presented with a course management system and told that a course needs to be developed and presented, the resulting course is likely to have minimal interaction and pay little attention to the development of a learning community, which promotes collaborative learning and helps to achieve learning outcomes. Instead, the instructor new to online learning is more likely to try to replicate what he or she has done for years in the face-to-face classroom. We discuss faculty training needs and good course construction in greater depth in chapters 2 and 5 and offer a template for faculty training in Appendix A.

## Current and Emerging Technologies

Although most course management systems now offer instructors the ability to customize their courses in many ways, emerging technologies are allowing instructors to move their classes out of the institution's system and enabling students to contribute content to an existing course. In addition, asynchronous discussions can be supplemented with the use of synchronous, or chat, sessions. Video and audio clips can be used. Instructors can post PowerPoint slides or other graphic illustrations of the material being studied. Support documents such as handouts, articles, and lecture notes can also be posted to a course site. Links to other sites of interest or to a digital textbook can be established. In whiteboard sessions, synchronous discussion can occur while graphics are annotated or brainstorming sessions are going on.

Learner progress can be assessed in new and different ways. For example, an instructor might have students create wikis or blogs and assess those as part of the course grade. Authentic assessments can be conducted through the use of audio or video in real time or through the posting of artifacts that students create. Students might create and submit a slide show by taking photos on their cell phones and uploading them to a site such as Flickr. Similarly, they may use the video recording function on a smart phone to produce an assignment for a course. Other applications allow audio recording or capturing a computer desktop and recording it with voice-over narration. The texting function on a cell phone can be used to respond to a poll or submit answers to instructor questions instead of taking a quiz in a course management system.

Many of these technological developments may be helpful in accommodating various student learning styles. An auditory learner, for example, may feel more comfortable listening to a brief audio clip explaining a concept than reading about it. A visual learner tends to do well in an environment that presents mainly text or uses video clips. A learner who is more kinesthetic may appreciate assignments requiring visits to other websites on the Internet and the incorporation of online research or the use of texting to submit material to the course. These techniques also help to keep things interesting for students who feel the need for more activity in a learning situation.

The use of mobile technology helps to diminish what has been known as the digital divide—not all students own computers. Many students, however, have access to cell phones. Despite this, we present the new technological developments with a caution: not all students can receive a course that contains all of these technological bells and whistles. A cell phone is not a smart phone, capable of audio and video recording, for example. When constructing a course using new technologies, the instructor needs to determine the technologies to which most students will have access and make accommodation for those who do not. As has been the case since online learning began, simplicity of design is the key.

In our experience, a well-constructed course is logical in its design, easy to navigate, and inviting to users. Generally a simply constructed and easy-to-follow course site will be better received by students than one that relies too heavily on elements such as multimedia and where access is slow due to slow connection speeds. Although many students now have access to high-speed connections and mobile technology, some live in areas where they are required to dial up to get Internet access and where cellular service is spotty. When we ask students to evaluate the effectiveness of their online learning experience, it is the ability to engage in discussion with their peers and instructor that they most value. Consequently, the choice of technology that makes it easier for students to connect with one another, enabling them to form a learning community, is critical.

## Emerging Issues for Both Faculty and Administrators

As development and acceptance of online distance learning continue to grow, critical concerns for both faculty and administrators have emerged, including planning for a solid technological infrastructure, intellectual property rights, review and development of agreements with faculty that reflect good understanding of work for hire and copyright, and choice of software for conducting online courses. Another issue is the use of mobile technologies and social networking, which bring concerns about privacy and other issues related to work outside the protected confines of the institution's system. Many of these concerns relate to the degree to which faculty are being involved in the planning and decision making that surround the implementation of online distance learning courses and programs.

Instructors argue that decisions should be made based on pedagogical need, but they worry that administrators are looking to the bottom line. Security concerns are also affecting how decisions about technology use are made. Table 1.1 outlines responses to common concerns. A brief discussion of each of these issues follows.

### TABLE 1.1 FACULTY AND ADMINISTRATOR RESPONSES TO COMMON CONCERNS ABOUT TECHNOLOGY

| Concern | Faculty Response | Administrative Response |
|---|---|---|
| **Technology decisions** Technology to be used in the delivery of online and hybrid courses. | Want to be involved in choosing technology that serves pedagogical needs. | Often want control over technology purchases for ease of support and maintenance. |
| **Governance decisions** Decisions about which courses and programs will be delivered online and who will teach them. | Want to have a voice in which courses or programs are offered online. Want to have the option to opt in or opt out of online teaching and have a voice in workload issues. | Want to maintain control over workload issues. Often use adjuncts to deliver online courses to deal with workload concerns. Generally hold the responsibility for deciding which courses and programs are offered online. |
| **Intellectual property** Who owns courses and what constitutes work for hire. | Want to retain ownership of courses developed or materials posted to an online course. Want adequate compensation for course development of their own courses or as work for hire for the university. | Generally see online course development as work for hire, property of the university, or part of the faculty role. Need to be involved in negotiating reasonable agreements with faculty. |
| **Instructor and student training decisions** Design and delivery of training programs for both faculty and students. | Need training in course design and development as well as course facilitation. Support the need for student orientation to online learning. | Support for training waxes and wanes with budget concerns. This needs to be a top priority, and training needs to be continuously supported. |

| Concern | Faculty Response | Administrative Response |
|---|---|---|
| **Course design decisions** How courses are designed and who is involved with course design. | Want to be involved with course design as subject matter experts or in the design of their own courses. | Need to support a team approach to online course design or support faculty through provision of instructional design services. |
| **Instructor workload** Decisions about how many online classes instructors should be required to teach. | Instructors realize that teaching online requires more time than teaching in the face-to-face classroom; some resist online teaching as a result. | Need to establish reasonable instructor loads, including teaching both online and face-to-face classes, along with other responsibilities. Overload situations for teaching online should be avoided. |
| **Regulatory environment** New regulations from the U.S. Department of Education are dictating the need to make courses and programs relevant to potential jobs or careers and to reduce time in program. | Instructors are feeling pressure due to the push to move students through programs more quickly and align courses more directly with students' career paths. | Need to communicate directly with faculty regarding regulatory demands and collaboratively seek proactive solutions. |

## Technology for Online Teaching Is Chosen Without Faculty Input

Interestingly, although this was identified as an issue early in the history of online learning, little has been written about this problem other than to cite it as one possible reason that faculty may resist engaging in online teaching (Allen et al., 2012). In 1999, Andrew Feenberg stated, "Professors aren't in the forefront of the movement to network education. Instead, politicians, university administrations, and computer and telecommunications companies have taken the lead, because they see money in electronic ventures" (p. 26). Unfortunately, this continues to be the case. The lack of faculty involvement in decision-making processes that directly affect the way in which online courses will be delivered potentially continues to widen the rift between faculty and administrators where online teaching and learning is concerned. Rather than excluding instructors from the decisions about which technologies they will use, involvement in the decision-making process required for the selection of course management systems can help elevate the level of faculty expertise required to teach online just by their testing out the various systems before they begin. This can give instructors a leg up in the course development process. Rice (2001) discussed the importance of participatory decision making along with a framework for planning to avoid costly mistakes. Bower (2001) defends faculty resistance as healthy skepticism, noting that many have simply been disillusioned by the technologies their institutions adopted without their input and without the ability to assess how the technologies will help them teach and help students learn.

If instructors are being asked and even expected to teach online courses, and the type of technology that they are expected to use can significantly affect the teaching and learning process, should they not be involved in its selection? Unfortunately, in our experience, rarely are they brought into the selection process in any meaningful way. Although administrators have the dollars and authority with which to spend them, instructors are the end users of the technology and should have something to say in its choice. Involving faculty will help them buy into the online teaching process and facilitate use of the software, thus allowing them to focus more on pedagogical than technical issues. Bates and Sangrà (2011) suggest that technology decisions should be made at a program and course level rather than an institutional level.

Administrators, along with faculty and students, need to be educated about the realities of online teaching and the impact that good technology can have on this process (Bates & Sangrà, 2011). The concern should be pedagogical, not budgetary. As we have already discussed, technology can be an effective enhancement to the face-to-face classroom. Well-constructed online courses can expand institutional offerings, thus attracting students who prefer this mode of learning. Online learning is not appropriate for all students, however, and is not likely to completely replace face-to-face classrooms.

## Governance Issues Have Emerged

As with the choice of technology to be used for online courses, the selection and design of courses and programs that will be taught online are also being made with little or no instructor input. In many institutions, department chairs are being asked which courses they will offer, and programs are being designed by administrators rather than faculty, adding to the level of faculty resistance (Bower, 2001). "When administrations in their hurry to launch potentially lucrative online programs forgo the usual channels of faculty consultation, quality suffers" (Maloney, 1999, p. 21). Concerns about quality continue to be primary contributors to faculty resistance to teaching online (Allen et al., 2012). Instructors also object to the creation and spin-off of for-profit arms of universities devoted to the development and delivery of online courses, citing poor quality.

Accreditation raises yet another set of issues related to governance. As courses and programs are delivered online, those charged with judging academic quality face the challenge of developing new standards. There is a belief that online classes cannot be evaluated through the traditional model of academic accreditation (Middle States Commission on Higher Education, 2011). As a result, new standards have been developed because online courses are not a reproduction of those delivered face-to-face. Barry Dahl (2012), an educator and online learning consultant, notes in his blog that although the newer accreditation standards evaluate online programs separately, they encourage comparison of online programs to face-to-face programs, thus indicating that somehow online programs will not measure up to their face-to-face counterparts. Additional fears are that quality standards are being bypassed, thus degrading public perception of the value of a college degree (Allen et al., 2012). Others, however, believe that new standards for the quality of online courses and programs should be determined through student feedback and institutional responsiveness, resulting in new sets of accreditation standards. Because national and regional accrediting agencies accredit whole institutions, they hold online courses and programs to the same standards as their face-to-face counterparts. However, there is a recognition that online teaching and learning are different, and that consideration has been built into current standards.

To complicate the picture, new regulations for both online and on-ground programs have been issued by the U.S. Department of Education. These regulations are meant to shorten time in program for students, thus reducing the level of financial aid debt required to complete a degree. Colleges and universities are also now required to demonstrate that the courses and programs they offer will support students in seeking and obtaining a job once they graduate. Finally, a regulation that will have a significant impact on institutions offering online courses and programs is that the college or university must be approved to offer education in any state where a student resides. Given that institutions offering online courses could potentially draw students from every state, concerns are emerging regarding the administrative load required to meet such a regulation. At the time of this writing, this regulation has been deferred, but institutions are well aware that they will need to prepare for it should it come to pass. For their part, faculty have a sense of increasing pressure to meet timely completion demands and also to increase the level of career relevance in their courses. This may not be as much of a concern to someone who teaches computer science, for example, but for an instructor who teaches literature, the concern is great.

Nothing takes the place of good planning in the creation of any new academic endeavor, especially in a new regulatory environment. Some institutions have bypassed a planning process in developing an online program, claiming faculty pressure to get courses online or the need to expand their market share quickly. However, as with the creation of a single course, planning with the end in mind will move the institution closer to a realistic use of technology to strengthen teaching and learning. What this means is that institutions should conduct assessments of the learning and programmatic outcomes they hope to achieve through online courses. The inclusion of faculty in this process should assist in creating a balanced approach focused on both pedagogical and budgetary goals.

Online learning will not save the academy by attracting large numbers of students while reducing infrastructure costs. However, through good planning and evaluation processes, institutions can avoid costly mistakes by developing realistic programs that address realistic student needs.

## Intellectual Property, Course Design, and Course Ownership Issues

Numerous articles appearing in journals and online discuss who owns courses developed by faculty for online delivery. Interestingly, this is rarely a subject of discussion when it comes to the face-to-face classes that faculty members have taught for years. When members of the faculty leave for another institution, their courses generally go with them, and another instructor is hired to develop and deliver the same course. Furthermore, it is usually not questioned that two instructors teaching the same course may choose to incorporate different concepts and material and are likely to approach the course very differently.

Online, however, a growing trend is for the institution to claim ownership of courses. Because online courses are generally housed on a university server and can be archived or kept intact indefinitely, the question of ownership has become a topic of contention. Some institutions are calling the courses "work for hire" and claiming ownership, whereas others have few policies regulating how online courses are viewed (Kromrey et al., 2005). In addition, many institutions are hiring faculty from outside the institution—people who are considered to be content experts—to develop courses or are purchasing or licensing such courses, which the institution's own instructors are then expected to teach. The quality of development and degree to which these courses can be customized is an issue that we discuss in more detail in chapter 6.

## Just Like Faculty, Students Need to Be Trained to Learn Online

Many of those we have spoken with around the country continue to believe that the key to faculty training lies in familiarizing them with the technology they will be using to deliver courses. As we have conducted our faculty training seminars, we have frequently encountered faculty who tell us that although they mastered the use of the course management system, they still wondered how to deliver the course effectively. Why were students not participating? Why was it that most or all of the interaction occurring in the class was between students and instructor rather than between students? Why was it that students seemed unwilling or unable to take the initiative in making the course "happen"? Both the problems and the answers may be related to one issue: faculty training in more than just the technology in use. Those who teach online need instruction in the differences in online teaching and what is required to build a learning community online. We return to this subject in chapter 2.

Instructors are not the only ones who need training. The same mistakes are made with students. Again, it is assumed that if students can navigate the course management system, they should successfully complete the class. In our experience, however, students also need training to learn what is expected of them in the online classroom. In chapter 7, we discuss the issues involved in working with virtual students.

Finally, administrators, politicians, and all those involved with decision making for online programs also need training. The financial realities and the ability of technology to resolve budgetary problems should be conveyed to the decision makers, along with the realities of online teaching and learning. Administrators and decision makers have been persuaded that online learning can replace campuses and faculty. This is a myth that needs to be dispelled so that faculty and administrators can work together to create pedagogically sound, learner-centered online programs.

## Instructor Workload

Managing instructor workload is a major factor in faculty resistance to teaching online and an enormous concern for both new and experienced instructors. Conceição and Lehman (2011) note that workload concerns generally emerge from administrative demands, the perception that online instructors are available twenty-four hours a day and seven days a week, inexperience with online instruction, and how to create a sense of presence with learners. The absence of training and support contributes to the problem of instructors feeling overloaded when asked to teach online.

Bower (2001) reported that faculty incentives in the form of reduced workload were not consistently offered to faculty to assist with this problem. In fact, in our conversations with faculty around the United States, many report teaching online classes in an overload situation.

We contend that providing institutional support and training to instructors is likely to reduce resistance and help them develop strategies to manage their work life when teaching online. This, coupled with institutional sensitivity to the need to better plan for and manage what is expected of instructors when teaching online, is likely to result in higher-quality online courses and programs taught by willing faculty who are skilled in online teaching.

# Recent Developments in K–12 Online Learning

Higher education professionals can begin their own learning process by taking note of the exciting developments occurring in K–12. Although technology has been used as an adjunct to elementary and secondary teaching for a while, virtual high schools and other virtual support services for school districts continue to emerge, bringing with them the development of standards for online teaching.

The delivery of online classes in the K–12 sector is increasing dramatically, promoting a need for training for online teaching in teacher training programs. Deubel (2008) reports that the demand for "virtual schooling" is increasing at a rate of about 30 percent per year, and with that comes the demand for experienced teachers who can teach online. Watson and Kalmon (2006) report that as of 2006, there were twenty-four state-led virtual schools with twelve more states in the process of developing them. Like their counterparts in higher education, teachers need training in the theoretical, pedagogical, and technical foundations of online work. They also need to understand how to effectively facilitate an online class, including the use of effective discussions, managing learners, incorporating collaborative activities, and conducting online assessments of student work.

For the most part, virtual schools rely on asynchronous technologies in order to accommodate school schedules and individualize pacing of the delivery of content. In some cases, a combination of technologies is used, with some tutoring and discussion held in synchronous virtual classrooms. Scheduling and pacing generally coincide with the school year, with some virtual schools operating on an open or year-round schedule.

Similar to higher education, student-teacher communication generally takes the form of e-mail exchanges and course discussion boards. Some virtual schools require regular phone communication between teacher and students or participation in synchronous sessions by virtual classroom or chat. Also similar to higher education are the many roles and tasks of the instructor, including facilitation of instruction using asynchronous or synchronous means, leading discussions, and assessing student performance. One difference is that online K–12 teachers are also expected to conduct regular tutoring sessions with students, which are generally held at scheduled times and generally run through synchronous media.

Virtual school programs can be fully online or hybrid (or blended) approaches. Three main models are used (Van Dusen, 2009):

- *Blended models.* This is the approach most often used by charter schools or homeschooling. The model allows students to work from home in online classes for the majority of their work, but they do come into a face-to-face classroom setting with the same instructor for a short period each week.
- *Supplemental models.* This approach allows school districts or multiple districts to fill in curricular gaps through the use of online courses. In this case, students are predominantly in face-to-face classrooms but may take an online course or two in order to move beyond what their school might offer. In general, this approach has been used to fill the gaps caused by budget cuts, which have predominantly affected the ability to offer electives, Advanced Placement courses, language courses, and the like. These models have also been used for the provision of summer school programs and for credit retrieval for students who need credit toward graduation.
- *Classroom-based models.* This approach focuses on technology integration in face-to-face classroom. However, it goes beyond simply

using technology to enhance classroom delivery by potentially using purchased online courses delivered in the classroom or engaging all students online while in the face-to-face environment.

The demands of online teaching in K–12 are likely different from those of higher education due to the developmental level of students, the ways in which the courses are offered, the nature of the curriculum, and the need to be responsive to multiple audiences (students, parents, schools, districts, states, and even the federal government). Because of this, standards for the development of online courses and their delivery have been developed and published by the International Association for K–12 Online Learning (iNACOL). To accomplish this task, iNACOL organized a team of experts consisting of online teachers, professional developers, instructional designers, researchers, course developers, and administrators to review these new standards and the new literature on the topic. The result is a comprehensive set of three categories of standards: National Standards for Quality Online Courses, National Standards for Quality Online Teaching, and Quality Standards for Quality Online Programs. Unfortunately, no such equivalent exists in higher education, so the quality of online courses and best practices in online teaching have been somewhat elusive concepts in this sector, leading to skepticism on the part of many instructors as to the value of online teaching (Allen et al., 2012).

The growing trend toward virtual high school education is one that we in higher education cannot ignore. The students who participate in online high school classes are likely to seek out the same forms of education when they enter college. They will likely be skilled in navigating the online environment and in working collaboratively with their peers. The question then becomes, Is higher education ready for them?

## The Effectiveness of Distance Delivery

A debate that we hoped would be resolved at the time of this writing but that unfortunately persists is whether online learning is as effective as the face-to-face classroom in achieving learning outcomes. Accompanying this debate are concerns that plagiarism and cheating are more easily accomplished online. Research on this topic continues to emerge with somewhat disappointing results and continues to indicate that instructors on the whole are not convinced that online learning is effective, despite the demand from students (Allen et al., 2012). The classic report released by the Institute for Higher Education Policy, *What's the Difference?* (Phipps & Merisotis, 1999), reviewed the research comparing the outcomes of online and face-to-face instruction. Because it is almost impossible to engage faculty in a discussion of online learning without this topic emerging, we feel that it is important to review some of that literature here.

Phipps and Merisotis, the authors of the report, in summarizing their review of the literature on the effectiveness of distance learning, noted that the studies conducted tend to fall into three broad categories: student outcomes (including test scores, grades, and comparisons to on-campus students), student attitudes about learning through these means, and overall student satisfaction with distance learning. One such study, conducted by Schutte (1996), randomly assigned students in a course on social statistics to face-to-face or virtual classes. Lectures and exams were standardized between the groups. The study found that the students participating in the virtual class had better results on tests. Schutte concluded that the performance differences could be attributed to the enhanced ability of students to collaborate in the online class: "In fact, the highest performing students (in both classes) reported the most peer interaction" (p. 4). However, Schutte noted that the element of collaboration is a key variable that needs to be controlled in future studies.

Phipps and Merisotis (1999) noted, "With few exceptions, the bulk of these writings suggests that the learning outcomes of students using technology at a distance are similar to the learning outcomes of students who participate in conventional classroom instruction" (p. 2). Others who have also compiled the research on distance learning have come to the same tentative conclusion (Hanson et al., 1997; Russell, 1999). Phipps and Merisotis offered this conclusion with a caution, however; noting that most of the research conducted on learning outcomes from distance learning classes is questionable. Many of the researchers, such as Schutte, noted variables that cannot be controlled, and many studies were based on qualitative rather than quantitative measures. In addition, the research did not define what is meant by *learning outcomes* or conceptualize what knowledge looks like (Boettcher, 1999). Consequently, much of the previous research attempted to paint the picture of "an illusory 'typical learner,' which masks the enormous variability of the student population" (Phipps and Merisotis, 1999, p. 5) and did not account for differences in learning styles. Despite problems with the research being conducted on effectiveness, Phipps and Merisotis offered important implications that have come out of it:

> Although the ostensible purpose of much of the research is to ascertain how technology affects student learning and student satisfaction, many of the results seem to indicate that technology is not nearly as important as other factors, such as learning tasks, learner characteristics, student motivation, and the instructor. The irony is that the bulk of the research on technology ends up addressing an activity that is fundamental to the academy, namely pedagogy—the art of teaching . . . Any discussion about enhancing the teaching-learning process through technology also has the beneficial effect of improving how students are taught on campus . . . The key question that needs to be asked is: What is the best way to teach students? (p. 8)

The 2012 Babson report illustrates that the issues outlined here have not been resolved: online learning has not been well studied as an entity of its own. Despite the criticism and skepticism, we now turn our attention to what it takes to assist faculty in developing high-quality courses. In so doing, we offer the following principles of good practice in undergraduate education. They were first published by the American Association of Higher Education in 1987 and reproduced at the conclusion of the Phipps and Merisotis report (1999, p. 32) as a guide:

- Encourage contact between students and faculty.
- Develop reciprocity and cooperation among students.
- Use active learning techniques.
- Give prompt feedback.
- Emphasize time-on-task.
- Communicate high expectations.
- Respect diverse talents and ways of learning.

These principles continue to form the backbone of a well-constructed online course because they encourage interactivity, active learning techniques, and the expectation that the instructor will be present and involved but not control the process. With these principles in mind, we now turn to the important topic of faculty training.

CHAPTER TWO

# THE ART OF ONLINE TEACHING

Teaching in the virtual classroom requires that we move beyond what have been considered traditional models of pedagogy, predominantly involving lecture, into new, more facilitative practices. Teaching online involves much more than simply taking tried-and-true models of pedagogy and transferring them to a different medium. Facilitation online requires practices that promote collaboration and discussion among learners and encourages them to work together to explore the content of the course. Unlike in the face-to-face classroom, attention in online education needs to be paid to developing a sense of community in the group of participants in order for collaboration to occur and the learning process to be successful.

In this chapter, we look at the myriad issues that instructors face as they move into the online environment: who should teach online; the frustrations of those who do make that transition and the need for more effective training; how to integrate technology into training; and the keys to success in the online environment, including ways in which to assess students and evaluate the online experience.

## Lack of Preparation

As we work with instructors and their academic institutions throughout the country, we continue to find that they are ill prepared to make the shift to online teaching and learning. We hear stories about poor student and faculty participation in courses, difficulties with course construction, and poor course evaluations by students.

A community college librarian told us about an experience of taking a required class for her teaching certificate in history. She chose to take the class online due to convenience. As the course progressed, she became increasingly frustrated and complained that she should have taken the class face-to-face. The instructor had set up the course simply by posting text-based lectures and lessons online. Students were expected to access the course site and read what was there, in addition to reading material in the textbook. They e-mailed their completed homework assignments to the instructor, with whom there was no other contact. They took exams online. There was no ability to interact with other students or even to know who else was enrolled in the course. When this student e-mailed questions to the instructor, she received no response and therefore felt that she was learning less and making less progress than if she had taken the class on campus. She did poorly on quizzes and exams and was confused by and frustrated with the whole experience. This may seem to be an extreme example, but we hear stories like this daily, and we have been asked why online courses continue to be developed in this way.

Such stories tend to discourage those who hear them from teaching online or suggesting that students take online courses and have contributed to faculty skepticism about online teaching (Allen, Seaman, Lederman, & Jaschik, 2012). According to Allen et al. (2012), some have even advised working adults returning to college to avoid distance learning programs. The concern stems from the reports of students in such programs who describe a sense of isolation and frustration, as well as an inability to gain exposure to a wide range of subject areas. And as for-profit universities predominantly offering online education have emerged, concerns have been raised by public sector institutions regarding the quality of such programs.

As we stress throughout this book, online learning can be powerful and effective if classes are constructed and conducted in a thoughtful manner, using the concepts and guidelines that we have developed and provide in this chapter. The key to well-developed classes is training instructors not only in the use of technology but also in the art of online teaching. Akridge,

DeMay, Braunlich, Collura, and Sheahan (2002) suggest that student retention online depends on three factors: selecting the right students for the
right program, using a highly learner-focused delivery model, and engaging
learners at a personal level. Hebert (2006) discovered that the responsiveness of instructors to perceived student needs helps to increase persistence
in online courses and creates a greater degree of satisfaction with the learning process. Whether the course is offered in a for-profit, nonprofit, or public institution, what is most important is good, solid online course design
coupled with highly effective facilitation. These are two elements that students cite when they talk about the quality of an online course or program.

## Who Should Teach Online?

Not all instructors are suited for the online environment, and academic
institutions are making some serious mistakes when deciding who should
teach. Those who may be resistant to making the transition to the online
classroom are being told that they have no choice and are being sent on
to develop courses with little preparation or training in how to do so. In
addition, choices about who should teach online are often based on faulty
criteria: it is usually either someone who is considered a content expert or
is deemed entertaining in the face-to-face classroom who is chosen. Brookfield (1995, 2006) notes that often, the most popular teachers who get the
best course evaluations are the ones who are able to entertain. This popularity does not translate well online.

In our book *The Excellent Online Instructor* (2011), we devoted a great
deal of attention to the characteristics associated with excellence online.
An issue-oriented white paper that was published following a conference
on virtual pedagogy (Kircher, 2001) noted the following characteristics:
organized, highly motivated and enthusiastic, committed to teaching, supports student-centered learning, open to suggestions, creative, takes risks,
manages time well, responsive to learner needs, disciplined, and interested
in online delivery without expectation of other rewards. Savery (2005)
offers the VOCAL acronym to describe the effective online instructor:

**V**isible
**O**rganized
**C**ompassionate
**A**nalytical
**L**eader by example

The Illinois Online Network (2007) adds to the list by noting that good online instructors have a broad base of life experience in addition to their teaching credentials; demonstrate openness, concern, flexibility, and sincerity (characteristics we have consistently equated with online excellence); feel comfortable communicating in writing (a characteristic also stressed by Kearsley, n.d.); accept that the facilitated model of teaching is equally powerful as traditional teaching methods; value critical thinking; and are experienced and well trained in online teaching. Kearsley (n.d.) also notes that having experienced online instruction as a student also helps, something that we support wholeheartedly. We suggest as well that additional skills that are significant in the emergence of excellence online include the ability to establish presence, create and maintain a learning community, and effectively develop and facilitate online courses.

Another important consideration is the instructor's willingness to give up some control in the teaching and learning process in order to empower the learners and build a learning community. An instructor who is open to giving up control of the learning process, using collaborative learning techniques and ideas, allowing personal interaction, and bringing in real-life experiences and examples and who builds reflective practice into teaching is a good candidate for teaching online. Certainly not all of these criteria need to be met, but a good measure of openness and flexibility is key to a successful transition to the online realm.

How do we find these instructors? At many institutions, this is being done through a process of attraction rather than coercion. Those who are interested in giving online teaching a try may develop or post a course or two. As they struggle but also succeed with the process, they will attract others to join them in this effort. The support that they need to make the transition successfully, however, rests in training and mentoring. Unfortunately, in these difficult budget times, training and mentoring programs are going by the wayside. Because of this, it is critical for online instructors to find ways to train themselves by attending conferences, reading journals and newsletters, and engaging in online communities devoted to online teaching.

## Training, Training, and More Training

Instructors cannot be expected to know intuitively how to design and deliver an effective online course. Although some courses and programs about the use of technology in education are emerging in institutions of higher education and are available to teachers in training, more seasoned instructors have not been exposed to the techniques and methods needed to make online work successful. Current course management systems (CMS) make it easy for faculty simply to transfer material to a course site. The lure to do this is bolstered by the fact that institutions, seeing online learning as their lifesaver in times of declining enrollment on campus, are enrolling such large numbers in online classes that the burden on faculty is enormous. The result is the development of poorly constructed classes, like the history class we described earlier in this chapter.

Providing training for instructors in order to help them get started and also to support their ongoing work in online teaching does help. In our experience, the pairing of those who are more experienced online with those who are just starting out helps to break down barriers and provide concrete examples of what works and what does not. We encourage the development of mentoring programs as an important component of training to teach online.

With the assistance of a grant, the University of Central Florida established a comprehensive faculty development program that addresses four key areas of readiness: the institution, faculty, courses, and learners. Institutional readiness looks at the following elements, which can be used as a checklist:

- The course or program is a good fit with the institution's character and mission.
- It is a good fit with learner characteristics of the institution.
- It has a clearly articulated mission and strategic plan.
- There is demonstrated faculty interest.
- There is a robust campus infrastructure to support courses and programs.
- There is leadership for the initiative.
- There are commitments to faculty support, course and program support, learner support, and assessment.

Faculty readiness is determined by a willingness to learn, a willingness to surrender some control over class design and teaching style, the ability to collaborate with peers, a willingness to change their traditional role, the ability to build a support system, patience with technology, and the ability to learn from others. Course readiness depends on faculty understanding of the technology in use, the pedagogy required for online teaching, and the logistics of the course production process. The readiness of learners is determined through informed self-selection, the ability to take responsibility for their own learning, an access plan for taking the course, awareness of their own learning style, some technical skill, the ability to build a support system, and the ability to deal with the uncertainties of using technology to take courses (Truman-Davis, Futch, Thompson, & Yonekura, 2000).

We have found that even experienced instructors have something to learn about the creation of a learning community online. An instructor who was participating in one of our training sessions asked why he could not get students to talk to him or include him in their conversations. Instead of seeing this as a good thing and evidence of a developing learning community that was able to carry on without his participation, he felt excluded and anxious. Another instructor bemoaned the fact that in the CMS her institution was using, there was no way to generate a transcript of the chat sessions (synchronous discussions) that were occurring during collaborative learning activities. The absence of a transcript and the fact that the instructor was not being asked to participate in the chat sessions left her feeling worried and uncomfortable. She was not in control of the learning process, which she felt was expected of her as an instructor. These examples illustrate that it is not easy to let go of traditional values and ideas in the academic arena. When instructors are given the opportunity to discuss their concerns and even fears emerging from their online experiences, it frees them to try new and better techniques to enhance learning and gain the involvement with students they seek.

Online training courses are another useful way to deliver training to instructors who will be teaching online. In an online training course, instructors can experience firsthand what it is like to be both an instructor and a student in the process. In our experience, the CMS to be used in the development and delivery of courses should be used in the training. As part of the training, instructors should be encouraged to develop a course or even a lesson that other participants can critique. The facilitator of the training, who is likely to be a faculty developer or a faculty member who has been trained or is skillful in the delivery of online instruction, should model good techniques for building a learning community and empowering the participants to explore both the medium and the material. In addition, exposing participants to new technologies (e.g., mobile technologies) as part of their training can spark excitement and creativity going forward.

We have found that it is best to include instructors who are about to embark on their first course when offering an orientation course for online teaching. Delivering such training to all faculty, whether they will be teaching online or not, tends to limit participation in the course. Those who are about to teach online are highly motivated to learn good techniques for doing so; those who are simply interested but will not immediately be using the material may not participate to the same degree. We have found that when the group is mixed, those who will not be teaching in the immediate future tend to drop away, frustrating those who are staying with the training and depending on the group in order to get something from it. But regardless of the form training takes, it is important to include techniques for course development, facilitating learning in the online environment, and building a learning community.

## Using Mobile Technology in Faculty Training

Changing teaching practice by engaging with new technologies is often carried out by those considered to be master instructors in online teaching (Palloff & Pratt, 2011). It is these instructors who are more likely to take risks and experiment with new technologies. The focus, however, may be more on the technology than how it supports pedagogical practice and learning outcomes.

By purposefully embedding the use of mobile technologies into faculty training and development, instructors may be encouraged to think differently about engaging their students through the use of these technologies in ways that support teaching and learning (Lefoe, Olney, Wright, & Herrington, 2009). In so doing, practice is modeled through the use of authentic tasks that instructors might use daily and are also considered daily practice for their students.

Providing faculty training through the use of mobile technology eliminates the issue of creating time and physical space for training as instructors can access training activities in just-in-time fashion. Scheduling becomes more flexible, and varied delivery options can be incorporated. Using everyday activities and the functions of mobile devices to capture those activities helps to create increased relevance in the training and then translates to the ability to create relevance in the teaching and learning activities instructors develop. In addition, they are able to remain more up-to-date in terms of new developments in technology as well as providing them offerings that align with the changing educational landscape.

Lefoe et al. (2009) noted in their work that the use of mobile technology in faculty training helps create awareness of the different contexts in which learning can occur, can promote group work and collaboration, increases instructor confidence with the use of technology, and can help to support assessment strategies. Not only does this approach provide a model of best practices, it also expands the resources available to instructors in their teaching practice.

## New Processes, New Relationships

In our previous books, we described in detail a number of techniques and ideas for building and sustaining an online learning community, in addition to discussing the importance of developing community in order to enhance and support the learning process. The attention to community is not just fluff, or something extra that already overburdened instructors need to pay attention to. It is a means by which students become empowered as learners, thereby taking charge of their own learning and, in fact, lessening the "teaching" burden on the instructor. Instead of increasing the teaching load, good online teaching serves to increase the instructor's responsibility as a learning facilitator. This is not a responsibility to be taken lightly, but rather than being a burden, it can be a way to infuse teaching with new energy and passion. Working online certainly takes more time than teaching face-to-face. However, that time is well spent if students are taking responsibility for the learning process.

Figure 2.1 illustrates the elements that are brought together in an online course that result in the development of a learning community: the people involved, the purpose around which they come together, and the process in which they engage. The outcomes achieved through the intersection of these three critical components include deeper levels of reflection, the ability for students to collaborate to create new knowledge and meaning, a stronger sense of having learned, and new ways of interacting with the learning process that transfer with that learner into every course taken.

Newer technologies have increased the range of what is possible online. Asynchronous learning environments allow students to read material and post to discussions on their own time schedules. The asynchronous environment allows students the luxury of time for thought and reflection on material, an important part of the learning process. In asynchronous mode, students can read assigned material, search out additional sources

### FIGURE 2.1   ELEMENTS OF THE LEARNING COMMUNITY

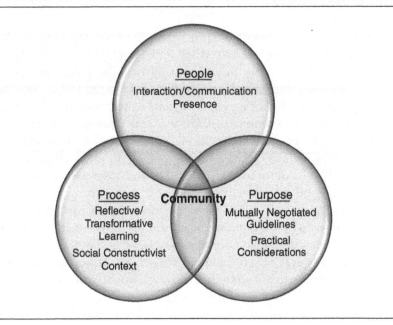

to complement what they are studying, engage in lively discussion with one another—discussion that demonstrates good critical thinking skills and the ability to do some research on a topic—and reflect on the material presented in the text by the instructor and by peers. The result is a greater ability to make meaning out of the material under study and to engage with it.

Supplementing asynchronous work with synchronous chat sessions, virtual classroom sessions, Skype conference calls, and assignments that involve the use of mobile technologies and other collaborative applications serve to create variety in the learning process. In addition, they allow students real-time interaction with the instructor and other students. Hearing voices and being able to ask a question as it occurs is invaluable to many students. Synchronous technologies allow that to occur as well as providing a platform for demonstrations and presentations. By incorporating mobile technologies and collaborative applications available on the Internet, students can also create content and presentations that the instructor and other students can see. Combining all of these approaches helps to create a robust approach to teaching and learning that is part and parcel of online pedagogy.

## Online Pedagogy

The online classroom is a potentially powerful teaching and learning arena in which new practices and new relationships can make significant contributions to learning. In order to harness the power this creates in education, instructors must be trained not only to use technology but also to shift the ways in which they organize and deliver material. Making this shift can increase the potential for learners to take charge of their own learning process and facilitate the development of a sense of community among them.

The shift to online learning poses enormous challenges to instructors and their institutions. As we noted earlier, many believe that the online classroom is no different from the face-to-face classroom and that approaches used face-to-face will surely work online. Many further believe that all they need to do to teach online successfully is to "convert" the course material by placing content on a website or in a CMS. Still others question the quality of what is being delivered online. We believe, however, that when the connection we have to our students is through words on a screen or through disconnected voices on a conference call, we must pay attention to many issues that we take for granted in the face-to-face classroom. It is our best practices that must follow us into the online classroom, and those practices are the basis for what we term online pedagogy, or the art of teaching online.

## Keys to Success

The transition to the online classroom can be successfully made if attention is paid to several key areas: ensuring access to and familiarity with the technology in use; establishing guidelines and procedures that are generated with significant input from participants; striving to achieve maximum participation and buy-in from the participants; promoting collaborative learning; and creating a triple loop in the learning process to enable participants to reflect on their learning, themselves as learners, and the learning process. All of these practices significantly contribute to the development of an online learning community, a powerful tool that facilitates the learning experience. We review each in detail.

### Ensuring Access to and Familiarity with Technology

In a sense, it is a mistake to begin with technology. Many institutions believe that all it takes to implement an online program is to install a fancy

CMS and train faculty to use it. Certainly an instructor needs to be knowledgeable about the technology in use and comfortable enough with it to assist a student having difficulty with it. An instructor should also be able to construct a course site that is easy for students to access, use, and navigate. However, the instructor's responsibility must not end there. The issue, then, is not the technology itself but rather how to use it in the design and delivery of online courses.

The most visually appealing course, complete with audio, video, and chat, is useless if a student is using old hardware or living in a remote area with limited Internet access. Although it may be hard to believe, there are still students who must dial up to access their online courses or have very slow Internet connections. As students enter online degree programs and courses, they are generally told that in order to access a particular course, they must have access to a certain level of technology. However, the most up-to-date computer technology will still not function well in areas with poor Internet access. Consequently, the CMS used for course delivery should have these characteristics (Palloff & Pratt, 2007):

- Functional, offering the functions necessary to design and deliver the course
- Simple to operate
- User-friendly, visually appealing, and easy to navigate

The increasing popularity of mobile technology has the potential to reduce the digital divide and overcome poor access to the Internet. Mobile technology allows students who might not have computer technology at home to access their online courses or participate in various activities using the functions and applications on a cell phone, smart phone, portable media player, or tablet. Activities using cell phones can be incorporated into face-to-face or online classes that support student collaboration and use the functions with which students are most familiar, such as texting. The simplicity of mobile technology helps to meet the functional and user-friendly criteria and thus provides a good adjunct to an online course.

As instructors become more adept at the design and delivery of online courses, the addition of multimedia elements can offer interest to the course that increases the level of engagement. However, a critical factor in the development of multimedia is to avoid simply videotaping lectures or incorporating more traditional course elements through the use of audio or video. Students quickly become bored watching a talking head video lecture on their computer screen. One of us participated in an online course involving fifteen-minute lectures in streaming audio and found that it was impossible to sit and listen for even that seemingly brief period of time without tuning out. Those who have written about the use of audio and video in online classes advise avoiding tapes of someone who is simply talking. And yet most attempts at using streaming video in online classes generally involve taping a professor delivering part of a lecture. The popularity of lecture-capture technologies has unfortunately supported this trend, as has misuse of the concept entitled "flipped classrooms" for hybrid class delivery, where lecture material is posted online with the intent of using class time for active learning and practice. Unfortunately, many instructors rely on the lecture and never quite get to the action learning component.

Kapus (2010) suggests five tips for the use of streaming media in an online course:

1. Post complete transcripts of all media, and encourage students to both watch the presentation and read the transcript.
2. Keep presentations relatively short, meaning fifteen minutes or less.
3. Plan the visual presentation before writing any accompanying narration to allow focus on key points.
4. Write out the narration before delivering it to allow better organization of thoughts.
5. Choose presentation technologies that allow editing audio and video separately in a few simple steps in order to make the presentation cohesive.

Nielsen (2010) studied college students' website use and found that they tend to multitask and work with multiple browser windows open simultaneously. Because of this, they are likely to miss important items they have visited the website to find, such as an assignment or announcement. Although Nielsen's research does show that users will scroll a web page if the content is engaging, most website designers suggest that important material be put at the top of the page, where users can find it easily. Nielsen's work has also shown that few Web users read more than one screen of text. Long web pages that require readers to scroll large distances and remember what was previously on their screens can be disorienting. Consequently, keeping it simple by using concise chunks of information or content is the best way to go (Smith, 2008).

Garrison, Anderson, and Archer (2001) found that chunking content helps students absorb what they need to complete assignments and activities, avoiding information overload and exhaustion. Brief informational posts or announcements that stimulate thinking and discussion serve the learning process well. Smith (2008) cites the benefits of chunking content as increased retention and understanding; more convenient access to course materials; and the likelihood that students will cover more material, results will be more measurable, and comprehension may be greater. Other studies have indicated that shorter modules are more likely to keep learners' attention, thus enabling them to complete the work (Pomales & Liu, 2006). Quality and depth of content do not need to be sacrificed through chunking of material. Instead chunking is a different way to think about and organize content for more efficiency of delivery.

Synchronous discussion refers to online conversation that occurs in real time and can take the form of chat sessions, virtual classroom sessions, and the use of Skype or Second Life or similar programs. All users are online at the same time and interacting in the same discussion space. It is best used in online learning to enhance collaborative learning experiences and enable teamwork.

In order to make the best use of synchronous discussions, groups should be kept very small, for example, ten to twelve students, and an agenda for the discussion should be distributed in advance in order to help keep participants on track. Otherwise it is too easy for a chat or virtual classroom session to wander off into areas unrelated to the course or the collaborative exercise. Small groups also create an environment in which all voices are likely to be heard. Because dominance in a chat session often goes to the fastest typist or the person with the fastest Internet connection, keeping a group small allows participants to keep up with the flow of conversation and enter when it feels appropriate. Similarly, a virtual classroom session where voice contact is possible can quickly mimic the face-to-face classroom where very few students participate. Consequently, it is important for the instructor to pay attention to what it takes to deliver a good synchronous session.

Finkelstein (2006) notes that instruction, collaboration, support, socialization, and extended outreach can be served through synchronous communication in an online course. He states that just as with any other form of technology use, the reason for including live, synchronous sessions must align with learning objectives. In other words, the session must serve a purpose in the online course and not be done just because it can be. And just as with all other learning that occurs online, careful planning should go into the facilitation of a synchronous session to achieve the goals for that session.

Some instructors are experimenting with the use of social media such as Twitter to conduct discussions, complete assignments, and deliver snippets of course information in real time. One of us has attempted to use Twitter for announcements and discussions. However, students were somewhat resistant to registering for a Twitter account. Consequently, the idea was scrapped. Schaffauser (2012) reviewed some successful experiments with social media in online and face-to-face classes and found that students enthusiastically engaged in the activities despite some glitches. The outcome indicated that as with all other forms of technology, finding ways to engage students through the use of social media is appropriate when it fits with course learning objectives. The age of the student may also play a role here. The Pew Research Center's Internet and American Life Project (Smith & Brenner, 2012) showed growing use of Twitter by younger people (those ages eighteen to twenty-four), with slight decreases in use among older adults and significant decreases among high school students.

Finally, the technology in use should be transparent to the students enrolled in the class. Instructors do not want to face technological struggles throughout the course in addition to working to build a good learning community. The instructors also need to be familiar enough with the technology to work around any difficult issues it might present. The technology, then, should serve only as a vehicle for delivering the course, allowing both instructor and students to pay attention to more important matters.

## Establishing Guidelines and Procedures

We cannot stress enough that an important beginning to an online course is to present clear guidelines for participation in the class, as well as information for students about course expectations and procedures. Guidelines are generally presented along with the syllabus and a course outline as a means of creating some structure around and in the course. If clear guidelines are not presented, students can become confused and disorganized, and the learning process will suffer.

Once the course begins, the instructor should also make an assessment of the group he or she is working with in order to determine what modifications to the guidelines might be necessary. One of us learned this lesson the hard way with a group of graduate students who were having difficulty making the transition to the online learning environment. A course was posted that the instructor had taught previously, using the same set of guidelines that had worked well with previous groups. This group, however, needed far more structure. Believing that they were asking for help, two students "flamed" the instructor on the course site, causing participation in the course to dwindle. (Flaming is when one participant in an online discussion sends to another any kind of derogatory comment. A flame is frequently interpreted as an attack rather than a discussion of the participants' positions. It is thus a very heated exchange.) Once guidelines and course expectations were clarified and the angry feelings of the students were attended to, participation increased, but it never reached acceptable levels for the remainder of the term. One student, Beth, responded to the clarification as follows:

> I have felt like I poured my personal self out online, and receive little to no feedback, so your prompting will help a lot. I was beginning to feel that this would be a course where I got the most from self-reflection, not the dialogue, but I would welcome a change in this. Sometimes I think the early online tensions in the course created some rifts. I think we are on our way to recovering as a group.

In evaluating their experience with this class, students commented that they learned more from the reading than from each other—a clear indication that learning objectives were not met with this group and that a learning community never formed.

The guidelines for an online class also should not be too rigid and should contain room for discussion and negotiation. "Imposed guidelines that are too rigid will constrain discussion, causing participants to worry about the nature of their posts rather than to simply post" (Palloff & Pratt, 2007, p. 20). Guidelines should not put students in the position of wondering, "Am I doing this right?" They should instead provide a safe space within which students feel free to express themselves and discuss material related to the course.

The guidelines can be the first discussion item in a new class. Doing this enables students to take responsibility for the way they will engage in the course and with one another, and it serves to promote collaboration in the learning process. We offer two caveats, however. First, the instructor should retain veto power—meaning that if a proposed change would substantially alter the course and send it in a direction that will not achieve learning outcomes, the instructor needs to step in and say no. Second, the instructor holds ultimate decision-making power in the area of assignments and grading. Frequently when we ask students for their thoughts on guidelines, we say that assignments and grading are not open for negotiation. Deadlines, however, are. If we have established an assignment deadline that conflicts with other courses students may be taking, we will certainly entertain the notion of changing deadlines. The second caveat is that if one student offers a suggested change, the other students should be polled to see if the change rests well with them. We will not change the way in which a course is structured based only on what one student wants. Because online learning should be collaborative, all voices should be heard when a change is proposed.

## Achieving Maximum Participation

Participation guidelines in an online course are critical to its successful outcome. As online instructors, however, we cannot make the assumption that if we establish minimum participation guidelines of, say, two posts per week, students will understand what that means. We must also explain what it means to post to an online course discussion. Posting is more than visiting the course site to check in and say hello. Posts should be considered a substantive contribution to the discussion: a student either comments on other posts or begins a new topic (Palloff & Pratt, 2007).

In addition to being clear about expectations for participation, we have found that the following suggestions for instructors can lead to increased participation in an online course (Palloff & Pratt, 2007):

- Be clear about how much time the course will require of students and the instructor in order to eliminate potential misunderstandings about course demands. Students sometimes assume that taking an online course is the softer, easier way to earn credit. They learn quickly, however, that this is not the case. If the instructor forewarns them through accurate information in an introduction to the course, students can make better-informed decisions about whether this is a course they can successfully complete. In addition, it helps to reduce or eliminate the possibility that they will drop out once the course begins. If some students are having significant difficulty managing their time as the course progresses and their participation is dwindling as a result, the instructor may need to work with them to assist them in establishing good practices to help them achieve their learning goals for the course.
- Teach students about online learning. Instructors and academic institutions assume that when students enter the online classroom, they will intuitively know what online teaching is about and how to learn in the online environment. We have found, however, that students need to be oriented to the online classroom and taught how to learn online.

- Be a model of good participation by logging on frequently and contributing to the discussion. The workload in an online class not only is significantly higher for students but also is significantly higher for the instructor (Seaman, 2009). Online instructors cannot post a course and then go on vacation for a week—unless they are willing to take a computer with them! An instructor is unlikely to keep up with student discussion by logging on once or twice a week. Furthermore, an instructor who does so is likely to see poor participation in the course. The instructor's role as a learning facilitator is to follow the discussion and gently guide and redirect it by asking clarifying and expansive questions. This practice keeps the discussion moving and also reassures students that the instructor is present and available.

The instructor also needs to maintain a balance between too little and too much participation. Grandzol and Grandzol (2010) note that the institutional practice of mandating high levels of instructor interaction through requirements to respond to every learner may be counterproductive, actually resulting in poorer rates of course completion. Because the learning community is a critical feature of the online course, the instructor need not respond to every student post but instead should determine the appropriate time to jump in, make a comment, ask another question, or redirect the discussion. Too much participation by the instructor can have the effect of reducing the amount of interaction among the students and create an unnecessary degree of reliance on the teacher. Too much instructor participation is often evident in the form of questions or comments being directed to him or her rather than to other participants or if the group waits for the instructor to post before they move on. Balance is the key to facilitating a good online discussion:

- Be willing to step in and set limits if participation wanes or if the conversation is heading in the wrong direction. Being a learning facilitator does not mean being uninvolved in the learning process. The instructor needs to act as a guide in order to ensure that learning objectives are met. Consequently, if students are headed down the wrong path, the instructor needs to let them know so that they can get back on track. We had an experience with a group of undergraduate students who, when asked questions designed to help them critically analyze the material they were reading in the textbook, responded with material directly from the text. When one student would begin the week's discussion in that fashion, the others would follow suit. We needed to step in often to push them gently to reflect on the material they were reading and move away from what was comfortable into territory that was new to them.

- Remember that there are people attached to the words on the screen. Be willing to contact students who are not participating and invite them in. When students drop away from the online discussion, the learning process of all participants is affected. Therefore, it is important to monitor the participation of each student and make contact either when there has been a change (e.g., someone has been a good participant but his or her participation wanes for a week or so) or when there has been minimal or no participation. Sometimes the reasons for nonparticipation have to do with technical problems and personal issues, and the instructor may be helpful to the students who are dealing with them. At other times, the instructor may find that the online mode of instruction simply does not suit the student. When this is the case, students should be encouraged to find other means to take the course, such as returning to the face-to-face classroom.

- Stress that good participation is essential. In the face-to-face classroom, the absence of one or more participants may not be noticed. But a student's absence from the online classroom significantly affects the quality of the online discussion and should be dealt with as soon as it is apparent.

- Create a warm and inviting atmosphere that promotes the development of a sense of community among the participants. During one of our presentations at a conference in Europe, an instructor from the Netherlands expressed concern that he was unable to get his online students to respond to him as a person rather than as an instructor. He was hoping to develop a sense of community with his participants and was finding this a difficult task. We encouraged him to share a reasonable amount of personal information with his students as a way of inviting them to do the same. For example, in an introduction, instead of simply telling students about academic accomplishments that demonstrated why he was competent to teach the course, why not include information about a spouse or partner, children, pets, and interests outside of academic pursuits? Sharing this information with students presents the instructor as a real person who is interested in hearing about his students as real people as well.

It is always important to remember that when we post to an asynchronous discussion, we present ourselves in text. Because this can be viewed as a flat medium, we need to make an extra effort to humanize the environment. In the face-to-face classroom, students have the opportunity to get to know one another as people before or after class, during classroom discussions, and in other campus locations such as the student lounge. In the online environment, we need to create these opportunities more purposefully.

If these suggestions are incorporated into the development of an online course, they will promote the development of a learning community and can also assist in the promotion of collaborative learning. Both potentially contribute to stronger learning outcomes and more satisfactory learning experiences for all involved.

## Promoting Collaboration

Collaborative learning processes help students achieve deeper levels of knowledge generation through the creation of shared goals, shared exploration, and a shared process of meaning making. In addition, collaborative activity can help to reduce the feelings of isolation that can occur when students are working at a distance (Palloff & Pratt, 2004). Jonassen et al. (1995) noted in their classic work on collaboration that the outcome of collaborative learning processes includes personal meaning making and the social construction of knowledge and meaning. Brookfield (1995, 2006) describes what he terms new paradigm teachers: those who are willing to engage in and facilitate collaborative processes by promoting initiative on the part of the learners, creativity, critical thinking, and dialogue.

Given the separation by time and distance of the learners from one another and from the instructor and given the discussion-based nature of these courses, the online learning environment is the type of learning arena that can facilitate the development of a shared goal for learning process, encourages students to bring personal motivating problems from their lives and work into the online discussion, and uses dialogue as the foundation of the learning process. Thus, collaborative learning assists with deeper levels of knowledge generation and promotes initiative, creativity, and the development of critical thinking skills.

Engagement in a collaborative learning process forms the foundation of a learning community and the formation of a solid learning community supports collaborative activity as depicted in our model of online collaboration. When collaboration is not encouraged, participation in the online course is generally low and may take the form of queries to the instructor rather than dialogue and feedback. Figure 2.2 illustrates the cyclical nature

### FIGURE 2.2   MODEL OF ONLINE COLLABORATION

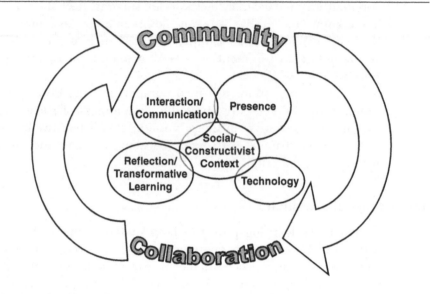

of the collaborative process: collaboration supports the development of the online learning community, and the presence of the online learning community facilitates more effective collaboration. Contained within the cycle are the important elements of the online learning community we have been discussing, all of them enhanced and supported by the cycle.

## Promoting Reflection

When students are learning collaboratively, reflection on the learning process is inherent. It involves self-reflection that includes the learning process and knowledge acquired about the content, how learning occurs online, the technology itself, and how users have been transformed by their newly found relationships with the technology, the learning process, and the other participants (Palloff & Pratt, 2007). In addition, when students are learning collaboratively online, reflections on the contribution of technology to the learning process are almost inevitable. They should be encouraged to reflect on their own learning process, how learning with the use of technology has affected that process either positively or negatively, and what they might have learned about the technology itself by using it to learn.

Constructing a course that allows these naturally occurring processes to unfold greatly enhances the learning outcome and the process of community building. It is more than reflection on the meaning and importance of course material. The reflection process transforms a participant in an online course from a student to a reflective practitioner and, ideally, sets in motion the potential for lifelong reflective learning. Purposeful facilitation of this process involves incorporating the following questions into a course (Palloff & Pratt, 2007, p. 199): "How were you as a learner before you came into this course? How have you changed? How do you anticipate this will affect your learning in the future?"

The following student post presents a good example of the reflective process. In her comments, Juliet reflects on the course, providing some "aha's" about online interaction. and her own learning style:

> A major realization was that the same leadership competencies such as vision, trust, building relationships, communicating, celebrating and rewarding, etc. are needed in the virtual and real world. These competencies are challenging to model in the real world and they take more effort and consciousness for leaders to model in the virtual environment. In virtual conditions leaders also need to be current and proficient in the many electronic tools available for leading.
>
> I now can understand how expressing a hidden or less used side of oneself in an online environment could provide an opportunity to work through emotional issues, not likely to be dealt with under more "real" conditions. It has been a learning experience, an opportunity to develop a less developed side of myself, and I have really improved my writing and analytical thinking skills.

The reflective process embedded in online learning is one of its hallmarks and most exciting features. If an instructor is willing to give up control of the learning process and truly act as a facilitator, he or she may be amazed at the depth of engagement with learning and the material that can occur as a result.

## The Final Transition: Assessing and Evaluating Students and Ourselves

Magennis and Farrell (2005) define teaching as "a set of activities that makes learning possible" (p. 45). Harasim, Hiltz, Teles, and Turoff (1996) in their early seminal work on online learning stated, "In keeping with a learner-centered approach, evaluation and assessment should be part of the learning-teaching process, embedded in class activities and in the interactions between learners and between learners and teachers" (p. 167). Good student assessment should provide the link between what was taught and what was learned. A self-assessment of our own teaching practice is embedded in the outcome of student assessment.

In the spirit of collaboration and reflection, assessment of student progress and performance should not fall to the instructor alone. Students should be encouraged to comment on one another's work, and self-assessment should be embedded in the final performance evaluation of each student. As the course progresses, we ask that students provide feedback to one another on assignments. In addition, at the end of a term, using a rubric designed for this purpose, we request that students send us a private e-mail with a descriptive assessment of the performance of their student colleagues as well as their own performance. We use this feedback, along with quality and quantity of participation and performance on assignments and in discussion, as measures of overall student performance.

Based on our experience, we believe that examinations may not be the best measure of student performance in the online environment. Unless an exam is well developed, it will not necessarily measure critical thinking skills appropriately. Rocco (2007) notes that instructors, due to expediency and the fact that most course management systems include a test and quiz function, may use tests and quizzes as their first choice for student assessment online even though this may not be the best choice. Well-developed exams are comprehensive, contextual, relate to the material being studied, and promote reflection and critical thinking rather than regurgitation of material. Rocco also notes, however, that most exams are not designed to measure the level of student mastery of the content that instructors hope to achieve. Given that most tests and quizzes are designed using true/false or multiple-choice questions, a student's ability to synthesize content, for example, would not be assessed. A student's performance online should be a better indicator of whether learning objectives are being met. When exams become part of the process, concerns about cheating emerge and, in fact, tests and quizzes given online may actually promote cheating (McNett, 2002). However, in a truly collaborative learning process, concerns about cheating become irrelevant because students learn from one another and together create higher levels of knowledge and meaning.

Assessment should not just be focused on student performance, however. Ongoing course evaluation should also be embedded in the learning process. Instructors should make means available to students through which they can express their opinions about the course, the way it is proceeding, and how well it is meeting their learning objectives based on the way it is configured. Course evaluation, then, should not be relegated to the end of the term and simply be a measure of instructor popularity. Instead, it should become part of the collaborative process of course delivery to meet learning expectations.

## Supporting Instructors to Make the Transition

Making the transition to the online learning environment means developing new approaches to education and new skills in its delivery. It means engaging in self-reflection as we determine our own comfort level in turning over control of the learning process to our students. It means promoting a sense of community among our students to enhance their learning process. And most of all, it means abdicating the tried-and-true techniques that may have served us well in the face-to-face classroom in favor of experimentation with new techniques and assumptions. In so doing, we will meet the challenges of preparing students to navigate the demands of a knowledge society and in the process learn something new ourselves, thus supporting our own quest for lifelong learning.

How to achieve all of this is one of the most challenging issues facing online instructors. To make it happen, instructors need good training, technical support, and the ability to participate in the process in the company of others. Nothing substitutes for the support of other colleagues as they make the same journey. Encouraging instructors who are teaching online to join discussion groups, attend conferences about online distance learning, and attend training sessions on campus can greatly assist them in making the move to the online classroom.

We close this chapter with some tips for successful online courses that summarize the essence of online pedagogy.

---

TIPS FOR INSTRUCTORS AND INSTRUCTIONAL DESIGNERS FOR THE DESIGN AND DELIVERY OF A SUCCESSFUL ONLINE COURSE

- Establish guidelines for the class and participation that provide enough structure for the learners but allow flexibility and negotiation.
- Mandate participation, and incorporate it into student evaluation and grading. A good idea is to require at least two or more posts each week.

Another good idea is to equate posting with the number of credit hours for the course; for example, a standard three-credit course would require three posts per week.

- Promote collaborative learning through small group assignments, case studies, simulations, and group discussion of readings and assignments.

- Have students post their assignments and encourage feedback to one another on their work. Although some instructors and students feel comfortable having grades shared on the course site, we feel that grades should be shared privately. Whether grades are shared or kept private can be discussed along with the guidelines at the beginning of a course; this also may be regulated or controlled by university rules and requirements.

- Set up a well-organized course site that includes a place for students to socialize.

- Include an area where students can reflect on what it is like to learn online, like a blog spot, and encourage students to self-reflect on their progress in the course at least at midterm and again at the end of the course through the use of rubrics.

- Encourage students to bring real-life examples into the online classroom. The more relevant the material is to their lives, the more likely they are to integrate it.

- Don't lecture! An online lecture can become just another article that students are required to read or a long and boring piece of audio or video. When constructing and incorporating lecture material, divide it into five- to ten-minute chunks that students can view or listen to quickly and that support the key points of the unit or week's study.

- When lectures are used, always provide a transcript of it to support disabled students or students who are visual learners.

- Stay present. Let your students know you are there by commenting on their posts and asking additional questions for them to consider. But also avoid being intrusive or overbearing. Balance is the key to successful participation.

- Become comfortable enough with the technology to be able to answer students' questions about its use and assist them when they run into difficulty.

- Act like a learning facilitator rather than a professor.

- Most of all, have fun, and open yourself to learning as much from your students as they will learn from one another and from you.

CHAPTER THREE

# ADMINISTRATIVE ISSUES AND CONCERNS

W hy, in a book that has been written primarily for the team of professionals engaged in the design and delivery of courses—faculty, instructional designers, faculty developers, and instructional technologists—would we devote attention to administrative issues and concerns? Consider the following two scenarios as a means to begin answering this question.

A university is using online courses to deliver its master's-level programs and certificates. Two different course management systems are being used, one significantly easier to use than the other. Students are expressing confusion as to why some courses are offered in one place and others in the other system. To complicate matters, other degree programs within the university are using only online delivery if the individual faculty member chooses to use the course management system. The faculty senate has determined that this is a problem, and a cross-university committee has been established to look at developing uniform technology use policies, incorporating the use of technology into the university's strategic plan, and determining faculty and student needs for training.

Another college has received a review from its accrediting body that indicated that its online courses are poorly designed and facilitated. In response, the university has decided that all faculty must be trained and certified in online course design and delivery, whether they teach online or not. The new expectation is that all faculty hired to teach in the university will also teach online. Faculty are expressing extreme resistance to this plan, however, and the college responded by paying them to sit through the training, whether they complete it satisfactorily or not.

As we have noted, colleges and universities are undergoing a significant transition. There are economic pressures from mounting costs, demands by the business world for graduates who are able to function in a knowledge society, and greater diversity among students who choose higher education. In addition, today's graduates are expected to be able to demonstrate good critical thinking ability, good analytical skills, and the ability to work collaboratively in a team setting and in distributed settings. What both of the scenarios point out is the need for comprehensive planning by a team of professionals, including administrative personnel, to deliver a coherent online learning program successfully. In developing a comprehensive plan for the institution, all participants in the delivery of the program must understand the needs and concerns of the other participants. In the next chapter, we discuss administrative and faculty concerns about the choice of technology and the creation of a technological infrastructure for the institution. These are not, however, the only issues administrators face as they seek to develop an online program or begin offering online courses.

Frequently as we present and consult, we are asked about issues such as compensation for course development and online teaching given the amount of time it takes to teach online courses. The issue of compensation is a controversial one, with no clear answers emerging to resolve it. In this chapter, we review current thought on this issue, as well as discuss other administrative issues and concerns, such as online program planning and development, faculty support and training, governance issues, and tenure issues. These concerns refer to issues of responsibility and control—in other words, who controls the development and delivery of online courses and who should be in control.

All of the issues embedded in the administrative arena are controversial and have been the cause of disagreement and even outright conflict between administrators and their faculties. They are, however, important issues for all elements of the institution to consider. The policies, which, ideally, are the outcome of the discussion of these issues, should become the foundation of a technological infrastructure in an institution. Bates and Sangrà (2011) describe the need for educational leaders to develop strategic frameworks to address the changing cultural, organizational, economic, and survival issues of the institution. They also note that leadership alone will not result in effective technology integration;

a wide variety of stakeholders need to support the strategy in order for it to be successful. Increasingly, we are seeing such plans developed by colleges, universities, and K–12 school districts as leaders realize their importance. All of the issues we have just outlined need to be included in such a framework. As Bates and Sangrà and others have noted, the demand for higher education is increasing, albeit with students who do not resemble the traditional students whom institutions have served in the past. In order for colleges and universities to rise to the challenge of delivering education with and through the use of technology, they must overcome the natural conservatism of their faculties and engage in the difficult discussions that will lead them to develop strategies to keep them fiscally sound while delivering high-quality educational programs. Administrators too must develop what Bates and Sangrà (2011) refer to as "compelling visions and goals for the use of technology" (p. 79) and move away from conservative views of how technology can support teaching and learning. This means is that administrators need to start working with and listening to their faculties.

We now examine each of the issues in the administrative arena and end with some tips for creating a sound technological infrastructure.

## Faculty Time, Compensation, and Questions of Tenure

A 1999 survey of sixty faculty conducted at Arkansas State University yielded results that appear to be the norm of faculty experience for those who teach online: 90 percent indicated that they needed substantially more preparation time to develop a course, 75 percent had not participated in any additional training opportunities other than what they needed to understand the technology in use, and more than 88 percent indicated that they were given neither additional compensation nor a reduced workload for developing or teaching distance learning courses (Dickinson, Agnew, & Gorman, 1999). More recent studies confirm that these are still issues. According to the report presented by the Association of Public and Land-Grant Universities (Seaman, 2009), chief academic officers have consistently felt that it takes instructors more time to develop an online course than to teach one. However, approximately 64 percent of faculty surveyed indicated that it takes "somewhat more" or "a lot more" effort to teach online (p. 6).

As online learning has grown in popularity, additional studies about the amount of time instructors spend teaching online have emerged.

Anderson and Avery (2008) found that instructors spend approximately 46.1 hours per credit hour teaching online. This figure does not include the time required to design and plan an online course. Bates and Sangrà (2011) estimate that developing an online course requires 12.5 days. Often these time demands go unrecognized. Considering these statistics, it is no wonder that some faculty resist the call to teach online.

An early study (Rockwell, Schauer, Fritz, & Marx, 1999) that was designed to look at what faculty feel are incentives for and obstacles to participation in online teaching found that primary incentives for faculty to teach at a distance were personal or intrinsic rewards rather than monetary ones. Included in the list of incentives was the opportunity to provide innovative instruction, use new teaching techniques, and receive recognition for their work. The main perceived obstacles correspond to the issues outlined in the more recent studies: the need for time, training, and support. Monetary rewards were seen as neither an incentive nor an obstacle to participating in online teaching. This was supported by findings of the Association of Public and Land-Grant Universities study (Seaman, 2009), which indicated that instructors cited student needs as their primary motivator for teaching online.

That is not to say that the time differences required for course development and delivery along with increased workload should not be considered when developing a reward structure for faculty. Bates and Sangrà (2011) asked a number of important questions: What counts as a cost in online learning? How does one cost out the extra work required of faculty? Should one cost it out? If the college or university sees online teaching as part of the faculty role and does not offer incentives for teaching online, Bates and Sangrà hypothesize that the cost of this stance will emerge in other ways, such as a reduction of research activity, less free time, fewer social activities, and less family time. They note, "At some point, these hidden costs become unacceptable to the instructor, and technology becomes rejected" (p. 158). Consequently, it is important to provide sufficient incentives and training in order to effectively engage instructors in online teaching and maximize the return on the technology investment.

When the educational landscape is changing as rapidly as it currently is because of the impact of technology, administrators, faculty, and all others affected by the changes need to be talking and agreeing on new ways of negotiating that territory. If, in other words, the outcomes and products of our engagement with online learning are shared, peer reviewed, published, funded, and presented at conferences, then these activities should be given the same consideration as the traditional criterion of research publication when rewards are made.

Instructors do respond positively and express interest in becoming involved in online work when appropriate incentives are put in place. Incentives such as the provision of in-house grants for course development, significant blocks of time off to engage in course development and training activities, reduced teaching loads while teaching online courses, and adequate support to assist with course development and delivery can help to allay the fears of faculty members who are entering the online arena for the first time. Incentives can also support master online faculty as they support the work of their peers who are new to online teaching. The Sloan Consortium (2012), in its discussion of the five pillars of quality online education, note:

> Personal factors contributing to faculty satisfaction with the online experience include opportunities to extend interactive learning communities to new populations of students and to conduct and publish research related to online teaching and learning. Institutional factors related to faculty satisfaction include three categories: support, rewards, and institutional study/research. Faculty satisfaction is enhanced when the institution supports instructors with a robust and well-maintained technical infrastructure, training in online instructional skills, and ongoing technical and administrative assistance. Faculty members also expect to be included in the governance and quality assurance of online programs, especially as these relate to curricular decisions and development of policies of particular importance to the online environment (such as intellectual property, copyright, royalties, collaborative design and delivery). Faculty satisfaction is closely related to an institutional reward system that recognizes the rigor and value of online teaching. Satisfaction increases when workload assignments/assessments reflect the greater time commitment in developing and teaching online courses and when online teaching is valued on par with face-to-face teaching in promotion and tenure decisions. A final institutional factor—crucial to recruiting, retaining, and expanding a dedicated online faculty—is commitment to ongoing study of and enhancement of the online faculty experience. (para. 4)

## Program Planning and Development

As the two scenarios at the beginning of this chapter illustrated, often the move to implementing online courses and the use of technology to support teaching is done without much planning. Planning should begin with instructional design and overall outcomes in mind. The technology tools that fit the needs of instructors, students, and the curriculum should then be chosen and integrated. Bates and Sangrà (2011) note that at many institutions, planning for the integration of learning technologies at the institutional level and academic planning at the department level are separate streams of activity. They contend that there should be coherence and coordination between these processes in order to provide the highest levels of support and innovation throughout the institution.

Cartwright (1996), with tongue in cheek, described four ways in which technology planning seems to occur on campuses:

- The End-of-Year Scramble, in which long-range planning is put aside in favor of honoring short-term budget requests before the end of the fiscal year
- Neo-Passe Chaos, where no planning process is evident but department heads are authorized with a budget to acquire hardware and software suited to individual needs; also termed the "faculty knows best" approach to planning
- Father Knows Best, where decisions are made by the technology administrator or a small, handpicked group made up primarily of technology professionals
- Pollyanna-Phillpanna Utopia, where all institutional activities are put on hold for several weeks a year while all departments engage in a consensus-building approach; this can result in a long-term plan with annual updates, but may result in no action

In summary, the mistakes that institutions make in the planning process revolve around lack of support or guidance from senior-level administrators, lack of knowledge or contact with the marketplace (i.e., students and their needs), a lack of specific action steps with which to implement plans, and an inability to implement plans rapidly.

Interestingly, the most comprehensive technology planning is occurring at the statewide level, primarily in the K–12 arena. Once again, higher education could benefit by reviewing the scope and intent of these plans in order to begin a comprehensive planning process on individual campuses. Some universities are beginning to address the need for the development of technology strategic plans and are publishing the results of their work online.

In addition to focusing on teaching and learning outcomes, a comprehensive technology plan for distance education should clearly identify the students the institution intends to serve and realistically assess the access to technology of that target group (Bates, 2000). Often institutions intend to use online learning to extend their reach without much thought about who those students really are, where they reside, or how they will access programs and courses.

We consulted with an institution that had this intent in mind. The thought was that offering distance learning to a nationwide audience would help to support and even save the institution economically. With no comprehensive plan in place, the institution used a combination of the faculty-knows-best approach to the development of courses and programs and the father-knows-best approach to the choice of technology the faculty would use. One department, after we provided some training, began offering a series of courses and experienced some success at drawing students from the local geographical region. When the department decided to expand its reach, however, the institution was unable to support it. For example, when students at a significant distance attempted to register for online courses, they were told that they needed to come to campus in order to do so. Despite intervention from the department, the registrar's office refused to budge. The obvious result was that the students at a distance did not take the courses. If the institution had developed a comprehensive plan in which all departments and units in the institution were represented, it would have avoided this situation.

Thinking through all aspects of the implementation of an online program or even a few online courses is critical to the success of that effort. Furthermore, the technology plan for the institution should not stand alone, but should be embedded in the strategic plan of the institution. Bates (2000) notes the outcome of a benchmarking study describing best practices in the use of technology on campus. The results of the study were not surprising and echo the best practices that we are encouraging throughout this book: the development of a strategic plan in which the implementation of technology in teaching plays a prominent role; investment in the technology infrastructure needed to support such an effort; support by senior leadership for the use of technology; support for faculty who use technology in their teaching; and support for students through access to computers, courses, and the Internet.

The best practices relate to the activities of teaching and learning, and not to the technology itself. Bates notes that although faculty development in this area is important, it is not the main strategy to be used in successful implementation of a technology plan. We will, however, now return to a discussion of both faculty and student development as important activities that cannot be ignored. But before we do, it is important to share one last thought on planning for the implementation of technology: although it is critical to plan institutionally to create realistic strategies consistent with the institution's mission, strengths, and available resources, it is also important to create plans and strategies that focus on the future and allow flexibility, growth, and change. As with all other activities related to the implementation of technology in teaching, balance is the key.

## Another Look at Faculty and Student Support, Training, and Development

The benchmarking report that Bates describes noted that in institutions following best practices in the implementation of technology, faculty development focuses on teaching and learning, not on the technology itself. Certainly instructors need to develop technology skills before they can move into teaching online. However, as we have been emphasizing, the focus in faculty development should be on pedagogical methods, not the technology in use.

Instructors who are presented with instructional design principles appropriate to online teaching often ask, "Where is the lecture?" Clearly this is an indication of the traditional approach to education wherein lectures have had a focal place. Unfortunately, lecture-capture technology has promoted the idea that the lecture continues to be central to the course, whether delivered online or face-to-face. For this reason, faculty training and development should incorporate concrete ways in which content can be presented without the use of lectures or with the use of different approaches to the lecture, such as short podcasts. Some of the techniques can include these:

- Designing WebQuests (or online scavenger hunts) that allow students to explore and seek out the content of the course
- Providing collaborative small group assignments
- Providing research assignments asking students to seek out and present additional resources available on the Internet and in books and journals
- Using simulations that allow students to practice the skills taught in the course using real-life examples
- Asking students to become well versed on a topic in the scope of the course and present that topic to their peers

- Using asynchronous discussion of the topics in the scope of the course material being studied
- Having students post papers to the course site and conduct peer review of those papers
- Incorporating brief (less than fifteen minutes) audio and video clips to support the content
- Links to YouTube videos or other Web-based content that supports the course
- Encouraging the use of wikis and other collaborative technologies that allow students to contribute content to the course while demonstrating their learning

What is important is to encourage and support instructors in developing creative ways to present course content, keeping in mind the technology to which students are likely to have access. Rather than relying on computer technology to deliver all aspects of the course, using the technology that almost all students have—cell phones and tablets—can help to reach and engage all students in the course.

Students need training not only in the course management system they will be using to access their courses but also in how to learn in the online environment. If the institution cannot provide this training or does not see this as a part of its technology plan, then incorporating suggestions for how to learn online becomes the instructor's responsibility. Instructors can do this in several ways—for example:

- Holding a face-to-face orientation, if possible, to show students the course site and discuss online learning
- Providing an orientation to the course somewhere on the course site or as a first discussion item in the course
- Providing students with a list of frequently asked questions and responses to those questions
- Placing basic information about how to navigate the course site on the welcome screen or course home page with a "Start Here" message
- Sending an e-mail message containing orientation information to each student enrolled in the course
- Creating brief video tours of the course site, course management system, and the course itself, which can be posted in the course or on YouTube

Regardless of how student orientation occurs, it needs to be considered an important element in the development of the course, yet it is often overlooked. Including information about this in faculty training can create awareness on the faculty's part of just how important this is.

As was noted in the benchmarking report, support for instructors and students is a crucial element in the construction of a good technological infrastructure. Administrators must keep in mind who their constituents are when they are developing a technology plan, and they must provide the fiscal and staff support necessary to keep an online program alive and well.

Two other issues that are critical to the successful development of an online program relate to the ongoing role of faculty in that program. Just as faculty need to be involved in decisions such as the choice of course management systems and other technologies, they also need to be involved in decisions about which courses are to be offered online and how those courses will be developed.

We now turn to issues of governance and return to the discussion of copyright and intellectual property issues as they relate to developing a plan to deliver online courses and programs.

## Governance and Intellectual Property

Who decides which courses are offered online and which degree programs are worthy of migration to the online environment? Should these decisions rest with department chairs, individual faculty members, the faculty senate, administrators, coordinators of distance learning, or a combination of these groups? Questions of who holds the decision-making power in distance learning and, of equal importance, who owns courses have become critical as the number and range of courses offered increase. And as with other issues pertaining to distance learning, these are not questions that are typically asked when it comes to traditional face-to-face classes held on campus.

Those who are writing about the impact of online learning on the academy, coupled with the current economic environment, have noted that distance learning has changed the economics of instruction, throwing institutions headlong into a competitive marketplace (Barone & Luker, 2000). Other worries stem from increasing budgetary concerns, federal regulations meant to reduce the burden of student loans, and a focus on tuition costs that often exceed federal student loan caps.

The response of many institutions has been to offer online distance learning programs and courses as a way to extend their reach, attract more students, and control costs. Some institutions are more prepared than others to participate in the distance learning market, and others have floundered because of a lack of vision or plan for successful entry or unrealistic hopes of "saving" the institution from financial ruin. More recently, those discussions have extended to the use of MOOCs (massively open online courses), which we discuss in the final chapter of this book, as a means to market what the institution might have to offer prospective students and provide no-credit online opportunities to a broad range of people at no cost.

Not surprisingly, the economics of distance education have changed the ways in which decisions are made about the courses and programs offered. On some campuses, departments and their faculty, in conjunction with faculty senates, are still making decisions about which courses and programs will be offered online. On other campuses, these decisions are being taken from faculty and made by senior administrative personnel, department chairs, or continuing education coordinators. In an environment that is already fostering the rift between faculty and administration, dealing with governance issues in this way cannot be helpful.

In response to this situation, institutions have engaged in a comprehensive planning process involving the faculty senate and administrators. The result of these planning activities has been comprehensive and detailed policies covering both administrative and faculty concerns that revisit agreements between faculty and administration and place concern for students at the forefront. The overall spirit of the policies is that online courses should be treated no differently from traditional ones. Quality measures in place for courses taught on campus will also apply to online courses, meaning that the curriculum committees of the university will review all courses; faculty will be hired in ways consistent with hiring on campus; the outsourcing of courses or programs cannot occur without the approval of appropriate university bodies; an adequate support structure will be put in place to assist both faculty and students; and prior to the offering of a course or program, agreements regarding copyright and intellectual property, as well as faculty compensation and use of revenue, will be completed in accordance with the university's existing policy on intellectual property.

Policies such as these are likely to be the wave of the near future. Such policies should include clear rules and guidelines regarding ownership of materials created for online courses. Bates (2000) offers an interesting perspective on this issue. As a matter of course, instructors who are hired to teach on campus are expected to write and publish independently. The university generally takes no ownership of or revenue from the materials its instructors publish. But when it comes to creating online courses, the picture changes. Bates (2010) writes, "Universities and colleges are now themselves funding the creation of materials and becoming major stakeholders in and producers of copyrighted materials" (p. 110). Consequently, if the course materials are created as part of the faculty's regular work responsibilities, then that material may in fact belong to the employer—in this case, the university. Complicating this picture is that courses increasingly are being created not just by one instructor but by a team comprising faculty, instructional designers, and programmers. The same, however, could be said for the writing and publication of a book: few faculty self-publish books. The books they write are produced with the help of a team. Consequently, the principle of fairness applies.

Hawke (2000) notes that universities are applying several models of course ownership. The first assumes that the faculty member owns the work and can assign ownership to the institution or grant the institution a nonexclusive license to use the work. The institution and the faculty member who created the course share the profits. The second model assumes ownership by the institution as work for hire. In this case, the faculty member may be given royalties and a license to use the materials elsewhere. The third model assumes that the faculty member who creates the work is an independent contractor who has ownership of the work and can assign or license it as in the first model. Universities most often adopt the last two models.

A good governance policy addresses the need to establish agreements before course development on the use of intellectual property and of the revenues derived from the delivery of courses. Prior agreements that are fair to all concerned can help to alleviate the concerns that can exist when instructors feel that their material is being used unfairly. Such agreements may include royalties to faculty who develop courses, inclusion of the delivery of courses into the standard teaching load rather than treating them as an overload, and revenue sharing once the courses have been delivered. There are no hard-and-fast answers yet, and few cases that address this issue are being tried in the courts. However, the potential for the development of case law in this area exists if universities and their faculties are not proactive about how materials will be developed and used. Once again, good planning is the key.

## Student Retention

Another important component of the new economics of distance learning, and one that seems to be consistently overlooked or ignored in both the planning and the delivery of distance learning courses, is the student. Many plans and policies do not address students, leading to concerns about attracting students to online programs and, more important, retaining them once they enroll. Phipps and Merisotis (1999) noted that "a large majority of institutions believe it somewhat or very important that their distance education offerings increase access to new audiences and increase enrollments" (p. 2). However, research that has sought to follow up on the impact of distance education on access, enrollments, and program costs does not conclusively show that if an institution offers distance education courses and programs, then enrollment will increase, although enrollment in online courses and programs has far exceeded campus-based enrollments (Allen & Seaman, 2011). Instead, students have simply come to expect that these offerings will be in place for them and are surprised when they are not. Complicating this picture is the fact that once students enroll in distance learning courses, the likelihood that they will complete courses and stay enrolled in online programs is lower than in on-campus courses.

Some research is available to help institutions understand why online students drop out more frequently. Reasons generally given for this relate to the demographics of the students who enroll, expecting that they tend to be older working adults with family obligations. The life situations that drew them to distance learning programs may also interfere with their ability to complete them. In general adult learners are twice as likely to drop out of online courses primarily because of professional constraints, personal issues, and institutional factors (McGivney, 2004). Park and Hee (2009), however, determined that demographics do not have an impact on persistence in online courses. Instead, they found that external factors as well as relevance of the course to the student's job or career plans were significant factors in persistence. Moore and Fetzner (2009) found that students persist in online courses and programs where good support is provided to both instructors and students and courses are designed using good learning effectiveness strategies.

What cannot be ignored, however, is that institutions often create technology plans without exploring their market or asking students what they want or need in an online program. Institutions tend to build online courses and programs based on instructor, institutional, or department needs and interests rather than what students need or want.

The traditional paradigm of education on college campuses is faculty centered. As we have argued, in order for online courses to be successful, the faculty-centered focus needs to change to a learner-centered one. The same is true when developing a plan for the implementation of technology into teaching and the construction of online programs: in order to be successful, plans, courses, and programs must be learner focused. To accomplish this goal, institutions need to engage in a planning process that includes good market research to answer these questions: Who are our students? Where are they located? What are their academic needs? What do they want in their education? How can we meet those needs?

Online courses and programs will not "save" academic institutions. However, technology in education makes sense when it is used to reach the increasingly nontraditional student body we now see in institutions of higher education and to meet their learning needs and objectives—needs and objectives that are different from the students institutions have traditionally taught. Online courses and programs also make sense to serve the needs of on-campus students who seek flexibility in their programs of study and demand up-to-date approaches to teaching and learning. Many of them have experienced online courses in their high schools and expect them to be available when they move on to colleges or universities.

## Some Last Thoughts on Administrative Issues and Concerns

Bates (2000) sums up the issues in the administrative arena well: "Large investment in technology-based teaching can be justified only if it leads to significant changes in the ways we teach" (p. 119). As we have been stressing, using technology to replicate the traditional face-to-face classroom is a waste of time, energy, and money. Technology should be used as a vehicle to assist institutions and their faculties in reaching students who might not otherwise be reached because of distance or learning style. It is also a vehicle to assist instructors in achieving learning objectives in new ways.

The introduction of technology to teaching is creating cultural changes in academic institutions that we cannot deny. Faculty and administrators alike are beginning to learn that the development of online courses cannot be accomplished by one person in isolation. It takes a team of committed professionals to develop high-quality online courses and programs. As a result, institutions can no longer do business as usual and must reexamine the ways in which faculty and administrators interact. Bates and Sangrà (2011) state that successful technology integration helps to increase the competitiveness of an institution in today's educational marketplace by allowing more flexible access to learning, better outcomes, better-prepared graduates, and higher-quality teaching and administrative services. Given these potential results, investment in good collaborative planning for technology integration seems worth it.

In the next chapter, we take another look at technology currently in use, particularly as it pertains to the planning process. Our focus is the development of a sound technological infrastructure designed to support the changes we are describing.

---

## TIPS FOR ADMINISTRATORS FOR CREATING A TECHNOLOGICAL INFRASTRUCTURE

- Create an inclusive team or committee to develop policies and plans for the institution regarding online courses and programs.
- Make incentives available to instructors for course development, including release time, reduced teaching load, and grants.
- Provide adequate technical support and training to instructors and students. Instructors not only need to know how to use the technology but also need to be able to explore new teaching methods and techniques. Students need to understand the technology in use and how to learn in the online environment.
- Reconsider agreements with faculty to include provisions related to the use of intellectual property that are fair and equitable for all concerned.
- Limit enrollments in online courses. If enrollments are to be high, provide graders, readers, or teaching assistants to reduce the burden on the instructor and allow the students greater access to the instructor.
- Work toward the development of a shared vision and strategic plan around the use of technology in teaching and learning. Plans should be fluid enough to allow inclusion of technological developments as they occur and not just limited to what is available at the time the plan is conceived.

---

CHAPTER FOUR

# THE TOOLS OF ONLINE TEACHING

Technology has changed dramatically since we wrote the first edition of this book and continues to do so at a rapid pace. The course management systems that were newly developing in 2001 have become the foundation on which most online courses are built now. However, that too is changing. Mobile technology is creating a stronghold in education and is being used in both face-to-face and online courses. Tablets such as the iPad and others are beginning to replace notebook and desktop computers. Many colleges and universities have invested in iPads, distributing them to new students and conducting iPad projects, a topic we discuss later in this chapter. Open source course management systems, which have been developed and are supported by communities of users, are quickly replacing the commercial course management systems that have ruled the online education world over the past decade.

Regardless, technology is not the focus of the online course and remains merely the vehicle for course delivery. The late Don Foshee, first president of the Texas Distance Learning Association, remarked in 1999 that the use of technology is only as good as the people and content behind it. He offered some lessons learned from the evolution of technology in education at that time, noting, "Good teaching is good teaching and bad teaching is even worse in a technology-based environment" (p. 26). And he stated what we cannot emphasize enough: nothing substitutes for good planning. Planning should cover the technology to be used, as well as programs to be developed and courses to be taught. These thoughts were true in 1999 and remain true today: technology is the vehicle, not the driver, of the online course.

In this chapter, we look at how technology is being used in education now, noting with caution that with the rapid development of both hardware and software applications, what we say today may not be true even by the time this book is published. We will, however, discuss how to work within the strengths and limitations of the technology available to us, thus assisting instructors in the planning process for their online courses and providing some suggestions for evaluating their technology needs. In addition, we explore ways in which online courses and programs can be developed and delivered when the institution has limited financial resources, which is so much easier today due to the availability of applications on the Internet and the use of mobile technology. We pay special attention to mobile technology: how it is affecting our work and how it can be effectively used for online teaching.

## Technology in the Twenty-First Century

In 1999 the National Center for Educational Statistics (NCES) published its first report (no longer available) that discussed the ways in which distance learning technology had advanced and changed. The report's authors noted that the key features of the technology in use were the increased level of interactivity between students and faculty, with the resulting ability to exchange greater amounts of information, greater variety in the types of information that could be exchanged, and significantly shorter amounts of time required for information exchange to occur. The types of online technology to which they were referring included e-mail, chat sessions, electronic bulletin boards, video, CD-ROM, audioconferencing, and desktop videoconferencing. The report cautioned that the use of advanced technologies did not necessarily mean better implementation of distance learning programs. Technology needs vary with instructional and learner needs. In other words, just because various technologies are available does not mean that they need to be used in the delivery of a course. One course may be delivered using only discussion boards, whereas another might make good use of chat or a whiteboard. There have been several updates to the NCES reports since 1999, many of which have focused on learning effectiveness through the use of technology and the degree to which technology is being integrated into teaching.

A survey conducted by Allen and Seaman (2007) revealed that more than two-thirds of forty-three hundred higher education institutions in the United States are offering some form of online education. In addition, 69 percent of traditional and nontraditional universities believe that student demand for online courses will continue to grow. As of 2007, 83 percent of the institutions already offering online courses expected their enrollments in these courses to continue to increase. The primary reasons cited for offering online courses and degrees is to improve student access and increase student completion rates (Allen & Seaman, 2007). Given constituent pressures on institutions in both of these areas, it is clear that online instruction will continue to expand.

A similar trend is happening in the K–12 sector. There are now online programs at the high school level in every state, and online programs are also being offered in every province in Canada. These programs especially serve students living in rural areas or provide access to courses no longer being offered by school districts due to budget cuts. Online education in K–12, also called virtual schooling, is growing at about 30 percent annually (North American Council for Online Learning, 2007). The North American Council for Online Learning and the National Education Association (n.d.) have both developed standards for quality teaching online and are advocating for states to create online teaching credentials.

A 2007 survey of K–12 teachers, administrators, and professional development trainers showed the disparity between the amount of preparation teachers receive to teach online and their preparation for other teaching endeavors. The variance in time devoted ranged from 0 hours to 270 hours annually. In addition, 62 percent of teachers reported having no training prior to teaching online (Rice & Dawley, 2007). Credentialing programs in all states require some competency in computer-assisted instruction, but no state has a credential specifically for online teaching.

Based on this level of demand, it is clear that the need for experienced faculty to teach these classes is very large and that institutions need to develop plans for recruiting, hiring, training, developing, and supporting online faculty (Green, Alejandro, & Brown, 2009). Training and development of faculty to teach online should include both discussion of the tools available to them, along with pedagogical strategy for their use.

Clearly the technology tools available to instructors to create and increase interactivity in online courses are varied and continue to be developed. As we noted earlier, the continuum of technology use in courses is no longer from zero to fully offered using technology; technological tools are generally employed in all courses taught today at all levels. Manning and Johnson (2011) note that the use of technology in education is a process by which we use those tools to address an educational problem. The tools, then, serve the function of supporting learning. Where we once made distinctions between the tools contained within course management systems and those we might encounter on the Web or elsewhere, those distinctions have now blurred. Manning and Johnson note that the proliferation of what are known as Web 2.0 tools (social media, wikis, blogs, and the like, all of which we discuss later) and the ability to link those to a course management system or use them to create the course outside of a course management system have moved us from what was a static approach to course development to a place where instructors can collaborate with students to share authorship for courses.

Again, however, we cannot stress enough that the availability of these tools does not dictate their use. Given that the tools are designed to support learning and address educational problems, instructors should design courses with learning outcomes and objectives in mind, building learning activities that allow students to reach those objectives using technology. The tools used should be chosen to match the outcomes and objectives and serve as a vehicle for reaching them.

We now look specifically at some of those tools—Web 2.0 technologies and mobile technologies—and along the way discuss how matching these tools to outcomes might be effectively done.

## Matching the Technology to the Course

The selection of distance learning technologies should involve the assessment of course content, learning outcomes, and interaction needs. No one technology is optimum for achieving all learning objectives, and conversely, instructors will rarely have the latitude to integrate all technologies into a course. Olcott (1999) provided what he called the five I's of effective distance teaching: interaction, introspection, innovation, integration, and information. They continue to be good hallmarks of ways in which to choose appropriate technologies to use in online or hybrid courses:

- *Interaction* refers not only to the communication that should occur between the student and the instructor and the student with other students but also the interaction between the student and the content of the course. Thus, asynchronous and synchronous communications, as well as the presentation of print materials and links to the Internet, form the technology needs of interaction.

- *Introspection* is the interpretation, revision, and demonstrated understanding of concepts. Discussion boards, graphics, and even audio and video can be effective technologies to encourage introspection.
- *Innovation* refers to the ability of instructors to experiment with technologies to address various learning styles and learning cycles students will go through during a course. Thus, combinations of audio, video, synchronous, and asynchronous discussion can provide various opportunities for students to learn. As important as using various technologies is implementing various modes of assessment of student work in a course. Reliance on one means of assessment, such as tests and quizzes, may not align well with the outcomes the instructor is hoping students will achieve (Palloff & Pratt, 2009). Instructors may even choose to offer students choices of ways in which they will be assessed, furthering the goal of student empowerment in the learning process.
- *Integration* reflects the integration of facts, concepts, theories, and practical application of knowledge. Using case studies, simulation exercises, the production of audio, video, or graphic presentations, and role-play can create a setting in which integration can occur. These collaborative activities can easily be accomplished in an asynchronous environment, and Web 2.0 applications and mobile technology can support their development.
- *Information* refers to the knowledge and understanding that is a prerequisite for students to move to the next level of learning. Instructors have traditionally thought of the transfer of information that occurs in a lecture. However, reliance on lecture in the online environment tends to reduce the dynamic capacity of an online course, while collaboration and interaction can effectively enhance it (Palloff & Pratt, 2004).

This discussion should illustrate that any form or forms of technology can be used to deliver a course. What is more critical to a successful online course is good learner-centered teaching. Consequently, the first consideration when choosing the forms of technology to be used in a course should be the outcomes to be achieved as well as the technology that students commonly use. All else should flow from there. In many cases, learning outcomes can be achieved with the least complex technology. This also allows the course to be accessed by the majority of users with little difficulty.

Access and accessibility continue to be important considerations in the development and delivery of a course, and mobile technology is helping to close the digital divide: students might not have computers at home or in their dorm rooms, but they are likely to own a cell phone. We now turn our attention to the impact and use of mobile technology in teaching and learning and how they are helping to increase access.

---

## Using Mobile Technology to Empower Student Learning

Cell phones are an integral part of the genre commonly known as mobile technology, which encompasses cell phones, personal digital assistants (PDA), iPod Touches, iPads, and numerous other devices. Devices of this nature have connectivity that allows access of information and both synchronous and asynchronous communication (Clough, Jones, McAndrew, & Scanlon, 2008; Traxler, 2010). We exclude laptops from the mobile device category because of issues of weight and battery life.

Mobile technology has "nearly infinite possibilities for education, networking, and personal productivity" (Lunsford, 2010, p. 66). Clough et al. (2008) stated, "With such near-ubiquitous market penetration, mobile devices have attracted the attention of researchers and educators through their potential both as learning tools that support and enhance the learning experience and as a disruptive device with the potential to interrupt and distract" (p. 359).

The near ubiquitous access of these mobile technologies may be the cause of a shift in thinking among educators in higher education, bringing distance or e-learning to prominence because of the technology's "ability to create and sustain communities of learners" (Garrison, 2011, p. 1). Mobile devices extend learning beyond the traditional classroom setting, whether physical or digital. The communication and data capabilities of the devices traditional classroom boundaries and move the classroom outside the norms of space and time (El-Hussein & Cronje, 2010; Yeonjeong, 2011).

### Mobile Technology in Higher Education

Although many in higher education see mobile technology as a disruptive influence, one that hinders education rather than enhancing it, mobile technology is quietly gaining a place among distance educators as an effective tool for bringing diverse communities of students together (Garrison, 2011; El-Hussein & Cronje, 2010). Palloff and Pratt (2007) indicate that an essential element of community building is social presence, defined as "the person we become when we are online and how we express that person in virtual space" (p. 28). Mobile devices allow individuals to post, comment on, and share information—in other words, to expand their social presence—regardless of geographical location or time (Engel & Green, 2011). With these technologies, individuals can contribute to their online presence at any given moment. In fact, mobile devices can go so far as to grant a "sense of continuous availability" (Koole, McQuilkin, & Ally, 2010, p. 61) to students in online communities.

In addition to opening new avenues of communication and strengthening social presence, the nature of distance in the online classroom is negated by the use of mobile technology, which can "amplify the flexibility of distance and online learning, reducing the significance of geographic location, all the while increasing that of contextuality"(Koole et al., 2010, p. 60).

### Contexts of Mobile Learning

Frohberg (2006) attempted to place mobile applications according to the learning context in which they are used—the free context, formalized context, digital context, and informal context. By doing so, he presented a model that others could build on and use as new applications are developed. In a free context application, context is not relevant for the learning activity. In other words, environmental and situational elements do not affect the learning activity. Free context applications include administrative applications, course management applications, calculators, dictionaries, and similar applications.

Frohberg (2006) defined the formalized context for mobile applications as "learning within a well-defined curriculum, being offered by some educational establishment and led by some central actor, i.e. a teacher, tutor, moderator, and the like" (p. 3). The relevant, contextual environment is the classroom, either traditional or virtual (Frohberg, 2006). This could include the use of an audience response application, like polleverwhere.com, for gathering data from students in the online environment. In addition, social networking tools like Twitter could be used in a formalized context for communication and community building. Applications like Twitter can give the learning community insights into the thinking of the community at a particular moment in time (Engel & Green, 2011).

*(continued)*

### Contexts of Mobile Learning

The use of mobile technology in the digital learning context is purely screen based and fully designed as an educational tool. Simulations and microworlds fit this context and are constructivist in design (Frohberg, 2006; Naismith, Lonsdale, Vavoula, & Sharples, 2005; Patten, Arnedillo Sánchez, & Tangney, 2006). "Educational microworlds allow learners to construct their own knowledge through experimentation in constrained models of real world domains" (Patten et al., 2006, p. 298).

Not many of these types of simulations exist yet due to the limitations of screen size and memory of the devices (Patten et al., 2006). However, new applications like geocaching and foursquare allow individuals and groups to become part of the simulation.

Elements of the digital context can flow over into the physical context as well. When simulations in the digital context break into the physical realm, they begin to have an impact on students in a new way, a way that becomes physical learning. This is a leading component of mobile learning where "the role of mobile technology is to enrich the physical environment in innovative ways" (Frohberg, 2006).

### Benefits of Mobile Learning

Informal learning, that is, learning outside the classroom, is foundational to true lifelong learning (Frohberg, 2006). Mobile technology is one bridge that can aid individuals in becoming informal, and thus lifelong, learners. Mobile technology "can be used within formal and informal learning contexts and therefore are a tool which may bridge life-wide and lifelong learning" (Beddall-Hill & Raper, 2010).

Because mobile technology is blended into people's everyday lives, it is the ultimate support for informal learning because it can be used at any moment, regardless of location and time (Naismith et al., 2005). The very mobility of mobile technology allows learners to roam and explore concepts freely without constraint—to manage information wherever they are. Newer applications on smart phones allow students to search the Web based on a picture taken on their phones. Other applications use augmented reality (a live direct or indirect view of a physical object or space that is augmented by a computer) to share information about a location or object. "Mobile technology has a high potential to support this management function in mobile settings, leaving a much higher flexibility, spontaneity, and ad-hoc adaptability than analog settings" (Frohberg, 2006).

Despite the benefits of using mobile technology in appropriate contexts, higher education institutions, like their secondary counterparts, have yet to embrace mobile technology as an essential part of pedagogical practice (El-Hussein & Cronje, 2010). A number of reasons exist for this. Ubiquity is one driving element for the lack of adoption of mobile technology (Engel & Green, 2011). The majority of college-age individuals do own a cell phone, if not a smart phone. Furthermore, a Pew poll indicates that minorities are even more likely to use the data and communicative applications of smart phones than nonminorities are (Smith, 2010). Another drawback of mobile technology is interactivity and screen size; market forces have addressed these issues. With the advent of tablets, screen size and usability of lightweight mobile technology have increased to a more usable size (Yeonjeong, 2011).

Beyond these physical limitations, others claim that safety and academic integrity issues brought about by mobile technology are too important to ignore; therefore, they say, the technology should not be used as part of pedagogy (Engel & Green, 2011). We agree that these issues are important and should be addressed. However, they should not be reasons to keep mobile technology out of instructional practice. Institutions should create guidelines governing the use of mobile technology that supports their pedagogical use while giving guidance with how to deal with violators of academic integrity and student safety rules.

Mobile technology is not a fad or trend of technology that will eventually go away: "Mobile learning is the harbinger of the future of learning" (Keegan, 2002). Mobile technology has the potential to change learning and teaching as we have known it. The use of this technology can empower students to become true informal learners that carry that knowledge through a life time of practice. Higher education stands on the edge of a great precipice of change—change brought about by mobile technology.[1]

---

[1] George Engel, State University at Albany and Clarkstown High School South, contributed this box.

# What Are Web 2.0 Technologies?

*Web 2.0* refers to the second generation of the World Wide Web, offering higher levels of user interaction and collaboration. Much of Web 2.0 emerged from the desire of young people for self-expression through creation of content posted on the Web, easy communication with peers, and ways to stay connected to friends. However, interest in and engagement with Web 2.0 technologies is no longer relegated to younger people or those who are technologically savvy. Adults are now using Web 2.0 technologies in greater numbers, and businesses are making use of these technologies for marketing purposes and to connect and communicate more effectively with consumers.

Web 2.0 tools range from those that allow personal expression to those that support community building. Educational applications of Web 2.0 technologies are increasing rapidly.

## Common Forms of Web 2.0 Technologies

Here we examine some of the more common forms of Web 2.0 technology currently being integrated into online courses, with examples of how they are being used.

***Blogs*** Blogs (Web logs) are online journals maintained by individuals, which are generally commentaries on particular topics. They are being incorporated into online courses in several ways. Instructors are encouraging students to set up blogs both inside and outside courses in order to serve as a journal of their reflections on the course and, in the case of journalism or writing courses, to experience the "blogosphere" that has become an integral part of journalism today.

Some instructors are using blogs as a means to conduct online courses, having students post assignments in the form of blogs, and asking students as well as experts in the field to comment on the blog postings. Instructors are also using blogs as a substitute for lecturing in that they allow instructors to reflect on course material and bring in additional perspectives.

***Learner-Generated Context*** Also known as *collective intelligence*, learner-generated context (LGC) is a system that collects the expertise of a group rather than an individual to make decisions and generate knowledge and can include wikis (defined separately), collaboratively generated digital content (such as through YouTube video content and Flickr graphic content), learning spaces, approaches to learning designed collaboratively by learners, and shared databases.

Learner-generated context is a collection of tools, information, and research conducted by others gathered by a group of learners to create a learning space that meets their needs. The interdisciplinary London Research Group is studying this form of technology and has defined it as "a context created by people interacting together with a common, self-defined or negotiated learning goal. The key aspect of learner generated contexts is that they are generated through the enterprise of those who would previously have been consumers in a context created for them" (Lukin et al., 2007, p. 91). LGC can include the development of wikis, Google Docs, YouTube video content, Flickr, and other digital technologies. It is being used as adjunct material to an online course, but we have not yet encountered a full course developed and delivered through LGC, although this is the goal of those studying this form of technology.

The downside to the use of LGC is that the instructor has limited control of the direction in which learners might go. The upside, as Lukin et al. (2007) noted, is that LGC breaks out of the boundaries of traditional pedagogy and significantly boosts collaboration among students.

**Wikis**  Wikis are systems that allow the creation and publishing of a web page or website. Wikipedia, is the most well known, but many other wiki sites exist. Anyone with access or permission can contribute to or edit a wiki.

The use of wikis is becoming increasingly popular in online courses, and the ability to create them is now built into many course management systems, although those wikis are not as robust as wiki applications found on the Web, which allow the creation of user accounts for the purpose of developing wikis. Students working on wiki assignments collaborate on gathering information and building a web page where that information is displayed. Students can add to or edit content if they have permission to do so.

Small groups in an online course can be working on multiple wikis simultaneously and can share the final products with the other groups, the instructor, or outside experts. Wikis can easily be added to portfolios for assessment and documentation of student work. Because of the ability to edit at will, wikis usually contain an accessible revision history that indicates the author of the edits. Due to this editing function, however, students need to develop "wiki etiquette" so as to keep collaboration primary and avoid possible conflict as content is deleted or edited.

**Podcasts**  Podcasts are audio or video recordings posted in an online course or on the Web that can be downloaded and played on a computer or an MP3 player.

Podcasting is another form of Web 2.0 technology that has gained significant popularity in online courses due to the ease of creation, download, and use. Podcasts are generally used for the delivery of just-in-time lecture content from the instructor and can be added to a course by file attachment, posting in iTunes or on YouTube in the case of video, or through an RSS feed, which we discuss in the next section. Given the availability of open source software for the creation of podcasts (Audacity) and vodcasts (iMovie, Windows Movie Maker, Jumpcut) and the ease with which the final products can be made available, students can also create podcasts and vodcasts alone or collaboratively to add content to courses or complete assignments.

**RSS** RSS (Really Simple Syndication) feeds refer to real-time information, usually in the form of news, blogs, or podcasts, that can be streamed to a website in real time.

Almost all course management systems allow the inclusion of RSS feeds. Instructors can choose to include them from outside sources that are relevant to course content or create feeds from blogs or any other updated content, such as podcasts as they are created. Students can also subscribe to RSS feeds on mobile devices. The feeds can help keep students abreast of new developments as they occur and students connected to the instructor and the class.

**Social Networking** Social networking sites such as MySpace and Facebook allow people to connect with a select group of people around personal or professional interests. MySpace is generally considered a place where younger people (mostly in high school) meet, while Facebook appeals more to college students and adults.

As of September 2012, it was estimated that over 937 million people worldwide were subscribed to Facebook (Internet World Stats, 2012) and 34 million young people were subscribed to MySpace (Social Compare, 2012). Users of social networks establish a list of "friends" with whom they communicate, share information about their lives, and in general connect socially and personally. Many academics are researching the impact of social networks, and some instructors are using social networks as a means by which to deliver online courses. Embedded within Facebook, for example, are applications such as wikis and groupware, useful for creating study groups that allow posting notes and sharing documents. Asynchronous discussion and the posting of files, photos, and other media are all possible with Facebook. Due to privacy concerns on Facebook, however, many instructors are turning to newer applications offered by Google and others, where membership can be restricted.

**Twitter** Twitter is a form of a social networking space that allows short (140 character) microblog entries known as "tweets." Tweets are delivered instantly to people who have signed up to "follow" a person on Twitter.

Known as a form of social networking, Twitter users, like Facebook and MySpace users, declare the list of people they choose to follow. Unlike Facebook or MySpace, where postings are limited to an identified group of friends, postings to Twitter (known as tweets) can be read by any Twitter user who chooses to follow a particular person. Although replies to Tweets are possible, this does not commonly occur (Angwin, 2009). A study of Twitter (Huberman, Romero, & Wu, 2009) concluded that Twitter users have a very small number of "friends" compared to the number of followers and followees they may have.

Twitter at this juncture is not being widely used in online teaching. However, some instructors are using it to communicate bits of information to students, including websites to visit, experts to follow, and what the instructor is currently reading or recommends for reading (Perez, 2009).

**Skype** Skype is an Internet-based phone service that also can be used for conference calling, document sharing, and text messaging. It is becoming a popular online teaching tool for teaching a variety of content areas and particularly in the teaching of languages where voice contact is important.

The ability to use Skype for voice, video, and chat helps instructors and students alike to meet a number of communication needs. When students are located all over the globe, Skype can make both individual and conference calling easy and carries no expense, a significant benefit. Skype also allows file transfers, file sharing, and whiteboarding.

**Second Life** Second Life (SL) is a virtual world in which users interact in real time through the use of avatars, which are graphical representations of themselves. It has its own economy and the ability to buy land; many universities own land in SL and are using it to deliver distance learning programs.

Second Life has not achieved the promise in online teaching that was initially predicted. There is a learning curve involved, and several orientation programs to Second Life, along with how to use it in teaching, have emerged to address this challenge. Users create avatars and interact in real time. Because classes are conducted in the virtual world and it is possible for students to speak at any time (versus threaded discussions, which occur in an asynchronous online course), instructors note that a new set of classroom norms needs to be developed to avoid chaos (Nesson, 2007). However, because SL is a virtual world in which instructors and students have physical representation, users believe that it helps to create a sense of community in an online class. The use of avatars has also raised questions about this, given that students can represent themselves as anything from human, to animal, to fantasy creatures. Additional concerns relate to the lack of security in SL: given that this is a virtual world that was not created for academic purposes, students can wander into less-than-desirable areas, creating possible liability issues for academic institutions.

## Using Web 2.0 Tools in Online Courses

As with any other form of technology, Web 2.0 technologies have both positives and negatives associated with their use. Some examples of concerns include the following:

- Because these technologies are available in the public domain for the most part, issues of copyright may emerge. Users of Facebook, for example, sign waivers acknowledging that Facebook owns the copyright to materials on the site.
- Another concern relative to the public nature of sites like Facebook and Second Life is that given that they are primarily social in nature, students can "wander" into areas that may be questionable. This raises possible liability issues for universities.
- Because materials are created on and posted to another site, there may be concerns about archiving and loss of content.
- Privacy concerns emerge in the use of social networking sites and Second Life.
- The use of social networking sites also blurs the lines of formality: some instructors object to being "friended" by their students.
- Instructors fear the loss of control that accompanies the collaborative and more social nature of Web 2.0 technologies and are discovering the need to develop new norms for their use.

These concerns must be addressed when using Web 2.0 sources for the creation of community or to extend the reach of an online course. The positive aspects of using these forms of technology, however, may outweigh the negatives. They do have the ability to support the development of an online community, thus contributing to more effective collaboration among students (Palloff & Pratt, 2004). Relying on any one of them to accomplish that task is a bit shortsighted; however, the inclusion of a variety of means by which community is developed in an online course can facilitate this task by increasing the means and amount of communication possible between students as well as between students and instructor. The sense of community can be significantly deepened, thus supporting the ability to collaborate online.

Web 2.0 technologies designed to connect people to one another also serve to increase the sense of social presence in an online course through these various forms of communication. The use of Web 2.0 technologies can help to reduce the isolation and distance that students often feel in an online course and thus are worthy of exploration.

## Choosing Technology Wisely

Despite the proliferation of mobile technology and Web 2.0 applications, instructors are required to use the course management system that their academic institution has chosen to deliver online courses or components of their face-to-face courses. However, often they do have the freedom to augment that system with other technologies, such as the mobile technologies or the Web 2.0 technologies we just discussed. How, then, can an instructor make good choices about what to use, given the wide array of what is available?

Manning and Johnson (2011) suggest some broad considerations to aid in these decisions and suggest that these elements be applied to any form of technology being considered for an online course:

- *The educational problem the tool is designed to address and solve.* Significant analysis should be devoted to this decision lest the tool end up creating rather than solving an educational problem.
- *The platform on which the course will be offered.* Is this a tool that will supplement a course management system, augment traditional classroom instruction, or be used with a hybrid approach?
- *What the tool is best used for.* Will it help meet the stated outcomes of the course?
- *The cost.* Will the cost be borne by the institution or the students themselves? Keep in mind that cost also includes staff time required to support the use of the tool.

- *The accessibility* of *the tool.* Aspects of accessibility include the various learning needs of students, technical competence, and the availability of the technology for students. In other words, do students need to acquire or download software in order to use the tool effectively? Is it easily accessed on the Web? Can students with disabilities, who may also be using assistive technologies such as screen readers, easily use it?

Course management systems have been grappling with these issues and working to make their systems accessible. When instructors go outside the course management system, they need to address these same issues themselves:

- What special technical equipment or technical requirements need to be addressed in order to use the tool, and what level of technical expertise, competencies, or skills will be needed to use it? If special equipment is required or students need a high level of competency to use the tool, the instructor must be prepared to offer technical assistance to students or have support staff available to provide the needed help. Manning and Johnson (2011) suggest that knowing the technical competence of students before the course even begins allows the instructor to avoid possible problems through the creation of tutorials or other training to support students in their use of the tool.
- Another evaluation concern for technical tools is whether its use is synchronous versus asynchronous. The use of synchronous tools, where students meet together to use the tool in real time, requires significantly more planning and facilitation than does the use of asynchronous tools, where students can use them at any time and from any place.
- When new technologies are used in a class, they tend to come with new vocabulary. Manning and Johnson (2011) note the need for instructors to learn the vocabulary associated with the tools in use so as to educate students to that vocabulary. Speaking the same language is important when introducing technological tools into an online or hybrid class.

A final and important consideration in choosing technology for online or hybrid courses is ensuring a balance between the tools in use and the outcomes for the course. It's enticing to incorporate all of the new technologies into a course to increase the level of engagement and excitement that they can potentially generate. Too many bells and whistles, however, can overwhelm and confuse students. An important lesson is to choose only the technology that serves learning objectives. Anything beyond that can create more problems than it solves.

## When the Technology Is a Problem

If an instructor is put in the position of using technology that was chosen by the institution and is not serving learning objectives well, creativity is the key. Supplementing it with the use of tools available outside the course management system may be appropriate in these cases. It is also important to respond to student concerns about the use of that technology without allowing the concerns to become the focus of the course. Setting up a discussion forum where students can work together on strategies for learning despite the shortcomings of the technology can let students be heard while keeping the focus on learning.

Faculty collaboration is critical to solving these problems at the institutional level. Communicating with one another about the problems experienced and brainstorming ways to solve those problems helps all instructors learn about the technology in use while supporting their students. It is important to convey concerns to administrators as well. It may not be possible to change the technology, but it may be possible to discuss the concerns with the software developer so that future releases can include modifications that are responsive to stakeholder needs.

## Evaluating Technology

Including faculty in the selection process of technology for the institution is critical. If at all possible, it is helpful to include students in the process as well. Although these appear to be obvious conclusions, often faculty and students, the prime users of the technology selected, are overlooked in the evaluation and selection process. Often technology-based decisions are made by technical personnel who base their decision on personal use, attendance at vendor-sponsored workshops, reading about it in trade publications, or having used other products from the same vendor or at other institutions. Clearly the ability of technical personnel to support the chosen technology should be one of the criteria used to evaluate what the institution adopts. However, this should not be the only means by which the decision is made. Technical personnel should be only one voice in the decision-making process; the faculty and students who are the users of the technology should hold the majority vote.

Because each institution has its own needs, requirements, and resources available—all factors in the choice of technology—there can be no standards for selection that cut across all situations. However, some common elements need to be considered regardless of the specific needs of the institution, its faculty, and students. Lawrence Tomei (1999) divided the common elements into three broad categories: use of technology, infrastructure, and instructional strategy. We consider each category and provide some questions to assist in establishing strategies for technology selection.

## Use of Technology

Purchasing computers and software without a sense of how they will be used either in or to support the work of the classroom is shortsighted. We recently consulted to an institution that purchased iPads for all of its faculty and students. Although this sounded like an exciting move, when we asked them how they intended to use them, they admitted that they had no idea. They figured that they'd get to that once everyone had the iPads in hand. Clearly not much planning went into the purchase, and it is likely that only confusion will result.

Here are some questions to consider regarding the use of technology:

- How do we envision using the technology? Will we consider it to be a support to the face-to-face classroom, will it be used to deliver classes and programs, or both?
- How will the technology meet the instructional needs in our institution?
- What do we see as the implications of the technology use in our institution?
- How extensive do we expect the use of the technology to be? Will its use be phased in, or will we move directly to offering full programs that require immediate implementation?

## Infrastructure

Many institutions embark on the delivery of online classes without first building a solid infrastructure to support the use of technology. The critical elements of the infrastructure are people, money, and resources, as illustrated in figure 4.1. The figure demonstrates the number of influences and even pressures that converge in the decision-making process. Accounting for all of the elements helps to support a solid infrastructure.

The people who should be considered while the infrastructure is being built are faculty, students, administrators, instructional designers (if the institution uses them), technology coordinators, and support staff.

## FIGURE 4.1   THE TECHNOLOGY INFRASTRUCTURE

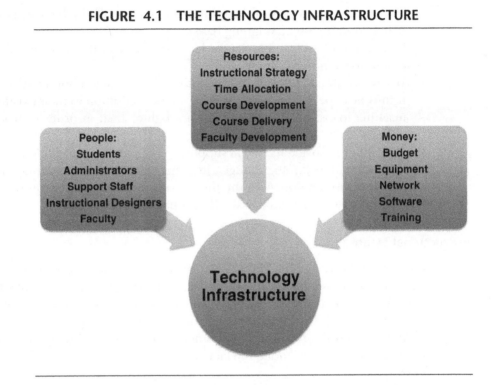

Simply identifying the stakeholders in the technology infrastructure is not enough, however. The training needs of each are also an important element here. The people and their training needs have a direct impact on the budget, or the money component, of the technology infrastructure. In addition to training expenses, budgetary concerns should include hardware and software purchases and upgrades, technical support and assistance, and incentives for faculty to develop online courses. The resources component of the infrastructure includes the allocation of time and effort necessary to make the use of technology viable. Release time for course development and delivery, and time for faculty and staff development, are important elements of the resources component. Questions to consider when building a technology infrastructure include these:

- How many faculty are interested in and ready to teach online classes?
- How many faculty will we need to train so that they can begin to develop and teach online classes? What levels of training do we need to provide for users (from novice to experienced)?

- How do we intend to provide training for faculty? What will it cost us to deliver training on an ongoing basis?
- What are student training needs? How will we meet them? What will it cost us to train our students?
- Will we be able to offer faculty incentives for course development? Will faculty be expected to teach online courses in addition to their existing teaching loads, or will they be given a lighter load in order to teach online?
- How will we provide technical support to both faculty and students?
- What kind of technology budget, in terms of both money and time, can we expect to develop? Will the institution support an expenditure for technology on an annual basis? If so, what will it look like?

## Instructional Strategy

As we have been emphasizing, decisions about curricular direction and learning objectives must precede those about the use of technology in teaching and learning. If hardware and software are selected without a good sense of the learning outcomes the institution is hoping to achieve, there may be resistance to the implementation of technology in the curriculum and poor use among the faculty for both the creation and delivery of courses.

We once worked with a small college that had received an endowment from one of its alumni that was earmarked to purchase technology for the school. The school invested in smart classrooms, computer labs, and other forms of technology without involving faculty and students in those decisions. The outcome was faculty resistance to incorporating technology into the delivery of their courses, minimal to no use of the resources available, and frustration on the part of administrators. There had been no discussion of the learning objectives that the use of technology might serve, and resistance was the result.

Once decisions about learning outcomes are made, appropriate choices of technology as a tool for learning and a vehicle to achieve outcomes can then follow. Discussion of how students will be evaluated should also be included during consideration of instructional strategy, because that has some influence on the technology chosen. Questions to consider in the area of instructional strategy are these:

- What programmatic, course, and learning outcomes are we attempting to achieve?

- How will technology assist us in achieving these outcomes?
- How will students' learning outcomes be evaluated? How will the technology selected assist us in evaluating students and their achievement of learning outcomes?

Planning is clearly the key component to an evaluation of technology purchases. It often appears that the rapid movement in the direction of online learning has sacrificed a good comprehensive planning process. However, nothing substitutes for a well-thought-out, comprehensive, inclusive approach that offers time for input from all stakeholders. Many of the institutional concerns that have been expressed about faculty resistance to teaching online can be overcome with good planning processes that allow them to have a strong voice in the technology that they will be expected to use, training in how to use it, and support once they begin to teach with it. In addition, planning and budgeting for a strong infrastructure to support an online learning endeavor can help to sustain it. Cutting corners in these areas amounts to nothing less than self-sabotage and needless expenditure of money. Obtaining the money to invest in online distance learning is a concern for many institutions. Consequently, we now turn to a discussion of means by which institutions can offer online courses when money concerns are very real.

## When Money Is an Issue

Many smaller institutions are finding that the purchase and maintenance of hardware and software for online learning can be costly. Although the cost for a license to download and run course management software may not be exorbitant, particularly if open source options are chosen, technical personnel are needed to configure and install it and provide ongoing technical support. There are also some course delivery vendors that do not offer the purchase of a license but instead require that institutions pay a fee for course development and hosting in addition to paying per student. Many institutions lack the budget or ability to purchase servers and licenses for software, hire support personnel, or pay high fees to a company that is willing to host and maintain their courses. How, then, can these institutions offer online options to their students and do so within their means?

Luckily, many low-cost or no-cost options now exist. Termed "open source," these options are often free downloads or provide the ability to create and access courses on a server that is not hosted or supported by the institution.

Another solution is that many textbook companies are providing digital versions of their texts with accompanying materials and exercises, as well as communication tools. Access to the materials is generally by subscription or an added cost to textbook purchase. In addition, the Web 2.0 technologies we have discussed are options. In order to enter online teaching, then, money should not be considered an obstacle.

## Accessibility Is a Major Concern

In contrast to financial concerns, access and accessibility issues are significant in online learning. Access can be a problem for students who own an older computer or own no computer at all. In addition, accessibility can be an issue for people with disabilities. Many mistakenly believe that computer technology serves all people with disabilities equally well. However, the use of computers is predicated on the ability to read what is on a monitor and type on a keyboard, watch video presentations, listen to audio presentations, or participate in synchronous sessions that involve both audio and video. Not all disabled people are able to accomplish these tasks. Assistive technologies exist, such as screen readers and voice-activated software, that are designed to help people with disabilities of varying kinds to use technology and access the Internet. However, this does not ensure that a website or course site will be accessible unless it is constructed with accessibility in mind. "In reality, an increasingly sophisticated Internet, one rich with graphics, multimedia clips and compressed text, has meant a less accessible Internet for the disabled" (Strasburg, 2000, p. B3).

Coombs (2010) notes that instructors do not need to be familiar with assistive technologies, but they do need to be familiar with principles of universal design, which allows for the greatest level of use by all users. These principles, which can be found on the website for the Center for Universal Design, include these components:

- *Equitable use,* meaning that the design should be appealing to all users
- *Flexibility in use,* meaning that the design accommodates a range of preferences and abilities
- *Simplicity and intuitiveness,* allowing users with all levels of experience, knowledge, language skills, or concentrations to use the site

- *Perceptible information*, that is, communicating necessary information effectively and easily
- *Tolerance for error*, which minimizes the potential for accidental or unintended actions
- *Low physical effort*, allowing users to move about easily and with minimal effort or fatigue
- *Size and space for approach and use*, allowing all users access to all components regardless of their body size or degree of mobility as well as accommodating assistive technologies

Designing online courses with these principles in mind can provide the highest levels of access for all students, not only those with disabilities, and thus are simply considered good practice.

• • •

Again, it is important to note that technology needs to be treated as just another learning tool. It is only a vehicle to meet learning objectives. When viewed in this way, the needs of the learners are kept primary, which is as it should be in the learner-centered online classroom.

---

### TIPS FOR CHOOSING APPROPRIATE TECHNOLOGY FOR AN ONLINE COURSE

- Choose technology for an online course with the learner and learning outcomes in mind first. Instructor or staff needs should come second.
- Do not use a technological tool simply because it is available. Use tools only if they serve learning goals.
- Synchronous tools or the use of lecture capture is neither the best way to deliver content nor the worst. Use these options judiciously, cautiously, and with specific learning goals in mind so as to increase access for all.
- Evaluate and adopt a course management system based on programmatic and learning goals, not sales hype. The system should be easy to use, transparent, and predominantly in the control of the instructor or an instructional team.
- Be wary of systems that promise "total solutions." If the technology is not under the control of faculty and the institution, concerns ranging from the ownership of intellectual property to the flexibility of use can arise and become problematic.

*(continued)*

- Allow faculty to augment the course management system with Web 2.0 and mobile tools to increase flexibility and levels of student engagement and assist with achievement of learning objectives.
- Include faculty and, if possible, students in evaluating and choosing technology for the institution. This not only helps to increase a sense of ownership and buy-in but also is more likely to result in a choice that more closely aligns technology use with learning objectives.
- Above all, keep it simple. A simply constructed course site with minimal use of graphics, audio, and video is more likely to be accessible to all users and cause fewer problems in the long run.

PART TWO

# TEACHING AND LEARNING ONLINE

CHAPTER FIVE

# TRANSFORMING COURSES FOR THE ONLINE CLASSROOM

As we meet with faculty around the country, we frequently find that both novices and seasoned instructors struggle with transforming a course that has been taught for years in the face-to-face classroom into one that will work well online. As we have stated previously, simply putting lecture material online is not the answer. Although current lecture-capture applications make this easy to do, we caution against this practice because lecturing online is not the best way to engage students at a distance. Indeed, instead of looking for ways to convert a course that has been successful in the face-to-face classroom, instructors are better served by approaching a course to be taught online as if it were a course to be taught for the first time—which in essence it is—while drawing on content knowledge and best practices for online teaching. This allows a sense of freedom in the development of the course, without a tendency to adhere to tried-and-true methods that may not work online.

Another issue for faculty is how far to jump in when considering online delivery of a course. Is technology enhancement of a face-to-face course sufficient? Should a hybrid or blended model be considered when 30 percent or more of the course is offered online? Or should the instructor take the plunge and work to deliver the course completely online?

We have had faculty apologize to us for their use of a Web-enhanced approach; they were feeling guilty that they had not moved directly to fully online delivery. However, many authors suggest that the most successful and satisfying course outcomes are seen in classes that are small and combine face-to-face with online interaction. These classes, they say, combine the best of both worlds in terms of using both face-to-face and online delivery (Albrecht, 2006; Bonk & Graham, 2006; Bourne & Seaman, 2005; Garrison & Vaughan, 2008; Marquis, 2004). Consequently, an important consideration in the development of an online class should be the degree to which technology can and should be used in course delivery.

Boettcher and Conrad (1999) presented three questions that form the foundation of good instructional design: Who are my students? What do I want my students to know, to feel, or to be able to do as a result of this course or experience? and, Where, when, and with what resources will my students be learning? We have incorporated these questions into a series of questions to assist faculty in translating course material for online work:

- Who are my students?
- Is this a course that will successfully transfer to the online environment?
- How do I define learning in this content area, and what do I want to see as the learning outcomes for this class?
- What do I want to accomplish through this course? What do I want my students to know, feel, or be able to do as a result of this course or experience? What course content will support these objectives?
- What guidelines, rules, roles, and norms need to be established for course completion?
- How do I plan to deliver course material? What will be expected of students in the learning process? Will I offer a combination of online and face-to-face options?
- How comfortable do I as an instructor feel about collaborative learning assignments, personal interaction, promotion of knowledge in learners, and releasing control of the learning process?
- How do I want to organize the course site? How much flexibility will I have in doing so? Do I have the freedom to develop this course in whatever manner I choose?
- How will I assess student performance in this course?
- How will I address attendance requirements?

We discuss each of these questions as we go through the process of developing a course. The course we develop here is an undergraduate course in sociology that we have actually taught online: Systems Theories. We chose not to display the course in any particular course management system because the development of content should occur outside the system and then should be able to be imported into the system in use as long as it has these characteristics:

- *It is functional.* It offers the functions necessary to design and deliver an online course.
- *It is simple for both faculty and students to operate.* Once users learn the system, it becomes transparent to the course delivery process.
- *It is user friendly, visually appealing, and easy to navigate* (Palloff & Pratt, 2007).

In addition, it should contain the ability to build wikis (collaboratively developed web pages) and be robust enough to allow the inclusion of audio and video content. (In fact, most of the current course management tools have this ability.) It will likely also contain a chat function to conduct discussion in real time. What we are attempting to do is illustrate the responses to the questions we posed regarding course design rather than promote a course management system. As we discussed in chapter 4, the tool is not as important as the learning outcomes or educational problem it seeks to support. Once decisions about learning outcomes have been made, the instructor can turn to the process of developing the course and choose the appropriate tools to support it. We now examine the considerations and decisions that need to be made.

## Starting Over: Considerations in the Development of an Online Course

Boettcher and Conrad (2010) suggest that two important decisions are made in moving a course online from the classroom: determining the vision (including the degree to which the class will be conducted online or through the use of technology) and envisioning the process. As instructors think about moving a course online and begin to consider the answers to the questions we presented earlier, it is important for them to maintain a vision of the course as a whole and the desired learning outcomes for students. With this in mind, instructors can then consider the process to be used to reach the desired outcomes in the context of what is possible online. Although the outcomes of a face-to-face or online course are likely to be the same, the process for reaching them differs in the two arenas. Assignments, discussions, and the tools used are likely to be quite different.

Too often instructors jump to the online process by posting lecture notes, a syllabus, or PowerPoint presentations without having a vision for the course as a whole and desired outcomes. Starting with the desired result in mind helps to shape the process needed to get there.

We next illustrate the course development process by presenting and answering a series of questions to consider in course development and illustrate the answers with our course example: Systems Theories.

## Who Are My Students?

We were asked to teach a semester-long course in systems theories in hybrid fashion, using three six-hour face-to-face intensive sessions, spaced one month apart, along with online discussion, to a group of ten to fifteen adult undergraduate students in health and human sciences. Although this may seem like a complete enough answer to the question of who we are teaching and how the course will be delivered, other questions about them surfaced:

- What other courses will they be taking while taking my course?
- Have they had any exposure to the content to be studied in other courses they have completed?
- Where does this course fit in the overall program of studies in which these students are engaged?
- How far away from the institution do these students live?
- Are they all working? Are they working full time?
- Have they taken other classes in this format, or will this be their first online experience?
- What technological capabilities does each student have, and what technology is available to them?

These questions were easily answered for us through a brief conversation with the department chairperson. Most students were taking an additional course in physiology, and some were fulfilling undergraduate requirements at other San Francisco Bay Area schools. We discovered that this would be the first exposure these students would have to systems theory concepts. Although some of their other classes might have touched on the topic, it was not covered to any great degree. All of the students who enrolled in the course were working full time, and most had family responsibilities as well. Many had long commutes to campus, but all lived in the Bay Area, where the college is located. Some of the students had online course experience in other courses they had taken, but the chair was unsure if all of them had taken an online course previously. Having this information assisted us in determining how much technology training and support we would need to provide, as well as what we might expect from the students enrolled in the course in terms of participation.

In developing a class for online delivery, it is important to get as full a picture as possible of the students to be served by the class before embarking on its development. In the face-to-face setting, an instructor would not design a basic survey class for upper-division students unless, for example, those students were in a degree completion program and had never been exposed to the material before.

Just as we would gather information about the group to be served in a face-to-face class, it is important to do so in an online group. This information helps us to determine process. For example, if most of the students who will enroll in the course live a significant distance from the institution, then the use of face-to-face sessions may not be viable. Once the class has begun, if we find that there are some differences in what we expected about the group enrolled in the class, we can adjust as we go to accommodate them.

## Is This a Course That Will Successfully Transfer to the Online Environment?

Most classes do transfer well to the online environment, particularly with the availability of the current technologies. Creative use of local lab and studio facilities and the inclusion of demonstration material using Power-Point slides and audio and video content that students can access on the course site or on YouTube may overcome the need for face-to-face contact. The issue usually becomes how to transfer the course and what technologies to use rather than if the course can be transferred.

We believed that systems theories would do well as an online course: not only could we create engaging discussion assignments, but there was strong potential for collaborative work, video, and the like. Content could be delivered through reading assignments and collaborative research assignments designed to push students to think critically and apply what they were reading. Consequently, we decided to use our face-to-face time for experiential exercises, such as case studies, simulations, and student presentations, and to use the online classroom for presenting assignments, preparing collaborative work, and discussing reading and other course-related material.

## How Do I Define Learning in This Content Area, and What Do I Want to See as the Learning Outcomes?

The response to this question is an important reflection on the overall process and is an important starting point in course design. How will I know that I have met the outcomes and objectives I have set for students? What does learning look like to me? Once these questions have been addressed, the instructor can then back up and design assignments of varying types that will help learners get to that desired end result.

In a collaborative learning environment, learning and learning outcomes are much more than simple acquisition of knowledge. The cocreation of meaning and knowledge that can occur in the collaborative online classroom can create a level of reflection that results in transformative learning, when students begin to reflect on the following question: How am I growing and changing as a learner and as a person through my involvement in this course? If the course has been designed to incorporate and invite life experience into the classroom, students can begin to explore the material being studied not just from an academic standpoint but also through the personal meaning they derive from it. As facilitators of the online classroom process, instructors can encourage students to engage in this level of reflection by creating assignments and asking questions that encourage students to apply material to their work or life situations. The following student quote from Systems Theories illustrates a successful learning outcome, the generation of transformative knowledge: "It seems that upon inspection, all systems have influences over others at some point. The weather [ecology system] or traffic [transportation system] could impact my work or family system, living in the Bay Area [community] may influence my being politically active affecting the government, etc. . . . There is no end!" It illustrates the ability of this student, David, to begin to reflect on what he was studying and apply it to his own life. David came into the course stating that he had little to no understanding of or much interest in studying systems. However, as the course progressed, he became intrigued with and excited about the number of systems he saw and interacted with daily. That brief comment begins to capture what he learned.

## What Do I Want to Accomplish Through This Course?

Beginning at the end by determining appropriate learning outcomes for a course is the best way to decide what content should be covered. The development of appropriate learning outcomes also begins to give the instructor a sense of what steps might be needed to move a student from the beginning of the course to the end and achieve the type of learning outcome that David's comments indicate. Instead of focusing on learning strategies first, such as lecture or lecture and discussion, deciding on learning outcomes, including what we want students to know, feel, or be able to do at the end of the course, helps us to determine how we might get there.

In developing learning outcomes for any course regardless of how it is delivered, it is important to ensure that the outcomes are measurable and written using action verbs. It is difficult to measure understanding; unfortunately we often see outcomes written with the word *understand*. Instead, verbs such as *articulate, describe, analyze,* or *demonstrate* can serve as measures of the degree to which a student understands a concept. Going beyond understanding to application of the concept moves students beyond basic understanding. Depending on the level of the course, this may be desirable.

Because we had found that our students in the systems theories class had little or no previous experience with the topic, we established the learning outcomes shown in exhibit 5.1.

Once we established the objectives, we were then able to move on and determine appropriate reading material and assignments so that students could achieve those objectives. Our course format was predetermined—a hybrid or blended format—so we could begin to decide what material to cover in face-to-face sessions and what to cover online. A phenomenon that emerged from K–12 teaching that can be considered in the delivery of hybrid classes is the flipped classroom. Attributed to two teachers from Colorado, Jonathan Bergman and Aaron Sams, the method began with recording PowerPoint-supported lectures and putting them online so that

## EXHIBIT 5.1 COURSE OUTCOMES

1. Investigate the historical roots of systems theory, trace its impact on the health care field, and describe the linkage of systems theory to health care.
2. Evaluate the relationship of patients and/or clients of the health care system with that system, applying theory to practice.
3. Identify and define the various systems theories, using systems terms, and articulate a preferred theory by applying it to professional practice.
4. Analyze issues of diversity, values, ethics, social and economic justice, and oppression from a systems standpoint and identify the impact of these issues on the health care system.
5. Identify populations at risk from a systems standpoint.

students could access them at any time. Using this model, the instructors present lectures online and support them with online discussion; they then use classroom time for active engagement with the content, other students, and the instructor (Strayer, 2011).

Given that lecture modality is not something we use in our face-to-face classes, we opted not to go in that direction for this class. As we developed our outcomes for the class, we searched for a text that had a companion website (one constructed by the publisher containing supplemental materials and exercises) but found none on the topic of social systems. Consequently, we decided to rely heavily on the books we chose, activities that encouraged students to explore the content in multiple ways, and videos and other supplemental material to convey course content. Weekly online discussions would focus on topics presented in the readings and additional material. Exhibit 5.2 illustrates the assignments created for this course to address the learning objectives.

## EXHIBIT 5.2 COURSE ASSIGNMENTS

There are four assignments through which your work in this course will be assessed.

### 1. Class Attendance and Participation

You are expected to attend all three weekend intensives and also participate in the online discussion between intensives, by logging on and posting to the discussion at least three times per week on three different days of the week. Attendance and participation are 40 percent of the grade.

### 2. Midterm Collaborative Assignment

You will be assigned to a small group for completion of this assignment. Everyone will read Kotlowitz, *There Are No Children Here.* Your small group will prepare an analysis of the book from a systems perspective. You may present your analysis in the form of a collaboratively created wiki or blog, a multimedia presentation using audio and video, a Prezi presentation [Prezi is a Web 2.0 tool that is an alternative to PowerPoint, allowing the user to create a "canvas" where the presentation can be viewed by panning, zooming, and moving around the presentation in predetermined ways rather than in linear form as in PowerPoint.], or a PowerPoint presentation. The following questions should guide your analysis:

- What systems were portrayed in the book, and how were they portrayed?
- How did the people in the book interact with those systems?
- How did the systems interact with each other, or did they?
- What were the obstacles faced by the people in the book and the systems with which they interacted?
- What was the outcome of their interaction with the systems in their lives?

Your group can feel free to interact in the group space created for you on the course site, on Skype, using chat, by phone, or, if you can make it happen, in person. Should you interact outside the course site, one person should be designated to post a report of the results of your meeting, along with who attended in your group space in the course. You will present and discuss your analysis at our second intensive meeting. This assignment is worth 20 percent of the grade.

### 3. Presentation and Annotated Outline

You are to choose a system with which you are involved. This can be anything from your family system, to the agency you work for, to a larger system such as the health care system or the welfare system. You are asked to prepare a twenty-minute presentation to present that system to your peers. Be creative! We want to see more than a lecture. Help us understand the system from within by using video, graphics, or an activity to help us really understand this system from within. You will also prepare an annotated outline that accompanies your presentation and shows that you used at least three references beyond the assigned reading for the course. An annotated outline is a topic outline that contains paragraphs that describe each element. This saves you from writing a full paper but pushes you to be more descriptive about your work. The outline should not necessarily be about your presentation, but about the system you researched for the presentation. You might also choose to use a mind map instead of an outline, but that mind map must also be annotated. You will present at the third intensive. The presentation is worth 20 percent of the grade.

### 4. Final Exam

A final take-home essay-type exam will be distributed at the end of the second intensive and is due along with your presentation at the third intensive. It is worth 20 percent of the grade.

### Grading

Grading rubrics for all assignments are available on the course site. Please refer to them to help guide your work as they contain the grading criteria to be used when assessing your work. The department grading scale will be used for this course:

| | |
|---|---|
| 90–100 | A |
| 80–90 | B |
| 70–80 | C |
| 60–70 | D |
| Below 60 | F |

All assignments need to be completed on time. Grades for late assignments will be reduced by 1 point per day for the first week and a full grade for the second week. Assignments more than two weeks late will not be accepted. If an emergency exists that prohibits you from turning in your work, you must contact us by e-mail or phone immediately. No incompletes will be given for the course except in emergencies.

## What Guidelines, Rules, Roles, and Norms Need to Be Established for Course Completion?

We cannot stress enough the importance of developing a good set of course guidelines, including rules for interacting with one another and expectations for receiving a grade. Course guidelines form the structure of the course and create a container within which students can learn together. Exhibit 5.3 gives the guidelines we developed for the systems theories class.

### EXHIBIT 5.3 COURSE GUIDELINES

Dear Students,

The following are guidelines to assist you in navigating this course successfully. Once you have read them, please post a message to the discussion board indicating that you have read them, understand, and are able to comply. If you have questions, please post those as well along with any issues or concerns you might have about them. We will try to accommodate as best we can!

Working online is fairly new to most of you, and to some, it's the first time you've taken an online class or have experienced online education. First of all, we are here to help you in any way we possibly can. Our phone and e-mail information is posted online. Please don't agonize over something that we can help you with. Either send an e-mail or pick up the phone and call.

**Discussion Week**

Our discussion weeks begin on Monday and end on Sunday at midnight PST. Assignments are due Sundays at midnight as well. We are flexible with this and will not count off for slightly late submissions. If it looks as if you may be significantly late, then send us an e-mail, and we can discuss it. You are adults in a degree completion program, and we will treat you as adults and as colleagues who are here to learn with us. We fully understand that life can get in the way. Don't hesitate to contact us if it does!

**Assignments**

There are one or two discussion questions posted weekly. You are expected to post your first response to the questions by Wednesday at midnight. Your responses to your peers should be posted by Friday and can continue until Sunday at midnight PST.

Assignments should be submitted by depositing them in the Digital Drop Box located on the left side of the course page. Pay close attention to the table posted in the Assignments area that outlines all due dates for assignments. Details for each assignment can be found in the syllabus and also under the Assignments tab on the left side of the course page.

You can expect to get feedback from us on a weekly basis on your discussion participation. Questions posted on the discussion board will be answered within 24 hours;

we will respond to e-mails within 48 hours; and we will provide grades and feedback on assignments within 7 days. At midterm and again at the end of the course, we ask that you reflect on the course rubric and send us an e-mail discussing how you feel you are doing in the course as related to the rubric. You can feel free to note your progress on the rubric itself by highlighting or underlining areas you feel pertain to you and then adding comments in the column on the far right of the rubric that has been provided for that purpose. You don't need to give yourself a letter grade at midterm, but we do ask that you tell us the grade you feel you've earned at the end of the course. We will respond to you and will also provide comments on the rubric, giving you feedback on your progress.

## Questions

If you have a question, post it either in public on the discussion board if it relates to the course or by sending us an e-mail if the issue is a private issue. If you send an e-mail and we feel it would benefit everyone to hear the response, we will ask you to post it on the discussion board and we will respond there.

## Using the Course Site

We strongly encourage you to go through the tutorial on the main page for the university that you will find when you log in. Post any questions you might have about the system on the discussion board. If one of your peers can't answer them or we can't, we'll direct you to technical support.

Don't forget to breathe, and let's have fun with this! We truly look forward to working with all of you!

Rena and Keith

---

The guidelines for this course created enough structure so that students knew what was expected of them. At the first face-to-face class meeting, which began the course, the guidelines were reviewed and modifications made based on student input. Students felt they needed the structure of knowing when the week's discussion question would be posted, along with a day or date by which their first responses to the question were due. They agreed that they wanted to see the discussion questions on Sundays, with first responses posted on Wednesdays, allowing them to read and reflect for a couple of days before answering. We generally consider due dates for discussions to be a negotiable item, whereas how grades are to be earned is nonnegotiable. It is important to ask students for their input on guidelines to a reasonable degree so as to increase their level of buy-in and to establish a contract for learning between the students and instructor.

## How Do I Plan to Deliver Course Material?

An instructor who is offering a course for the first time may choose to take small steps in online course development by offering a technology-enhanced version of a class. In so doing, a flipped approach might be considered, putting lecture material online along with directions for assignment completion and potentially some amount of asynchronous discussion. Thus, the instructor can conduct face-to-face sessions that are made up of active learning activities allowing the application of the theory being studied. Other ways to begin experimenting with online learning are to place course-related information on a course site and receive assignments on the site without requiring online discussion or to use a text in an electronic format or a companion website to the text.

Whether the course is to be conducted completely online or is technology enhanced, the instructor needs to decide how students will acquire their knowledge of the content. If lectures are not the mode of choice for imparting information and content, then how will students access material that will provide them with the same information? Here are a few suggestions:

- A digital textbook that has interactive study guides and activities
- Assignments that develop research skills and empower students to find articles, websites, and other resources that pertain to the content being studied, perhaps posting their findings to a wiki
- Collaborative small group assignments that enable students to learn from one another and that deepen the knowledge acquired
- WebQuests (otherwise known as online scavenger hunts) where students seek out material in a structured way in response to guiding questions or directions and post that material to the course site
- Assignments that turn students into experts in one area of the content being studied and ask them then to teach their colleagues (including the instructor) what they have learned (also known as a jigsaw approach to the content)

The university had predetermined that our systems theories course would be offered through a combination of face-to-face and online sessions. We chose not to use the face-to-face sessions to deliver lectures and so had to decide how students with little or no understanding of systems would gain that knowledge. When we looked for a digital text and found nothing that suited our requirements, we opted for a standard text that approached the subject from a human systems perspective because these were students in health and human services. In addition, we assigned the work of Fritjof Capra, a well-known author in the area of ecological systems, to give them a broader base of theory, and assigned a nonfiction book describing a family living in poverty who come in contact with numerous social systems. We asked students to analyze this book from a systems perspective. Discussion of the readings took place online for the most part. In the face-to-face sessions, we used video, simulations, and student presentations as learning exercises to help students apply what they were learning.

## How Comfortable Am I in Releasing Control to the Learners?

The success of collaborative assignments in an online course rests with the instructor's willingness to empower students to take on the work with clear expectations for completion and then step out of the way. In addition, because of the amount of work involved for students in completing collaborative assignments online, spacing out the assignments judiciously and using a combination of intensive and less intensive assignments helps with successful completion and meaningful acquisition of knowledge. For example, assigning a weekly group project involving research and compilation of results is likely to be too much, but assigning two to three such assignments during a semester is more manageable. These assignments can be interspersed with discussion of readings and other material, giving feedback on each other's assignments, alternating facilitation assignments, and using other collaborative processes that keep the spirit of collaborative learning alive.

We consulted with one instructor who complained that her students were unable to complete collaborative assignments online. When we visited her course site, we noticed two things. First, she was involving herself in the small group discussion around collaborative assignments, and second, she was assigning intensive small group projects every week. Students were complaining that the workload was too heavy and that they were not getting much out of the assignments. We suggested that she eliminate some of the collaborative assignments, giving students more time to complete the remaining assignments. We also suggested that she remove herself from the negotiation and small group discussion of the collaborative groups because we thought that her involvement was complicating their group process. Small groups should have the option of asking the instructor to intercede if the group is not working well together. However, the instructor should not make himself or herself an integral part of the group process.

In developing our course in systems theories, we chose to use our allotted face-to-face time for intensive collaborative work. These sessions were interspersed with online discussion of the readings and other topics related to systems. The schedule is presented to the students in such a way as to create a checklist of sorts: students can see what is required of them each week and make sure that all assignments have been addressed. A portion of the schedule for the course is shown in exhibit 5.4.

### EXHIBIT 5.4 COURSE SCHEDULE AND ASSIGNMENTS

| Teek | Topic | Readings | Assignments |
|------|-------|----------|-------------|
| 1 | **First Intensive** Review syllabus and course expectations A beginning primer on systems: definitions, types, and theories Video: *Turning Point* Case study work in small groups | Handouts: Syllabus and glossary of systems terms Kotlowitz: Read the whole book to prepare for the assignment for the second intensive | Attend first intensive and complete case study 1 in small groups. |
| 2 | Living systems, systems thinking, and world systems theory as a conceptual framework | Capra: Parts 1 and 2 Alexander, Chapters 1 and 2 | Participate in online discussion |
| 3 | Self-organization, complexity, and social structures and problems | Capra: Part 3 Alexander: Chapter 3 | Participate in online discussion |
| 4 | Microsystems: the family | Capra: Part 4 Alexander: Chapter 4 | Participate in online discussion |
| 5 | Meso- and macrosystems: groups and organizations | Alexander: Chapters 5 and 6 | Participate in online discussion |
| 6 | **Second Intensive** A model of social systems Kotlowitz presentations Video: *Mindwalk* Case study work in small groups Discussion of final presentation | Handouts: Systems model | Attend second intensive, present collaborative assignment, and complete case study 2 in small groups Take-home final distributed |

## How Do I Want to Organize the Course Site?

Many institutions have adopted course management systems that they ask faculty to use in order to simplify and unify course management and to minimize technological headaches for faculty, instructional technologists, technical support staff, and students. Current course management systems generally allow faculty to upload a syllabus that has been created using a word processor and create asynchronous discussion areas for large and small group discussion and places where students can post assignments. They also offer e-mail and grade books, in which faculty can record grades and students can monitor their progress in the course. Other features might include the ability to use audio and video and a whiteboard in a virtual classroom application, wiki and blog functions, and the ability to engage in synchronous chat.

The presence of these technological tools should not be considered an open invitation to use them, of course. Depending on the technical expertise of both the instructor and the students enrolled in the course, as well as the learning objectives for the course, the use of audio, video, and chat may not be appropriate. Most often a simple course site that is easy to navigate leads to the most successful experience. This doesn't preclude the use of other technological tools. As always, good planning is the key.

The institution for which we were teaching had a course management system available for our course and also granted us considerable freedom and latitude to develop the course in the prescribed technology-enhanced format. This does not always occur, however. Many faculty have told us that they have been required to use technology that did not serve their learning outcomes, thus limiting their ability to deliver the course in the way they saw fit.

We tend to rely fairly heavily on basic discussion forums as the main means of conducting the class. Consequently, we set up an organized discussion board to support student work. Figure 5.1 shows the discussion board that we created for the class.

## How Will I Assess Student Performance in This Course?

Just as in a face-to-face course, decisions about how student performance will be evaluated are made during the planning stages of the course. What is the most effective means of determining how students are mastering content and applying it appropriately? Often in the face-to-face classroom, the instructor uses tests, quizzes, and papers to evaluate knowledge acquisition. There may be additional requirements, such as attendance, that

## FIGURE 5.1   SAMPLE DISCUSSION BOARD

---

 ⌂ › Systems-101 › Discussions

# Discussions

 Questions for Drs P&P                                    Jul 30 at 5:07pm
Rena Palloff, PhD

Use this area to ask any course-related questions.  If one of you has a question, usually all of you
have the same question!  :)  If you have questions of a personal nature, please send those via
email.

---

The P&P Cafe                                             Jul 30 at 5:06pm
Rena Palloff, PhD

Use this area to socialize, tell a joke or two, inform us about your travels or time away, and
generally just hang out and relax!

---

Meso and Macro Systems – Groups and Organizations                    Jun 28 at 7:36pm
rpalloff@fielding.edu

After completing the reading for this week, consider a group or organization of which you are a part
and discuss your role within it.  Do you consider this group or organization to be caring and
inclusive?  What suggestions might you make to the group or organization to more humanize it?

---

Micro Systems – the Family                                      Jun 28 at 7:32pm
rpalloff@fielding.edu

Analyze your own family as a social system. What elements do you see at play within the structure
of your family system? It might help to discuss your family in comparison to the families of friends
or colleagues, to see where they are the same and where they are different.  What important
resources does membership in a family provide each member? In exchange for those resources, what do
we give up? Use your analysis of your own family to help answer this question.

---

Self-organization, Complexity, and Social Structures and Problems          Jun 28 at 7:29pm
rpalloff@fielding.edu

This week we looked at how systems and social structures can act as impediments for some
groups of people. Choose a social problem that particularly bothers you.  What systems interact to
impact that problem positively or negatively?  Relate this to the theories we've been reading about
and discussing.  You can also find an article or website that addresses this problem and discuss it within
this context.  What does this tell you about the nature of systems change?

---

Living Systems, Systems Thinking, and World Systems Theory             Jun 28 at 7:25pm
rpalloff@fielding.edu

How does the reading you completed for this week reflect your own thinking about the world and
the systems within it?  How did it challenge your worldview?  Please cite the reading in your
discussion and respond to at least one other person in the group reflecting on their worldview.

---

students are expected to meet. In the online classroom, however, there needs to be careful consideration of how well any of the traditional means of evaluation will work. Tests and quizzes may not be the best measure of knowledge acquisition and application online.

Many institutions continue to require that some form of examination be used to evaluate students. Most of the course management systems available for online courses allow secure administration of tests and quizzes, often with a link to the grade book embedded in the application. Answers to test questions can be entered into an encrypted file that is then available only to the instructor. Just as in the face-to-face classroom, however, the question of cheating emerges when tests and quizzes are used. Because students in an online course are often working at a distance, there are additional concerns. How will the instructor know that the test answers he or she received were really given by the student whose name appears on the test? Studies, however, have revealed that there is no more cheating in an online class than there is in a face-to-face class (Rowe, 2004; Varvel, 2005). It is important to remember, though, that since students are working at a distance from the convenience of their home or dorm room, it is unrealistic to expect that they will not use books and materials to complete the exam (Major & Taylor, 2003). Consequently, we advise that all exams and quizzes be considered open-book tests and be constructed as such.

Nevertheless, there are some ways to minimize the possibility of cheating online. For example, a test might be administered at a proctored site with a requirement that the student show identification before being allowed to take the test, students might be required to take the test on campus, and students taking an exam can be monitored through the use of a webcam. Although these are not ideal solutions and we do not recommend them due to their inconvenience and the fact that they will not completely eliminate the possibility of cheating, they may help to reduce that possibility if that is a concern.

The use of a collaborative process in delivering the course, with minimal use of tests and quizzes and maximum use of authentic application activities, allows an instructor to build trust in students' abilities to do the work, gives the instructor ongoing evidence of the work they are capable of producing, and, most important, empowers students to engage in their own learning process.

An advantage of teaching online is that as the course progresses, instructors learn to recognize the unique writing style of each student. The advantage in the online course is that students not only submit papers but also post written responses to online discussions. Therefore, any variations in a student's writing become more obvious and can be addressed by the instructor. Plagiarism detection applications or running a few sentences through a search engine can also help to reassure the instructor that the student is doing his or her own work and is paraphrasing and citing appropriately.

An online course has yet another advantage in evaluating students that the face-to-face classroom does not. In an online course, students must participate in some fashion in order to complete it successfully. This means that the instructor can see on a regular basis how students are analyzing and applying course material, especially if they are being asked to respond to questions that encourage them to think critically. Consequently, a good means of evaluating student performance in an online course is to require a specified number of substantive posts each week. A substantive post responds to the question in a way that clearly supports a position, begins a new topic, or adds to the discussion by critically reflecting on what is being discussed or moving the discussion in a new direction. Simply logging on and saying "I agree" is not a substantive post. Consequently, evaluation guidelines for student performance in an online course can include the quantity, content, and quality of posts. Thus, concerns about cheating are eliminated as students engage in a collaborative learning process.

Written papers can serve as another means of engaging in collaborative learning in an online course. An expectation can be that papers be posted online and that students comment and respond to one other's work. In a course on addiction studies that one of us offered, students were asked to post brief papers every week in response to a case study. A portion of the week's discussion was then devoted to reflection on the responses, which frequently took the discussion to a deeper level. In the responses to one of the case studies that follows, the interchange between the students illustrates what we mean when we identify a post as substantive and also how reflecting on each other's work deepens the learning process.

*Steve:*  I agree with you except for your last sentence. I think it's good to start with education in our session as well. But, I feel that the higher level of treatment, the more forcefully the denial may be dealt with. He may brush off what I have to say in the therapy session, but when he is in a room of other alcoholics or in a rehab center it is going to be harder for him to attribute his problems to "stress" only. He will hear his own story in those of the other recoverees and hopefully identify. With more intensive treatment he may be more confronted with the reality of the severity of his problems. Also the PhD in Psychology indicates to me that he may tend to intellectualize, and probably already knows something about substance abuse from this mental level. Ron needs to really get it.

*Kathy:* I understand your position. But after reading the discussion I think there is a good possibility that his major problem is his PTSD [posttraumatic stress disorder] and that the alcohol and marijuana addiction has been his way to deal with it. I think the whole family needs to be brought in so that it can be evaluated in terms of his wife's possible addiction and how to provide support for increased symptoms of PTSD when he detoxes. I meant to also say that with some view of the family situation there will be some possibility of doing a more effective confrontation. There should be more evidence of how the alcohol and marijuana use has been detrimental and how it would be helpful to detox in order to deal with the PTSD more effectively.

*Steve:* I agree with you that the PTSD is also a large problem which he has probably been covering up with alcohol and drugs. And I also agree with you about family involvement. But, for me there was enough evidence in the case study that the alcohol and drug use needed to be treated first or in conjunction with the PTSD. Thanks.

Exhibit 5.2 set out how we decided to evaluate our students in Systems Theories. Because the course was hybrid rather than delivered completely online, we used the face-to-face sessions to initiate, complete, and discuss assignments. Instead of having students post papers online, we determined that they would be turned in at the face-to-face sessions and discussed at that time. We were required to give some form of a final examination for the course. Consequently, we decided to assign a take-home essay exam that required students to reflect on the material being studied. Exhibit 5.5 shows the exam we developed. We determined that the exam would account for only 20 percent of the total grade because the ongoing online discussion would provide us with a good idea of how well students were understanding and applying systems theories.

## How Will I Address Attendance Requirements?

Accounting for attendance becomes more difficult online to some degree. Yet many institutions are requiring faculty to account for attendance just as they would in the face-to-face classroom in order to meet guidelines for state, federal, and financial aid. Therefore, we have established a rule of thumb for our online classes. In order to meet attendance requirements, students must log on and post something to the discussion an equivalent number of times to that which the class would have met on a face-to-face basis. For example, an undergraduate class that would normally meet three times per week equates to at least three posts per week. A graduate-level

## EXHIBIT 5.5 SAMPLE FINAL EXAM FOR SYSTEMS THEORIES

Please briefly, but thoroughly, answer the following three questions. Your answers should be double-spaced and in APA format. If you use references, please cite them, and include a reference list at the end of each question. There is no page expectation for your answers, but please don't submit a 20-page paper! You should be able to answer each question in 2 to 3 pages. Your take-home final is due on Saturday of the last intensive. No late papers will be accepted. Please feel free to contact us if you have any questions, problems, or concerns. Good luck, and try to have some fun with this!

1. During the first week of the online discussion, we asked you to describe the most influential system in your life. Looking back over the reading and discussions for this course, talk about all (or as many as you can think of) the systems you encounter on a typical day. What are they? What do they look like? How do they interrelate, or do they? (Remember—there are virtual systems, too!!)
2. Think about a system that bothers you. This could be the political system, the health care system, the education system, or any that comes to your mind. Describe and analyze it. What is it about this system that disturbs you? What changes would need to be made in this system that would make it less disturbing? When talking and writing about the system, make sure you discuss the participants, makeup, boundaries, etc.
3. Briefly answer the following:
   - What did I know about systems when I entered this course?
   - What have I learned?
   - Has my learning changed me in any way? If so, how? As you list the changes, try to identify them with the system that might have influenced that change.

---

class that would have met once per week for two hours requires two posts per week to the online discussion.

In a blended or hybrid course, accounting for attendance becomes an easier task because there are required face-to-face sessions. Some hybrid classes may require one or more in-person sessions each week, with additional work online. However, it is still a good practice to mandate a certain number of posts to the online component of the course weekly. Our hybrid class required three weekend sessions and three online posts per week. Regardless of the configuration of sessions, attendance in a hybrid class is usually made up of a combination of presence at required meetings on campus coupled with presence online.

## The Process of the Course

Now that we have moved through the planning process to create an online course, we can begin to consider the process of the course itself. How do online courses actually work? What does the process look like? Once a syllabus has been created and posted to the course site, how do we get started? Boettcher and Conrad (2010) suggest that online courses move through four phases: beginnings, early middle, late middle, and closing weeks. They also describe the tasks in each phase for the learner and the instructor, the content in each phase, and the environment. Here we divide the process into three phases: beginnings, once the course has started, and endings.

## Beginnings

The beginning stage involves ensuring that the tools to be used for the course are in place and that students know how to use them. This phase also involves the start of community building through posting introductions, photos, and the use of icebreaker activities to help students connect to one another and the content. Some academic institutions have created their own online orientations, which help students practice with the tools they will be using but also learn about online learning itself. When an instructor does not have an orientation program available to students, one can be created in the course. The syllabus should contain tips for successful completion of the course, along with guidelines for completion and for respectful interaction, also known as netiquette. Some instructors post frequently asked questions in order to provide an orientation for students.

Once the orientation has been developed and delivered, there are two important steps to take at the beginning of an online course. The first is to create a welcome message that repeats some basic orientation information for students and remains on the course site. This can also be e-mailed to students, creating some redundancy and ensuring that the message is delivered in one way or another. A portion of a welcome message follows. In addition to the welcome to the content, specifics for getting started and for successful course completion can be included. This is the introduction one of us (Rena) made at the start of a course:

> Hello all! I'm excited to begin this exploration of groups and group process with you all. As many of you may know, working with online groups is not only my interest but also my passion—particularly groups that come together online for the purpose of learning together. We have the opportunity here to act as our own "laboratory" if you will—we can learn about online groups by forming our own. My hopes for this term are that we all will learn something about how groups form, develop norms

together, and work together online. But more important, I hope we all can learn something about how we as members of that group and how we as individual members contribute to that process. I also hope that we all will be able to apply this new knowledge and skill development in the workplace and certainly in your other classes. What we're doing is groundbreaking stuff, which has tremendous implications for distributed and networked organizations and in team building. I'll post more of an introduction later. Just wanted to say hello and that I'm looking forward to taking this collaborative journey with you—I hope you're all willing to join me and have some fun in the process!

Posting introductions is the second important step to take when a course begins. Most course management systems allow both students and the instructor to create simple home pages, often including a picture that remains on the course site. We have heard students and instructors comment on how useful this has been to them. These pages serve as an initial way to get to know one another, and because they remain on the site, students and instructors find themselves visiting the home pages frequently as a reminder about what students look like or what they said about themselves. In addition to being a good community-building tool, this helps everyone in the course understand why someone else might be coming from a particular place or take a particular position in his or her postings.

It is not uncommon for us to set aside the first week of an online class to get to know one another; in fact, we refer to this week as Week Zero. We avoid getting heavily involved with the content and focus more on building a learning community. In addition to asking students to post their introductions, our first questions for the course generally address stating their learning objectives for the course or beginning to discuss the course as it relates to their lives outside the online classroom. For example, our first question in Systems Theories was this:

> Following up on our discussions in class about the fact that all of you know more about systems than you think, we'd like you to think about all the systems you come in contact with on a daily basis. What are they and how can you describe them? What are their elements and the relationships between those elements? What constitutes their boundaries? Think about the reading you are doing and our discussion of the video we watched together—*The Turning Point*—and then describe in some detail the system that most influences you daily. Please comment on and discuss each other's descriptions.

David's quotation that follows is an indicator that this series of questions was successful in helping students to get to know one another:

> Thank you everyone for your system descriptions. It is nice to know more about you and to know important influences upon your lives—we are, after all, a system that will live on through our lifetimes. We are classmates who will enter new professions once we complete our education. Hopefully, we will continue our connections with each other and the faculty through the College Alumni Affairs Office and College-sponsored events. Additionally, we may call upon one another as a network of knowledge, professional assistance, and friendship. It's a nice thought.

Additional items to discuss in the first week are learning objectives for the course and course guidelines. The discussion can be incorporated into the introductions. For example, students can be asked to present information about not only themselves but also what they hope to get out of the course. They can also be asked to comment on course guidelines to determine if they will assist them in reaching their learning objectives. This should not be the only time that the guidelines are discussed, however. If students find that the guidelines are not meeting their needs in some way, they should feel free to raise this as a topic of discussion, and the guidelines can be renegotiated at that time. We generally do not change guidelines until we hear from all of the students involved with the class to make sure that all will benefit from the change. The following example shows such negotiations:

*Jane:* Now that we are only responding to the week's case study and we are about halfway through the term, I thought I'd clarify academic expectations (I am nothing if not prompt:-}). We each have used varying styles in posting responses to the case studies. Some have followed the more traditional format noted in the guidebook, others have shared their thoughts that the case study brought up for them, while others have answered discussion questions noted at the end of the case. I haven't noted any performance feedback from you (either positive or negative) on the way you would like to see these postings continued. Is there a particular style you would like to see? Is there a way you consider best or most appropriate in how we approach the cases for the rest of the term?

*Rena:* Thanks for asking this question, Jane. It's been kind of a free-for-all up until now due for the most part to the confused discussion expectations to begin with, and for that I apologize!! As for the remainder of the term, what I'd like to see is for you to use the case study guidelines I posted at the beginning of the term if they work for you—for this week's case, they may not. If not, use what seems appropriate from those guidelines and rely on the questions at the end of the case. Whether you use the guidelines in whole or in part, the questions should be somehow addressed in your response. Have I muddied the waters even more, or does this make sense??? Rena

*Jane:*   Clear as mud!:-) No, that's great. It sounds like we should first use the guidelines unless another approach makes more sense. If another approach makes more sense, you would like us to ensure that we work to include all applicable facets of the case study guidelines in our response. Is this close?

*Rena:*   You got it, Jane!!!:-)

This bit of discussion illustrates that clarification of guidelines is an ongoing, important process in an online course. All students need to accept the guidelines in order for the course to progress smoothly. These students clearly felt empowered to raise the issues that were important for them and to clarify issues for each other. At times, revisiting the guidelines is helpful in order to ensure that learning objectives are achieved.

## Once the Course Has Started

Once introductions have been made and the course has begun, how does the instructor move into course content and stimulate participation? The key to good participation and dynamic discussion is asking open, expansive questions that promote critical thinking and analytical responses. When students begin to work with expansive questions, they also learn to ask questions of each other in the same way. The momentum generated through lively discussion of the topic being studied generally can be carried through the remainder of the course. Boettcher and Conrad (2010) note that in the early middle phase of the course, learners begin to fall into a rhythm of reading, posting, and responding. Once they move into the late middle phase, they should be engaging well with course concepts and better able to handle complex issues and problems.

To facilitate this, the instructor needs to master good questioning techniques. There is a difference, for example, between saying, "Give three examples of systems in your life," and the questions we used to begin our systems theories class: "Think about all the systems you come in contact with on a daily basis. What are they, and how can you describe them? What are their elements and the relationships between those elements? What constitutes their boundaries?" The first question encourages students simply to generate a list of systems with little or no reflection about what that means. The second series of questions encourages students to reflect more critically on the systems they encounter daily and describe and analyze them using material they are reading for the course. The second approach not only expands the thinking process of the group but also begins to get the students in the course to engage in systems thinking, a learning objective for the course. The responses to the questions also generate a broader range of feedback possibilities among the students. It's very difficult to comment or give feedback on a list, less so when discussing more complex concepts.

Often we have found that when instructors worry about lack of participation in an online course, one of the problems stems from the way in which they are asking questions. When instructors learn to reframe their questions to be more expansive and include examples from the students' lives, participation increases dramatically and the course becomes more relevant as a result. In order to move the process along, students should be encouraged to bring real life into the online classroom as much as possible. Asking questions that relate the course material to their lives or asking them to engage in real-life research—such as, "Would you describe your work organization as a self-organizing system? Why or why not?" or, "We'd like you to go to your local Walmart. From a systems perspective, what did you see there?"—helps students begin to make sense of the material on a personal level.

As the course progresses, it is important to continue to pay attention to the development of the learning community. Allowing the sharing of important personal events helps students and the instructor to bond as people, builds trust among them, and serves to enhance the collaborative process. For example, as the Systems Theories course was in progress, one of us reunited with his son, whom he had not seen in many years. He shared that information with the group. Following is some of the discussion surrounding that event:

*Keith:* Just wanted to let everyone know what a great weekend it was for me even though the Raiders lost the football game. Both my sons arrived and in good condition. We spent the weekend getting to know one another and just all-around having fun. We were on the front page of the *Fremont Argus* on Monday and they told the story pretty well. Its really scary how much we all are alike, not being together for 26 years. Hugs.

*Polly:*   Keith, That is so awesome! Congratulations!!! I'm sure it was a weekend you will not soon forget.:)

*Sara:*    Many heartfelt congratulations to you!! It was nice to hear all went well. Take care you Proud Dad!

*Gracie:*  That's great! I'm going to have to get a copy of Monday's paper so I can read the story.

The comments are brief but supportive. The emoticons—symbols used to convey emotion online—help to convey a sense of warmth and the happiness the students were feeling about this event. Although not related to the academic material being studied, this event helped the group to coalesce into a learning community. They had shared something important on a deeply personal level that served to assist them in working more closely together in the learning process.

## Endings

As a course draws to an end, it is important to allow time for reflection on what has been learned and whether learning objectives have been met. If there is a final face-to-face meeting, as we had in our Systems Theories course, some of that time can be devoted to discussion of this topic. If not, allowing time for closure online is important.

Frequently we use the last week of the class for online discussion of learning objectives and an evaluation by the students of how they experienced the course. We also post some feedback to the group as a whole on how we thought the course went. We ask students to send us an e-mail evaluating their performance using the course rubric and then send individual e-mail messages to students to give them feedback on their work and contribution to the course. Because we met face-to-face with the Systems Theories group at the end of the course, we used some of that time for an evaluation of the experience. Here is an example of closure in another master's-level online course:

*Rena:*    Hello everyone and welcome to the end of our time together for the term! As you think about what you've learned and gained from this class, I wanted to post a thank you to all of you for your enthusiastic participation. All of you have been thoughtful in your responses and have done a wonderful job of responding to one another. The dialogue has been lively and definitely interesting!

Leo, thanks for usually being first out of the box with beautifully thought-out and written responses to the cases. I continue to appreciate your ability to think in metaphor and your ability to weave that in as appropriate.

Mike, thanks for your sense of humor, responsiveness to your teammates, and wonderful ability to think critically and to analyze material. I enjoyed working with you for yet another term!

Jane, it was a pleasure meeting you this term! I appreciate your critical thinking skills, your warmth, your willingness to engage in dialogue and to pursue points that needed pursuing! Your papers were always well written and thought provoking—looked forward to reading them!

Liz, I enjoyed working with you in another context! It was great to see your confidence grow this term and to see your willingness to offer another viewpoint that might not agree with the others. Good for you! Don't lose that courage!

Lynn, again, a pleasure to work with you! I enjoy your sense of humor immensely! Coupled with it is your ability to think deeply and critically and to respond in a creative and sound way to the material we've discussed.

I also want to express my appreciation to all of you for hanging in and renegotiating the course design when it looked like it wasn't working. It is always difficult as an instructor to take over somebody else's course and to try to get into their logic of design and material. All of you helped me do that and I thank you!

*Mike:*  Hi everyone, Thanks for your assessment of everyone, Rena. We think the same pleasant thoughts about you too! The following are my ending thoughts on our learning experience.

Thanks again everyone for your sharing, caring, and insights! Virtual Leadership was the name of the course, but we really covered the gambit, didn't we? I believe what we learned followed a natural progression for subject matter that broke new ground for all of us. In an effort to learn how to lead in a virtual environment, we first had to understand the idiosyncrasies of that environment. Going back through some of our postings, it seems that all of us at one time or another referred to a self-revelation that opened our eyes to both the similarities and the differences found between our normal work environments and our virtual environments . . .

I appreciate the idea of learning how to be more flexible and adaptable by understanding our strengths and being aware of our weaknesses. I do believe that all of us are very optimistic concerning the relationships and level of friendships that can be created and fostered within the virtual environment. I think in our organizations that we need all the help we can get in evolving a friendlier and a happier work environment. Maybe this medium offers an aspect that can propagate the idea of improved and enhanced social connections and interactions . . . Even more than leading though, are the aspects of all of us "being" a part of this environment and the recognition of our own "doing" as we participate within this environment. Rena and group thanks for another great learning experience!

Mike's assessment of his learning experience demonstrates not only that the learning objectives for this course were met, but also that transformative learning occurred for him too. Others in the group shared similar observations and reflections, indicating that the course was a successful learning experience for them and that they felt they had created an effective learning community.

The ending reflections shared by this group of students are what we hope to see. They are an indication that the planning and delivery of the course was effective in moving students not only toward their learning objectives but also toward what we view as real learning. They also illustrate what Boettcher and Conrad (2010) offer as the highlights of this phase: that learners are digging deeply into concepts and resources, supporting one another, and reflecting on and identifying their personal outcomes from the course.

The end of a course is also the time to communicate grades to students, although it is preferable for students to have a sense of how they have been doing throughout the course by ongoing feedback from the instructor. Communication of grades can occur through the use of the grade book in the course management systems or progress and grades can be communicated by e-mail. We recommend that both be used so that feedback can be communicated along with the grade. One of the practices we routinely use is to have students self-assess using the rubric for an assignment or discussions and add their own comments to that rubric. We then review it and add our own comments to theirs. An example of this practice is illustrated in exhibit 5.6. Regardless of how the communication of grades occurs, it should be private between the instructor and the student. Grades should not be posted publicly on the course site.

In this chapter, we have reviewed and described with course examples ways in which to move an existing face-to-face course to the online environment. Increasingly, however, institutions are hiring faculty to develop courses that other faculty will teach or purchasing already-developed courses for the same purpose. In the next chapter, we examine this in more detail and suggest ways in which instructors who are charged with delivering courses they have not developed can do so effectively. We also discuss rolling admissions in online courses and how to create community and monitor progress in these circumstances.

## EXHIBIT 5.6 SAMPLE RUBRIC

| Criteria | Nonperformance (0) | Basic (1) | Proficient (2) | Distinguished (3) | Comments |
|---|---|---|---|---|---|
| Includes and applies relevant course concepts, theories, or materials correctly with citation of sources when appropriate. | Does not explain relevant course concepts, theories, or materials. Does not provide citation of sources where appropriate. | Summarizes relevant course concepts, theories, or materials. Provides appropriate citation some of the time. | Applies and analyzes relevant course concepts, theories, or materials correctly. Generally provides citation when appropriate to do so. | Evaluates and synthesizes course concepts, theories, or materials correctly, using examples or supporting evidence. Consistently provides citation when appropriate to do so. | |
| Responds to at least two fellow learners on time, relating the discussion to relevant course concepts and providing substantive feedback. | Does not respond to fellow learners. | Responds to fellow learners without relating discussion to the relevant course concepts. Provides feedback, but it is not substantive. Response is not timely. Responds to two other learners. | Responds to fellow learners, relating the discussion to relevant course concepts. Feedback is substantive most of the time. Most responses are posted on time. Responds to more than two other learners. | Responds to fellow learners, relating the discussion to relevant course concepts and consistently extends the dialogue through provision of substantive feedback. Responses are consistently posted on time. Consistently responds to more than two other learners. | |

(continued)

**EXHIBIT 5.6** (*Continued*)

| Criteria | Nonperformance (0) | Basic (1) | Proficient (2) | Distinguished (3) | Comments |
|---|---|---|---|---|---|
| Applies relevant professional, personal, or other real-world experiences. | Does not contribute professional, personal, or other real-world experiences. | Contributes some professional, personal, or other real-world experiences that may or may not relate to course content. | Applies relevant professional, personal, or other real-world experiences. | Applies relevant professional, personal, or other real-world experiences and extends the dialogue by responding to the examples of peers. | |
| Supports the development of a learning community through collegial and collaborative interaction. | Does not demonstrate collegiality and does not collaborate with peers. | Generally supports the development of a learning community through collaboration and professional communication. | Consistently supports the development of a learning community through demonstrated collaboration and collegiality. | Demonstrates consistent support for others, works to include all group members, is professionally responsive to group members, and demonstrates consistent ability to engage others in collaboration. | |

## TIPS FOR SUCCESSFULLY TRANSFORMING A COURSE
## FOR ONLINE DELIVERY

- Develop as comprehensive a picture as possible of the students who will be enrolling in the class.
- Begin with the end in mind by developing learning objectives first.
- Determine the best fit between the course and the degree to which technology and online delivery will be used.
- Develop a good set of initial guidelines to create a container in which all participants can interact.
- Include collaborative learning assignments, the ability for students to interact on a personal level, and other means for developing a learning community.
- Give as much control of the learning process as possible to the learners themselves. Be creative in developing means by which content can be delivered without the use of lectures.
- Provide clear expectations for performance in the course, including how assignments will be evaluated, the degree to which participation will be evaluated, how attendance will be taken, and how overall evaluation of student performance will be conducted.
- Use rubrics to clearly communicate learning objectives and grading criteria for each learning activity in the course and incorporate them into student assessments.

# CHAPTER SIX

# TEACHING COURSES DEVELOPED BY OTHERS

Increasingly, online distance learning instructors are being asked to deliver a course they did not develop or design. There are several reasons for this trend, but the main one is that institutions are discovering that creating an effective online course requires more than just transferring classroom materials online. Creating high-quality online courses that promote the achievement of learning outcomes is time-consuming and expensive. In addition, larger institutions find that having courses developed individually each term is not a sustainable model as enrollments increase. Some institutions are offering training and incentives for instructors to develop courses. However, once the course is developed, the instructor who designed it may not be the one to teach it.

Instructors are teaching courses designed by others for a number of reasons:

- An instructor may be asked to develop a course for online use and then leave the institution. Another instructor may then be asked to take over the course and teach it as it has been created.
- Institutions are hiring instructors as content experts specifically to design—but not deliver—online courses. This may be done to create

a uniform look and feel to all courses that the institution delivers or to save money on costly course development time.

- Institutions are purchasing or licensing courses from another organization whose business it is to develop courses for online use.
- Instructors are opting to use digital textbooks, which provide text material, exercises, quizzes, a grade book, and the ability to hold discussions on a website that belongs to the publisher.
- Some institutions are contracting with organizations that specialize in what are termed total solutions: instructors submit material to the company to be converted into an online course. The course is then installed on that company's server, and other instructors from the academic institution can use it as well.
- There may be a need to offer multiple sections of the same course. In order to create consistency across courses and work toward the same learning outcomes, the same course design and materials need to be used.

Regardless of how the course is created, many instructors now find themselves being asked to deliver such a course to students, and, in fact, many of the larger online institutions are hiring instructors to do just that. The issues that emerge for these instructors include how to build community into the process, as well as how to add material that they deem to be important and work with material they consider unimportant.

An additional development has been the use of rolling enrollment in some institutions. In this model, a course is ongoing for a period of time, generally anywhere from six weeks upward. However, enrollments occur monthly. Consequently, one student may have been in the course for thirty days when more students are added. This model creates additional challenges for creating community and the efficient delivery of material.

In this chapter, we explore these issues and make concrete suggestions about how instructors might work with and personalize the material, as well as how to create community and foster collaboration. In addition, we consider ways to evaluate good course material and packages. Ideally, in such situations, instructors should be able to

- Use or emphasize the material they feel is most important
- Omit or deemphasize material they feel is unnecessary
- Include collaborative activities
- Promote interactivity and community building

## A Focus on Content

Often when an online class is developed by an instructor who will not be teaching the course, the focus is on content rather than pedagogical process. We have made the case that teaching online requires another form of pedagogy, one that is more focused on the facilitation of a collaborative process than on the delivery of content. Thus, simply hiring a content expert to develop a course will not address the issues involved with online teaching. Pairing the content expert with an instructional designer who understands online teaching and can assist in the course development process by asking questions that are central to good course design can help to alleviate the problem. An instructional designer might move the subject expert away from a focus on content by asking how to achieve learning outcomes for the course. In other words, what exercises, readings, case studies, and so on would be useful to students in gaining an understanding of the material being studied? A content expert who can be coached to focus on ways to apply the material online is more likely to develop a course that can be transferred to another instructor.

Because many instructors do not receive training in online teaching, they might not create an online course with that form of pedagogy in mind. Furthermore, the receiving instructor is frequently not privy to the thought process and logic of the person who developed the course. In addition, the receiving instructor may not know how to deliver a course using methods appropriate to online teaching. Because the receiving instructor may not have online facilitation skills either, the importance of good training once again becomes an issue.

One of our former supervisors once remarked that a good instructor can teach almost anything if he or she has good preparation. Thus, a receiving instructor who is practiced in delivering an online course can make it work.

A course can be beautifully constructed, but if the instructor does not teach using techniques appropriate to the online classroom, the course experience will not be a good one for the instructor or the students. Instructors can be given all the resources they need to teach the course, but a successful outcome comes down to their pedagogical approach.

One of us was asked to teach a course on cultural competence written by a subject matter expert with the assistance of an instructional designer. The course contained a debate activity that spanned three weeks of the twelve-week term. Instead of designing the activity so that it occurred on the discussion board, the design team suggested that students be paired up and post their responses to the debate in the assignment drop box and then "publish" the assignment so that the whole class could see it. They were then to rebut the argument of their partner in the same way the following week. In the third week, they were to choose the argument of one other class member and rebut that argument. The approach led to chaos, where students were confused not only by the posting and publishing process but by the whole process of the debate. Consequently, in the middle of this process, the assignment was moved to the discussion board, where the pairs had their own discussion thread to use with an additional area for the third phase of the debate. A suggestion was made to completely rewrite the activity for following terms and was accepted because what had seemed like a good idea in concept didn't work in online teaching practice.

## Ability to Adjust the Course

The initial reaction of an instructor who is being asked to teach a class he or she did not create is often, "How much can I customize it?" Consequently the most critical issue in the use of a course created by another instructor is the ability to adjust it. The central issue in customizing an online course is knowing what is involved with its successful facilitation and what elements should be considered when revising and adapting it. Adjustment may take the form of adding discussion forums for the purpose of building community. The receiving instructor may decide that some material included when the course was developed is unnecessary or that some of the discussion questions in the course don't adequately address concepts, or he or she may choose to add more collaborative activities or change the suggested assignments for the course.

We recently talked to an instructor who teaches science and whose institution had purchased an online science course that he was asked to teach. His first reaction to the course was dismay that there were no labs; the first adjustment he made was to add labs by asking students to conduct simple lab projects at home and report the results, make arrangements to visit the science labs at a local university to conduct some of their work, or come to campus to complete lab assignments. The lab work he assigned was simple enough that students could complete it on their own, but it added a practical element to the class that assisted with the achievement of learning outcomes.

The need for adjustment may not be initially apparent to the receiving instructor. Therefore, the ability to make adjustments as the course progresses is also critical to successful delivery. An important consideration, then, is the flexibility of the course management system. Does it allow the insertion of topics not originally included in the course? Can topics easily be deleted? Can the discussion board be modified in any way? The instructors who are teaching the course must also have enough knowledge of the system to be able to make these changes should they so desire or have support staff available who can assist with this. This type of flexibility, accompanied by an understanding of the course management system, allows instructors to adapt the course in whatever way they see fit and makes the use of another instructor's course more manageable.

## Examples of Customization

One of us was asked to teach a course created by another instructor when that instructor left the institution two weeks before the start of the term. Students were already enrolled, had received copies of the syllabus, and had bought the books. The course site had not yet been established, however, which meant we could do a significant degree of customization for delivering the material. The possibility of adding reading material in the form of journal articles and book chapters also existed. However, the department chair asked that all else remain the same if at all possible, including the topics to be discussed.

At first, the task appeared relatively easy because delivery could be altered to fit the instructor's usual teaching style. However, after reviewing the assigned readings, course assignments, and topics for discussion, the instructor found the course to be somewhat confusing and found that it did not cover many topics that she would have included had she created it. The task therefore became how to include relevant readings and topics without confusing students in the process.

The course design as it was originally configured also proved confusing for the students. They were asked to work collaboratively with a case study every week and respond to a set of discussion questions. Having two types of collaborative assignments weekly was burdensome, and the students kept asking which set of questions they should focus on (the ones included in the case study or the separate discussion questions based on the readings) because the questions focused on related issues and appeared to be closely intertwined. Around the third week of the course, students asked that the course design be reconsidered. This request from the students actually came as a relief to the instructor. It then became necessary to renegotiate the way in which students were proceeding, and the final decision was that they would prepare and respond only to case studies that they themselves developed, each of them taking a turn with presenting the case. Once that adjustment was made, the course proceeded smoothly.

Although working with a course that someone else has created offers challenges, if it is constructed with customization in mind and the training is provided to the instructor, the challenge is lessened and the instructor can focus on delivering a course more in line with his or her own style of teaching.

## When Customizing Is Not Possible

What happens, however, when an instructor is unable to customize a course to any significant degree? Many times an institution will ask an instructor to teach the course as is, at least the first time it is offered—and sometimes every time it is offered. This request raises some important questions: Is this a violation of the instructor's academic freedom? How often does a department chair ask an instructor teaching face-to-face to teach a class in exactly the same way someone else taught it? Most faculty view as objectionable a directive to make no changes in a course. Nevertheless, this request is frequently made when instructors are asked to teach online. In fact, uniformity in course design and delivery is an element that accreditors look for when evaluating a new online program. There is logic behind this: students feel more comfortable and can more easily move from course to course in an online program when courses have the same look and feel. In addition, they have a better idea of what to expect in terms of weekly work-load and assignment completion. The hope, of course, is that instructors will be asked to teach well-designed courses that need little modification. When that is not the case, colleges and universities often provide a means by which instructors can make requests to implement minor changes in the course as it is being delivered and even in future offerings of the course.

In fact, some instructors entering online teaching for the first time can be relieved to receive a course that is already developed. Even when they are given permission to customize, some teach the course without any revisions at least the first time. As their level of comfort with online teaching increases, they are more likely to seek modifications to the courses they teach.

When customizing a course is not possible, the instructor may still be able to extend the use of discussion boards or make good use of multimedia or Web 2.0 applications to supplement the material in the course. Both can help point students to material that was not included initially or suggest they pay minimal attention to material that the instructor feels is irrelevant. Good use of outside resources should help lessen the confusion while moving students in a direction that is more in line with the instructor's orientation. A university for which one of us teaches encourages such practice on a weekly basis. The instructors are encouraged to seek out material beyond that included in the course, such as YouTube videos, websites, and additional articles, and to present those to students weekly along with their own interpretation of the week's material, which can be done in text, audio, or video. Students often express appreciation for this practice because they can see and hear the expertise of the instructor, and instructors appreciate the ability to demonstrate their content expertise in this way.

Through course discussion and by asking probing questions, the instructor should be able to empower students to seek additional resources and share what they find with their peers. The instructor may choose to give a research assignment to the entire group, asking each member to focus on a particular area or topic in the course and then report to one another. Another technique is to divide the topics included in the course and ask small groups of students to seek resources on a topic and then report back. Assignments like these help students develop their research skills, improve their ability to find additional reference material, and build collaboration into a course where none was present previously. Instructors who make creative use of technology resources that the institution might not provide can successfully deliver a course that at first glance appeared to have little room for customization.

## Building Community into the Process

A more critical factor in teaching a course that another instructor has created is finding ways to build community during the process of delivering the course. Because most courses developed by another instructor or entity focus on content rather than process, the development of a learning community is often neglected. Yet it is a key component in the successful achievement of learning outcomes. How, then, can an instructor build a learning community into a course that lacks it?

Regardless of the content and schedule of the course, the instructor can still use the first week to focus on community building. He or she can encourage students to begin communicating with one another on a personal level; for example, having students post introductions at the start of the course helps them connect with others in the course. We make it a practice to respond to every student introduction and find something to comment on. For example, we might say something like, "I see you have a dog that you love. I have a dog as well, and she absolutely rules our family!" The instructor may also ask all the students to engage in icebreaker activities even if those activities are not included in the course design. We often create a social space in the course where students can share important news and jokes and support one another as the course progresses. Creating this forum becomes a perfect place to conduct a beginning icebreaker or to use one as the course is in progress to help students continue to connect and to relieve the tension that can occur as the course progresses.

An instructor once contacted us because she had been asked to teach her first online course using a website on which another instructor had placed course content. She had no ability to create a discussion board associated with the course or to customize it in any way. She decided, after talking to us, not only to use Twitter to create discussions but also to create subgroups of students for the purpose of collaboratively working with case study material. Although she found this approach cumbersome and a bit primitive, she was able to create a more collaborative approach to the course and received feedback from students that the outcome was successful. Based on that first experience, she has since requested her institution to allow her to make significant changes in the way in which the course is constructed by using a different course management system so that collaboration and discussion can be built into the course site.

## Evaluating a Course Developed by Another

A recent important development is an attempt to create a list of quality benchmarks by which to measure online courses. Toward this end, a number of years ago, the Institute for Higher Education Policy released a list of twenty-four quality assurance benchmarks for online education (Merisotis, 2000). Following this, in 2003, the University of Maryland Online began what is known as the Quality Matters Project, designed to create quality standards for online courses that could be replicated across institutions.

Quality benchmarks become particularly important when deciding whether to adopt a course developed by another entity and also when a course is developed by a subject matter expert in an academic institution and will be delivered by a number of instructors. However, in and of themselves, benchmarks mean nothing; they must be couched within a good planning process for an overall institutional online program. The benchmarks related to online course development and teaching and learning make common sense and reflect the practices we have been promoting. These benchmarks, which Merisotis (2000) put forth, are reiterated by the Quality Matters Program:

- Learning outcomes, not the availability of existing technology, determine the technology being used to deliver course content.
- Instructional materials are reviewed periodically to ensure they meet [institutional] program standards.
- Courses are designed to require students to engage themselves in analysis, synthesis, and evaluation as part of their course and program requirements.
- Student interaction with the instructor and other students is an essential characteristic and is facilitated through a variety of ways, including discussions, activities, or e-mail.
- Feedback to student assignments and questions is constructive and provided in a timely manner.
- Students are instructed in the proper methods of effective research, including assessment of the validity of resources.
- Students are provided with supplemental course information that outlines course objectives, concepts, and ideas, and learning outcomes for each course are summarized in a clearly written, straightforward statement.
- The program's educational effectiveness and teaching-learning process are assessed through an evaluation process that uses several methods and applies specific standards.
- Intended learning outcomes are reviewed regularly to ensure clarity, utility, and appropriateness. (Merisotis, 2000, pp. 2–3)

It is important to note that all of the quality benchmarks related to course development and delivery have little to do with content. Instead, the benchmarks focus on constructing the course in a way that facilitates good delivery—in other words, on the process of online teaching and learning. Consequently, as institutions and instructors evaluate a course, they should be concerned first and foremost with how well the process of the course will assist students in meeting learning objectives. Although both content and process can be customized, if the basic structure of the course allows an interactive, learner-focused delivery process, it will provide a solid foundation on which to customize content. We offer some additional criteria that we use when evaluating the effectiveness of online courses that include content, process, and facilitation:

- Course fits with the curriculum.
- Course is learner focused.
- Course is accessible.
- Relevant content is included.
- Collaborative activities, including case studies, small group work, jigsaw activities, simulations, and rotated facilitation are included to stimulate critical thinking.
- Course is interactive.
- All course elements are in alignment and are cohesive.
- Learning styles and culture are addressed through the use of varied activities and approaches to the topic.
- Clear instructions about course expectations and for assignment completion are included.
- A reasonable workload balances reading, posting, assignment completion, use of e-mail, and the like.
- The technology in use serves learning objectives.
- Course pages are designed with one screen of text and graphics, requiring limited scrolling.
- The use of audio, video, and synchronous media is appropriate.
- The use of introductions, profiles, and bios is included.
- Icebreaker activities are included at the start of the course.
- Experience-based activities and exercises are included.
- A social space is provided in the course or social networking technologies are included.
- Clear guidelines for communication, including netiquette, are included.
- Clear expectations about posting requirements, timelines, and assignments are communicated in the course.
- Open-ended questions are used to stimulate discussion and encourage reflection.
- Assessment and evaluation activities that are in alignment with learning objectives and course content are used. (Palloff & Pratt, 2007, pp. 154–155)

## Issues of Intellectual Property

When we were writing the first edition of this book, instructors and their institutions were struggling with issues related to intellectual property in online courses. Intellectual property issues, or the debate about who owns online courses, continues to receive attention as online learning grows. This is particularly so when institutions ask instructors to develop and teach a course online for the first time and then switch the teaching responsibility to another member of the faculty, or when they adopt courses developed by other entities that they then modify, unless clear agreements are in place regarding course ownership.

Intellectual property issues do not belong entirely in the realm of administrators and their lawyers. Instructors also need to be concerned with the ownership of intellectual property and as they create courses for online delivery. Among the important issues to address are these:

- Is an agreement in place between instructor and administrators that spells out who owns courses housed on the university's server?
- If one instructor develops a course that another member of the institution teaches, is there a provision for royalties, or has the developing instructor member been adequately compensated for "work for hire"?
- Do instructors own the courses they develop, and can they use those courses in other ways, such as teaching them at other institutions, placing them on their own private websites, or selling them to a private entity for delivery elsewhere?
- If the institution has an agreement with a course developer and a member of the institution is asked to submit course material to be placed on that company's website, does the instructor still own the course material?
- If the instructor leaves the institution, does the course he or she developed go along, or does it remain on the institution's server and become the property of the institution?

There are still no hard-and-fast answers to any of these questions, which are not applicable to the face-to-face classroom at all. The American Association of University Professors issued a statement regarding distance education and intellectual property in its May-June 1999 issue of *Academe*. It noted that online education "invariably presents administrative, technical, and legal problems usually not encountered in the traditional classroom setting" (p. 41), which result in difficult issues of ownership of materials designed for distance education. Although written many years ago, this statement holds true today.

A 2005 study (Baron et al., 2005) noted dramatic changes in policies and practices regarding intellectual property as applied to online courses. All of the universities studied by these authors had a published intellectual property rights policy that included the rights of instructors to their work. They noted that although 93 percent of these policies designated that professors should have control of their traditional scholarly works, 71 percent of these universities specifically listed exemptions to this policy. Many claimed these exemptions included scholarly work that was created through the use of substantial university resources. In these circumstances, Baron et al. noted that the universities generally offered royalties to instructors for their use. They noted as well that a substantial majority of universities claim the intellectual property rights for materials that faculty are given specific assignments to produce, are specifically hired to produce, or are commissioned to produce as this is considered work for hire.

In addition to these potentially contentious areas, the study revealed some other areas of growing concern. Although half of the universities gave control of syllabi, tests, and notes to faculty, only 31 percent of these institutions also included materials posted to the course site as part of the delivery of the course. Often one of the ways in which instructors customize a course is to add their own material to it, and with this type of policy, this material would then belong to the university. Another area of concern is that 57 percent of universities make some claims in their policies to work developed within the scope of employment or according to the copyright law for works-for-hire. Under this type of policy, anything the instructor writes or creates could potentially be claimed by the university as its property.

The issue, then, is that instructors need to be aware of and ask the questions presented here as they move forward with course development rather than move blindly into uncharted territory. It is dangerous to assume that intellectual property issues will not apply to the work they are creating or modifying. Consequently, instructors and their institutions need to come to an agreement about how courses and additional materials will be used and, most important, who owns them.

## Courses with Rolling Admission

Courses with rolling admissions are relatively new in online learning and can pose some interesting challenges to instructors and students alike.

Generally rolling admission courses are prewritten courses that allow students to start at any designated point, often at the start of a month or middle of a month. This means that some students may be finishing their course requirements while others in the same course are just getting started. In such situations, we have been asked how to go about establishing a learning community or facilitating collaborative assignments. Both of us have taught rolling admission courses and offer the following suggestions based on our experience:

- Include an area for introductions or bios to allow newer students to jump in and introduce themselves as well as quickly get to know the others in the course.
- Structure some form of icebreaker activity at the points in the course when new members will be joining the group to assist with the integration of new members. These icebreakers can be part of the content so as to maintain the flow of the course.
- Use students who are further along in the course as buddies or mentors for students who are just beginning.
- Leave discussions from past students up and available for a designated period of time. This gives newer students in the course some perspective about how others have viewed course material. Interestingly, we have had students get very excited about the posts of students who have preceded them and sometimes reach out to those students to extend the discussion beyond the parameters of the course.
- Use smaller groups for collaborative work and shorter time frames for the assignments to ensure that all students who are enrolled in the course at the same time can begin and complete the work together.

Apart from the obvious challenges of integrating new members and facilitating the development of community and the use of collaborative work, time management for both students and the instructor can be an issue. Instructors in this situation can find themselves feeling like perpetual grading machines as they endeavor to stay on top of all assignments that are coming in from both ongoing students and newer members. It is also possible that instructors in this situation will not get breaks very often, which can lead to burnout. If there is an option to skip a month at the start of a course, we advise that instructors take advantage of it periodically. Having a few weeks without students coming and going in a course is important in helping instructors recharge and prepare for future offerings of the course.

## Final Thoughts on Teaching a Course Developed by Another

Our discussion of the use of courses developed by another entity or instructor member, along with discussion of rolling admission courses, is not intended to suggest that these practices be inhibited, particularly given how pervasive they have become, but rather that good planning is needed when moving in this direction. Given the amount of time for training, development, and support that is needed to create a new course, the use of predeveloped courses can be cost effective. Building an online course is similar to writing a textbook and developing associated learning materials: it is a process that takes a tremendous amount of time and energy.

When predeveloped courses are well designed and focus on the process of delivering the material rather than the content, they can be a high-quality means of moving into online teaching. As with any other online course, however, the focus must remain on instructor and student training in order to be able to move through the course successfully and give support when problems occur. Purchasing courses does not relieve the institution of its obligation to provide a strong infrastructure for its online program.

• • •

With these thoughts in mind, we now turn our attention to the learners, who should be the central focus of all online efforts. In the next chapter, we explore the roles of learners in the online learning process as well as what learners need in order to become successful online students.

---

TIPS FOR SUCCESSFULLY TEACHING A CLASS DEVELOPED BY ANOTHER

- Evaluate the material in the course to determine its relevance for students, and make modifications as needed. Add material through readings, Internet research, lab assignments, fieldwork, Web 2.0 applications, social networking, or any other creative means in order to customize the course if so desired.
- If the original course includes little or no interactivity among the students, add a means by which this interactivity can be achieved: discussion boards, collaborative assignments, social networking using Twitter or Facebook, and other forms of networking for example.

- Facilitate the building of community among the students by encouraging personal interaction such as sharing introductions and creating a social space either on the course site or through the use of Web 2.0 or social networking.
- Get training in online teaching and ask for help when necessary. Don't feel you need to muddle through alone.
- When developing a course that another instructor is likely to teach, ask questions about intellectual property and the ongoing use of the course.
- Make sure to determine who owns any supplemental materials that you add to an online course.

# CHAPTER SEVEN

# WORKING WITH THE VIRTUAL STUDENT

Successful learners in the online environment need to be active, creative, and engaged in the learning process. Nipper (1989) described successful online learners as "noisy learners," or learners who are visibly engaged with one another and with the generation of knowledge. This description of the successful online learner persists today. Dabbagh (2007) noted that the profile of online learners has changed from those who are older, employed, place bound, goal oriented, and intrinsically motivated to a more diverse population that is younger and technologically oriented. Aslanian and Clinefelter (2012), in their survey of fifteen hundred adults who were either enrolled in online programs or planned to enroll, found that the average student who is seeking postsecondary education online is white, thirty-three years old, female, and working full time in a high-paying career. This does not account for traditional undergraduates who are taking online classes as part of their on-campus program, however. Aslanian and Clinefelter estimate, based on their findings, that approximately 40 percent of online students are younger than thirty years old and that 20 percent are under the age of twenty-five.

Our experience, along with the demographics of online learning, tell us that all of the profiles presented now hold true: online learners range from younger students who have grown up with technology to older adults who are returning to school and seek the convenience of online learning. The Illinois Online Network (2010) provides the following list of characteristics of the successful online student:

- Open-minded about sharing life, work, and educational experiences as part of the learning process
- Able to communicate in writing
- Self-motivated and self-disciplined
- Willing to speak up if problems arise
- Willing and able to commit four to fifteen hours per week per course
- Able to meet minimum requirements for the program
- Accept critical thinking and decision making as part of the learning process
- Have unlimited access to a computer and the Internet
- Able to think ideas through before responding
- Feel that high-quality learning can take place without going to a traditional classroom

But are online students simply "born" with these characteristics, or are these characteristics that can and should be developed and encouraged through participation in an online course? Some students who are not noisy learners in the face-to-face classroom flourish online because they have the luxury of time for reflection and response and do not have to compete with more extroverted students in order to be heard (Pratt, 1996). However, it cannot be assumed that students will engage with one another in the learning process or possess all of the characteristics in the Illinois Online Network list; these abilities must be taught. Preparing students to enter online distance learning courses is the focus of this chapter.

## If We Build It, They Will Come

As academic institutions rush headlong into online distance learning, at least two key assumptions are being made: that teachers will know how to teach in the online environment and that students will instinctively know how to manage the learning process. Our experience in teaching online courses and in consulting with faculty, faculty developers, and administrators across the United States and around the rest of the world is that the opposite is true: faculty need training and assistance in making the transition to the online environment, and students too need to be taught how to learn online. Learning through the use of technology takes more than mastering an application or feeling comfortable with the hardware being used. Students in online learning courses need to come to an awareness that learning through the use of technology significantly affects the learning process itself. Furthermore, they need to realize that for the most part, the online learning process occurs through the formation of a learning community and is reflective in nature.

Students may begin an online course expecting to be educated by a content expert, just as in a traditional classroom. When they discover that the most profound learning in an online course comes through interacting with other students, they may become confused and sometimes feel "cheated" by the process. Our culture has led students to believe that education happens through exposure to the sage on the stage, as many describe the traditional academic. In the online environment, in contrast, the instructor acts as a facilitator, or a guide on the side, enabling students to learn collaboratively from one another. For many students, this is a significant shift and one for which they need to be adequately prepared. Furthermore, although younger students have essentially been weaned on technology, they do not necessarily have the experience of using technology for academic learning. Making the transition from playing games or interacting on social networks to the online classroom is a process that needs attention. They need to learn what it means to be an online student and how learning online differs from their previous experiences using technology.

As we consider the collaborative learning process that occurs online, some questions emerge. How can the characteristics of successful online learners be developed? What is the role of the learners? How do instructors facilitate online courses in order to maximize the potential of online learners? And how can instructors teach their students to use the online environment effectively for learning? We explore each of these questions in an effort to provide instructors with ideas and suggestions to assist them in working more effectively with virtual students.

## The Successful Learner in the Online Classroom

Some students take to the online classroom easily and successfully. Others struggle. Some students believe that the online classroom more closely supports their learning style than the face-to-face classroom does, particularly if they need time to think and reflect before responding to questions and ideas. Some may find that they express themselves more effectively in writing than verbally; some are adept with the use of multimedia tools or Web 2.0 applications and find that those support their learning process and help them demonstrate what they have learned. The following comment by a student addresses this issue:

> I . . . am an introvert [and] am much more "outspoken" through the written word than through speaking. In part, I think this has to do with my more reflective nature. Written communication provides me with the opportunity to reflect, collect my thoughts and respond before the topic has changed like it often does in face-to-face communications.—Jane

Much of the research done on successful students in distance education programs suggests that older students who are attracted to this form of education share certain characteristics: they are voluntarily seeking further education, are motivated, have high expectations, and are self-disciplined. These students tend to be older than the average student and have a more serious attitude toward their courses, education, and learning. Aslanian and Clinefelter (2012) note that their primary motivation for enrolling in online courses and programs is career advancement. They are what most would consider to be nontraditional students. We have found, however, that this description does not and should not exclude traditional undergraduate students, particularly because few of today's undergraduates can truly be considered traditional. Estimates are that only one-fourth of the undergraduate population is made up of eighteen to twenty-two year olds who are attending school full time and living on campus. Most students today are older, are working, and need flexible schedules. They are not necessarily looking for campus-based educational and social opportunities. Consequently, they bring with them a different set of assets and expectations to the learning process. In addition, many traditional undergraduates are seeking the flexibility of online learning so that they can engage in other activities, such as a job, sports, or social activities, at any time and also address their studies.

Successful online students tend to enjoy learning for learning's sake. They become energized by the ability to be set free to explore a topic with peers. These students demonstrate good thinking skills, an ability to work and do some amount of research independently, and an ability to work with a minimal amount of structure.

In the past, online learning was seen as most successful in adult and continuing education. However, more universities are using this delivery method with all groups of students regardless of age or level of educational experience, and we're seeing growing acceptance and development in the K–12 sector as well. Dabbagh (2007) notes, "The concept of the independent, place-bound, adult, self-motivated, disciplined self-starter, and goal-oriented learner, which largely characterized the classic distance education learner, is now being challenged with socially mediated online learning activities that de-emphasize independent learning and emphasize social interaction and collaboration" (p. 219). Our own experience with younger undergraduate students has shown us that the students in that age group who do well online are looking for flexibility in their busy schedules, are more independent than the average undergraduate, and may feel lost in large face-to-face classes. The online classroom allows them to express themselves in ways that the traditional classroom does not.

In our experience, online learning can successfully draw out students who would not be considered noisy learners in the traditional classroom. It can provide an educational experience that helps to motivate students who appear unmotivated in another setting because they are quieter than their peers and less likely to enter into a discussion in the classroom. We are also discovering, however, that the interactive skills learned in the online environment can be carried over to the face-to-face setting. In other words, once students are acknowledged for their contributions to the class, their thinking skills, and their ability to interact, they gain confidence in their ability and tend to use these newly discovered skills in other settings. Liz, a student who recently enrolled in one of our online classes, makes this point:

I have found through the learning environment that I have somewhat changed personally and continue to develop another side of myself. Most explicitly, confidence continues to develop within. Also, because I am more of an introvert, I tend to be more direct with my staff and peers. Yet, as I communicate online, I don't have to worry and do find myself toning down at work. I am not as impulsive and I tend to think more before I speak.

The online classroom can provide an alternative that may be quite useful for some students. However, students must not be forced into the online classroom because it is not effective for everyone. Understanding different learning styles can help illustrate why that is the case.

## Addressing Different Learning Styles

Litzinger and Osif (1993) define *learning styles* as the ways in which children and adults think and learn. They break down thinking and learning processes into cognition, or the ways in which people acquire knowledge; and conceptualization, or the ways in which people process information, and motivation, which includes decision-making styles, values, and emotional preferences.

A number of authors have attempted to categorize the ranges of learning styles people possess based on the basic processes. Probably the best known is Kolb (1984), who identified four predominant learning styles:

- Convergers, who like to reach closure quickly by finding concrete solutions to problems and making decisions
- Divergers, who have an awareness of meaning and values and enjoy brainstorming and imagining alternative solutions
- Assimilators, who like to take in lots of information and build theoretical models based on that information
- Accommodators, who are more action oriented, taking risks and teaching themselves through trial and error

Although from our description thus far, it may appear that accommodators are most suited to the online classroom environment, the reality is that all learning styles can work well there. Kolb described a cycle of learning that begins with one's own experience, followed by observation and reflection on that experience, leading to the formation of abstract concepts and generalizations, which leads to the development of hypotheses to be tested in future action, leading to new experiences. Everyone develops a learning style that has some strong and weak points. For example, a person might jump into new experiences without taking the time to reflect on the lessons to be learned from those experiences. Because all students move through this cycle in the learning process and embrace parts of it to a greater or lesser extent, all learning styles can be adequately accommodated online. Creating learning experiences that allow students to experience all portions of the learning cycle enables them to develop more fully in areas where they might be weak, and thus develop a new learning style. Knowledge generation through interaction with peers, plus the development of a more reflective approach to learning as influenced by the use of technology, facilitates this process. The result of the process is a more reflective style, indicating that the transformative nature of online learning has taken hold. We thus refer to this new learning style as *reflective transformative*.

To complicate the understanding of learning styles further, it has been theorized that people tend to learn predominantly through one of their senses: they are auditory, visual, or tactile (Barsch, 1980). Auditory learners tend to retain more of what they hear, visual learners tend to retain more of what they see or read, and tactile learners tend to retain more when they are using their sense of touch—when taking notes, for example. Many published articles seem to indicate that in order to accommodate various learning styles in the online classroom, various forms of technology must be used, or the same concept needs to be taught in various ways. But an online course that uses different types of assignments and approaches to learning can accomplish the same objective without using more complex technologies or multiple versions of the same activity. For example, in addition to asking students to read and engage in discussion online, instructors who use simulations, case studies, Internet research, and collaborative group experiences help broaden the learning experience and accommodate various learning styles. Because it is difficult for instructors to know the learning styles of their students before the course begins, creating a course that is varied in its approaches can help to motivate all students and keep them involved.

## Recognizing and Working with Those Who Do Not Succeed

Should we expect all students to succeed in online classes? Although a student who might not be successful in the face-to-face classroom may do well online, it is unrealistic to expect that all will do well, just as all instructors will not be able to adapt their teaching styles for effective online teaching. How does an instructor determine when a student is not doing well in the online classroom? This is a more difficult question to answer when the instructor cannot see the nonverbal cues that usually indicate when a student is confused. Nevertheless, online students provide evidence to indicate that they may be in trouble. Here are some signs to look for:

- *Changes in level of participation.* A student who had been participating well but suddenly disappears from the online discussion for a week or two may be having difficulty with the course or course material. It is important for the instructor to contact a student who drops away for more than a week to determine the cause and seek solutions.

- *Difficulty getting started.* Some students simply have difficulty getting started online. The instructor may get e-mail or phone calls from the student about technical or other difficulties with the course. The student may continue to express confusion with course procedures and guidelines despite the instructor's explanation.
- *Flaming.* When students are frustrated or confused, they may inappropriately express these emotions by lashing out on the course site. The instructor needs to respond quickly to an outburst online, just as he or she would in the face-to-face classroom. We return to the topic of dealing with disruptive behavior in the next chapter.
- *Dominating the discussion in inappropriate ways.* Some students attempt to dominate the discussion, moving it to personal or other concerns that have little to do with course material. Again, as in the face-to-face classroom, the instructor should attempt to work with the student on an individual basis to redirect this behavior.

When students do not do well online, as evidenced by any of these behaviors, they should be given the option to return to the face-to-face classroom or offered proactive measures, such as tutoring or technical support, to help them better understand what they need to do as online learners or assist them with the course. Their performance should not be considered a failure, but simply a poor fit or perhaps an indication of a different learning style or preference. Not all students do well online and may need more structure and face-to-face contact with an instructor and other students in order to succeed. Once again, this approach to problems with participation differs significantly from the traditional way in which these issues might be resolved. In the traditional academic setting, a student might be asked to drop a course or transfer to another section. Flexibility in moving that student to a completely different learning environment did not exist until the advent of online instruction. Consequently, the online environment provides instructors with a new means by which to assess and work with student capabilities, learning preferences, and performance.

## The Role of the Learner in the Online Learning Process

One of the hallmarks of the online classroom, and one that differentiates it from face-to-face learning, is the need for students to take responsibility for their learning process. In so doing, students play various roles and take on various functions. All the roles—knowledge generation, collaboration, and process management—are very much intertwined and interdependent.

## Knowledge Generation

The instructor in the online classroom serves as a gentle guide in the educational process. Consequently, the "recipient" of that guidance, the learner, has a responsibility to use that guidance in a meaningful way. Garrison, Anderson, and Archer (2000) note that students in an online learning community can and do take on part of the teaching function. These learners are responsible for going beyond a summary of reading or information contained in the subject area under study to analyze the material critically and present it to their peers and the instructor in ways that demonstrate critical thinking, analytical, and research skills. Thus, the learners in the online classroom are together developing original thought and realizing the preferred learning outcome: the construction of their own knowledge and meaning. Students may express their thoughts tentatively at the beginning of a course, as the following student post illustrates, and should become more assertive as a course progresses:

> This assignment has me baffled and I hope that you can help me. I have not enjoyed the readings by Negroponte and haven't been able to tie in his readings with this assignment. I then began the readings by author Jackie Kostner and found her readings notably enjoyable and easier to tie in to this assignment. I am somewhat baffled because I don't quite know what the realm of virtual media is. I picture virtual media as a form of electronic communication through computers. Do I have a limited perception?

Liz was tentatively expressing an opinion that was different from that of her peers. The response she received from them was warm and supportive, which encouraged her to become more confident in her opinions as the term progressed.

The following post, which appeared toward the end of a different course, shows the level of assertiveness that students can attain. Although it may be difficult for some to read, it illustrates the level of comfort in a learning community that this student was experiencing. He knew, because of the interaction with his peers, that his post would be received in the spirit with which it had been created. Steve did not post this material in an attempt to upset his colleagues. Instead, he demonstrated a willingness to question long-held beliefs and go beyond assigned course material to analyze information and present an opposing viewpoint. This post is not atypical of those that an instructor might see in an online course, because the relative anonymity of the medium allows students the freedom to express what they might not in a face-to-face setting:

> NOW's (The National Organization for Women) slogan for breast cancer is "If breast cancer targeted men, emphasis on research leading to a potential cure would have taken on an added sense of urgency." The CDC [Centers for Disease Control] reports that there were 210,203 new cases of breast cancer in 2007/2008; there were 233,307 new cases of prostrate cancer. In 2007/2008 40,589 women and 390 men died from breast cancer. In that same period 29,093 men and 0 women died from prostrate cancer. The American Cancer Society estimated they will spend $872 million on breast cancer research and $399 million on prostrate cancer. [I feel] the NOW slogan slanders men, accusing them of not caring about women where as in reality women receive the vast majority of benefits in our society especially in the important areas of emotional and psychological care. Take a look around you at [our university], who are the minorities? What group is the most under represented in psychotherapy, if you guessed men you guessed right! Think about it!!!

Some learners gravitate easily to the knowledge generator role, sharing many resources with their student colleagues as the term progresses, along with critical reflection on their work. One of us had a student in the knowledge generator role who commented on every draft of a final project posted by her peers and suggested additional reading or resources for each one. Her peers were extremely grateful for her input and actively sought it as the term progressed.

## Collaboration

Students in the online learning environment should not feel alone and isolated but instead that they are part of a learning community that is working together to achieve learning outcomes and generate knowledge. The failure of many online learning programs stems from the instructor's inability or unwillingness to facilitate a collaborative learning process. If course material is simply placed on a website or in a course management system for students to access with little to no means by which to interact with the instructor or other students, contact with professors and peers is not likely to spontaneously occur and the course is not likely to lead to better learning outcomes. Rovai and Barnum (2003), as well as other researchers, have noted that the interaction of the instructor with learners, together with the development of highly interactive course activities, helps learners not only to achieve learning objectives but also increases their perception of having learned.

In the online environment, students should be expected to work together to generate deeper levels of understanding and critical evaluation of the material under study. They should also be expected to share the resources they are finding with the other members of the group. For example, an instructor might consider creating a space on the course site to house the material that the students are discovering. Providing assignments that encourage students to seek additional resources is a good way to increase their research ability and knowledge of how to use the Internet as the vast source of information that it is. Some discussion of or information about search and research skills and techniques can be included on the course site to assist students in this process.

One joy we have found in working with instructors as they explore online teaching is their discovery that the online classroom is the perfect environment in which to encourage collaborative learning. Including collaborative assignments in an online course helps build a learning community and enable achievement of the goal of generating new knowledge and deeper levels of meaning. The mistake that some instructors make is that as a result of their excitement about collaboration, they may include too many collaborative assignments in a course. Students find collaborative work time-consuming as they strive to "meet" together in creative ways and negotiate the roles and tasks necessary to complete this kind of assignment. Consequently, an instructor should allow some breathing room between collaborative assignments. If a term is fifteen weeks, then a maximum of three collaborative assignments is about right. In an eleven-week quarter, one to two may be all there is time for. And in a shorter intensive course of six or eight weeks, there may be time for only one collaborative activity.

Students should be encouraged to use creative means to communicate with one another while completing a collaborative assignment. They might use synchronous discussion through Skype or chat to work together on an assignment or have a question-and-answer session with the instructor. They might be encouraged to make extensive use of e-mail, have a whiteboard session, or have a designated group area in the course site for their asynchronous discussions. The instructor should relinquish control over the learning process during the time when a collaborative assignment is in progress and not feel the need to participate in every discussion. Students should be empowered to get the job done and report results to the instructor and the rest of their class.

In addition, students should be guided and encouraged to give one another meaningful feedback on their work. When a collaborative assignment has been completed, they should be encouraged to evaluate their own and their teammates' performance. Evaluations should be shared privately with the instructor so that students feel more comfortable completing them. We generally have students send us an e-mail that discusses their own performance on the assignment, the grade they feel they deserve, and an appraisal of the work of each member of the team and the grade they would give were they the instructor. We take this feedback seriously, although we retain veto power should we suspect that a group member is being treated unfairly.

Another means by which to achieve collaboration is to have students post all written assignments to the course site and ask them to provide feedback to one another on that work. The feedback, however, needs to go beyond a pat on the back for good work done; it should comment substantively on the ideas presented and question any gaps, omissions, or inconsistencies. Providing feedback to one another helps students develop the critical thinking skills necessary to engage effectively in their knowledge generation role.

One of the advantages to working over the Internet is that groups of students working together in a class do not need to be isolated. They can engage in dialogue between learning communities. By this, we mean that instructors who are teaching similar courses in either the same or different universities can encourage and even facilitate discussion between the participants in those classes. Instructors may even consider team teaching through this approach. As students gain confidence and ease in their ability to study online, their interest can be stimulated in doing additional collaborative work. Students may connect, using the Internet, with experts in their field of study, other universities and learning communities, or discussion groups that have formed around interest in the area under study. As they do this, their ability to use these skills while working in other course areas also increases.

## Process Management

Instructors frequently ask us what the process manager's role looks like. It is the student role that most significantly sets this form of learning apart from the face-to-face classroom, and it is also the most difficult for many instructors to accept. Students as active learners are expected to participate with minimal guidelines and structure. We also expect them to interact with one another and take responsibility for the direction of their learning, as well as the formation of the online learning community. With increasing use of collaborative Web 2.0 technologies, this task is becoming easier to facilitate. However, in order for this to happen, the instructor must empower learners and then step out of the way to allow them to do their jobs—much as a business manager would empower employees. All students have the ability to become process managers in an online course. The reality is that one or two of them will step up to this role. Once that happens, the other students in the group are likely to look to the student leaders to assist them in managing the learning process. Evidence that the process management function has emerged exists when one or two students begin to answer questions that might otherwise be directed to and answered by the instructor.

The instructor's response to the development of the process management role needs to be a willingness to leave behind the traditional power boundaries that exist between instructor and student. The online classroom has been described as the great equalizer—essentially eliminating the boundaries that exist among cultures, genders, and ages—and also eliminating power differences between instructors and students. Dabbagh and Bannan-Ritland (2005) noted that today's online students represent a wide variety of cultural and educational backgrounds and that the globalization of education has allowed students from all over the world to engage in learning activities together. In order to achieve this state, however, instructors must be able to relinquish their power over the educational process and let the learners take on their process management role. Clearly instructors hold the extra edge in the process because they assign a grade for the course. However, in the area of process management, instructors can and should play an equal role. The following student's post illustrates her understanding of the process management role:

> Virtual leaders have less managerial authority than face-to-face leaders. Earlier I wrote about the lack of control faced by virtual leaders and how it is best to embrace loss of control rather than fight it. I think that roles in virtual teams are also more flexibly defined. Authority can more easily be distributed in a virtual team. I think this flexibility results from the looser dynamic. When a leader is in a face-to-face meeting, subordinates expect the leader to assume an authoritative role throughout. In a virtual meeting, those expectations are less strong, because the leader's loss of

physical control is a given. The virtual leader's power, so to speak, comes from her ability to keep the team connected, because that is essential to the team's success. The focus on connections is much more facilitative than managerial, I think. At least in the conventional sense.

I think that's why teachers act much more as facilitators online than they do in a face-to-face learning environment. In a face-to-face environment, students primarily address themselves to the teacher/professor and not to their peers. And it's hard to break that, because of the physical location of the teacher at the head of the class, etc. [Seminar] classes do that to some extent, but the teacher is still obviously the authority.—Liane

By relinquishing our traditional power role as teachers, we frequently find that we learn as much from our students in an online course as our students learn from us. In a workshop we were presenting recently, an instructor stated, "I'm an expert in my field. What could I possibly learn from an undergraduate student?" Our response to him was that we hoped he was not serious. When instructors participate in learning communities, they must be open to the promise that learning emerges from multiple sources and is a lifelong process.

Flexibility, openness, and willingness to relinquish control are characteristics that, when shared by both instructors and their students, make for a successful online learning experience. If we all can maintain an attitude of "being in this together," with instructors holding an equal role in the learning community that has been created, the ability to create deeper levels of meaning and knowledge exists. Instructors, then, must be willing and able to empower students to take on the roles necessary to facilitate educational success in the online classroom. The roles are likely to emerge naturally in an online course. However, some instructors, as a means by which to facilitate their emergence, may choose to assign them: each week there may be a new process manager in the group or someone who is assigned to oversee the collaborative work in which the group is engaged. When a small group collaborative assignment is part of the course, we often ask students to take on the roles to help the small group achieve its task.

## Maximizing the Potential of the Virtual Student

Even when students are empowered to take on the necessary roles, they may not assume their responsibilities unless they are prompted and encouraged. In addition, some students in the group may take on more responsibility than others. This often leads to frustration on the part of learners with collaborative activity and resistance on the part of instructors to include them as a result. Instructors must take steps to draw out students who are not fully engaging with the course and the other students. Just as an instructor might spend additional time with a student who is not responding well in the face-to-face classroom, he or she needs to spend additional time motivating learners to join the online learning process. We offer some suggestions that instructors may take to maximize the potential of all learners enrolled in an online class. Although these suggestions may sound time-consuming for instructors, the time they spend on these may be well spent if it results in active participation and the achievement of learning objectives for all students enrolled in the online course.

### Use Best Practices from the Face-to-Face Classroom to Promote Participation Online

Instructors need to assess the tricks of the trade that have served them well in motivating students and working with problem students in order to find those that might work online as well. Asking, "What would I do in this situation in the face-to-face classroom?" is the best way to do this. If, for example, an instructor has traditionally set up a private tutoring session for a struggling student, she should do the same with an online student. The session might occur through synchronous discussion online, a telephone conference with the student, an intensive e-mail exchange, or a face-to-face session if distance allows. Nothing should be left to chance or assumption simply because the instructor cannot readily see her students. Consequently, in teaching an online course, instructors need to stay actively involved, diagnose problems as they occur, and seek solutions to keep the course moving and students motivated.

### If a Student Is Absent for a Week, Contact Him or Her to Determine the Reason

Just as in the face-to-face classroom, attendance and presence should contribute to the grade in an online class. In a large face-to-face class, a student's absence may go unnoticed. But in the online classroom, a student's absence is quite noticeable and also has a detrimental effect on the other members of the group. Instead of assuming that a student's absence is the result of a lack of motivation, instructors need to investigate the reason for the absence and attempt to bring the student back into the online classroom as quickly as possible. Sometimes a brief e-mail message or phone call can make all the difference for students who may be struggling with the technology in use, the material under study, or other life issues and concerns, allowing them to reenter the learning process without losing significant ground.

## If Students Have Technical Difficulties, Offer Support or Connect Them with Tech Support

Instructors need to be knowledgeable enough about the technology in use for an online course to be able to answer basic questions for students in their classes. In general, students may struggle a bit during the first few weeks of a class as they acclimate to the technology and to learning through the use of technology.

An instructor with whom we were consulting sent us an e-mail requesting our assistance because he was unable to generate a sufficient degree of discussion in his online class. He asked us to "lurk" in his classroom to see if we could help him diagnose the problem. When we visited his class, it became immediately apparent that part of the problem was the technology.

The instructor was using a good course management system, but he had constructed his course and was asking questions in such a way that students were required to move forward and back continually in order to read and respond to what was being posted. Some were finding that simply reading what was there was taking them more than an hour before they could think about or post their own responses. The instructor in this situation responded in two ways. First, he modified how he was asking questions in order to minimize the need for students to look in several places before they determined what they needed to respond to; second, he became more familiar with the system so that he could instruct his students on the best ways to use it and minimize their time online.

## If Conflict Hurts Participation, Intercede with the Students Involved

Disagreements and differences of opinion should not interfere with good participation. However, nothing stifles good participation in an online course like unresolved conflict. Just as in the face-to-face classroom, if a student is acting out, other students may fear becoming the object of that student's negative attention and will withdraw from active participation. In the online classroom, the fear of being attacked is likely to result in reduced participation and reduced interest in the class itself. The experience we described in chapter 2 is a good example. Flaming occurred early in the learning process and the instructor was unable to resolve it satisfactorily. Consequently, students were reluctant to engage with one another for fear of reprisal, and they felt unmotivated to participate. The result was dissatisfaction with the entire learning experience for all involved.

Again, this is a situation where best practices should prevail. Instructors should determine how they feel most comfortable in dealing with conflict in the classroom and with students who are acting out. Just as in the face-to-face classroom, if conflict resolution assistance is available through the institution, the instructor should make use of it. If all else fails, the student or students involved should be asked to withdraw from the class so that the learning process can continue for the others. When this happens, however, it is advisable to have a discussion with the remaining students so that they understand the efforts that were made to ameliorate the situation and why the final decision was made. Often a conference call or a virtual classroom session will help the remaining students understand what happened and allow them to express their concerns and feelings about it.

## If Security Breaches Cause Nonparticipation, Report Them Quickly to Reestablish a Sense of Privacy

We have found that as students form their learning community online, they create for themselves a false sense of privacy. They believe that because the class is password protected, others will not be able to access their discussions. Although this is generally true, there are times when other students might hack their way into a course or it may be discovered that others are lurking, that is, observing what is happening, in the online discussions without making their presence known; someone might have shared a password with another who is not enrolled in the course, allowing that person unauthorized access to the discussions. This can be upsetting to students participating in an online discussion, particularly if they have been sharing material that is sensitive or of a personal nature. Consequently, every attempt to maintain security should be made. If an unauthorized person gains access to the course site, students should be notified and new passwords issued. The instructor should also alert the institution immediately.

Students should be informed if there will be observers in the classroom and what the nature of their presence might be. In a course we recently taught, the discussion turned to the institution in which the students were enrolled. One student posted a message asking who had access to the discussion forum because this would significantly affect the nature of her participation. When she was reassured that no one from the school had access to the discussion, she expressed her relief and felt that she could freely express her opinions without fear of repercussion. Had she not received this reassurance or if someone from the school was observing the class, she would have felt betrayed. Trust is an essential element in building a strong learning community. There should be no surprises where privacy is concerned.

## Log On to the Online Classroom Three or More Times a Week (Daily If Possible!) to Keep the Discussion Moving

Logging on often allows the instructor to keep up with the discussion as well as to deal with any problems and move the discussion in another direction should that become necessary. The importance of an appropriate level of instructor participation should be obvious. By providing a good role model, the instructor demonstrates what "acceptable participation" means. In addition, we have found that students voice anxiety if the instructor is not obviously present.

Regardless of the student centeredness of this mode of education, students still seek guidance and approval from the instructor as they move through the course. If that guidance is not forthcoming, they begin to worry that they may be headed in the wrong direction. We let our students know at the beginning of a class that we intend to log on daily. We may not post a comment daily, but we want our students to know that we are there. One of us was contacted by a department chair five weeks into a ten-week course and asked to rescue a class where the instructor had logged in during the first week and never returned. No assignments had been graded and no feedback had been given to students. An intensive three or four days ensued of assuring students that there was a new instructor present who would grade all assignments and catch up on feedback to them as well as facilitate the remainder of the course. The students, who had been complaining bitterly to the university, were not only relieved but also felt supported by the school and department. Good participation by the instructor is not only good teaching practice but also generates goodwill for the institution.

Many times the instructor may log on and find that there is no need to actually participate in the ensuing discussion. Nevertheless, making some comments at least a couple of times a week reassures students that all is well and that they are on track. Comments should be made regularly and consistently.

## Learn How to Ask Broad Questions That Stimulate Thinking to Promote Participation

Knowing how to ask good, expansive questions is an art, and it is one that can be developed with practice. There is a difference between a question like, "Name and describe three social systems theories that apply to community development," and, "What theory of community development did you find yourself relating to most? Why? How would you apply that theory to our learning community?" The response to the first type of question simply yields a list and requires little critical thinking ability on the part of the students. The second series of questions requires that students evaluate the theories they are reading about and apply them to the context in which they find themselves. It also has the potential to stimulate discussion among the students as they find themselves agreeing or disagreeing with the choices their colleagues make. As we demonstrated in chapter 5, instructors who find a discussion falling flat should reassess the question that has been asked to begin the discussion and either refine that question or ask another one that might serve to stimulate more discussion.

## Include Humor in Your Posts to Help Students Feel Welcome and Safe

Although many believe that communicating in text in the online classroom creates a flat medium in which little emotion is apparent, an increasing body of literature points to the ability to communicate emotion online (Menges, 1996; Pratt, 1996; Palloff & Pratt, 1999, 2007). In addition, adults tend to learn best in situations where they can relate what they are learning to the life they are living (Brookfield, 1995; Knowles, 1992).

Therefore, instructors do not necessarily need to feel that teaching online is a completely serious business. It is important to create a warm, inviting course site where students can feel comfortable expressing themselves and relating course material to their everyday lives. Just as in the face-to-face classroom, humor can add personal warmth to the online experience. When students feel comfortable expressing who they are without fear that this might not be relevant to the course, the likelihood of developing a strong learning community is greater.

Instructors need not fear sharing themselves in the service of developing a learning community. When students are able to see the instructor as a real human being, their willingness to explore and bring in new ideas increases.

### Post a Welcoming Response to Student Introductions to Help All Join More Successfully

We strongly believe that an effective way to begin any course is to have students post an introduction along with their learning objectives for the course and any experience with the subject matter that they might have. It is also important, however, to acknowledge the posting of introductions. In fact, this is the only time during an online course that we will respond to every student post to a discussion.

The instructor can and should be the first to welcome students as they enter the class, once again providing a model for other students to follow. This may well open up ways in which students can connect with one another around common interests and can be a first step in the creation of a learning community. In addition to welcoming students individually, most course management systems allow the instructor to create and post introductory messages. These might be in the form of a brief welcome video or audio message posted to the course or a link to the instructor's website where introductory material might be housed. Once again, this invites students to participate in the course by presenting a small amount of information about it and making them feel welcome. The instructor should also post her introduction and bio as a way of presenting herself as a real person, thus taking the first step to creating a warm, inviting course atmosphere.

## Teaching Students to Learn in the Online Environment

For the most part, students are unaware of the demands that will be placed on them as learners when they opt to learn online. They may enter a non-traditional learning setting with traditional expectations—that is, that the instructor will "teach" and they will "learn" from the material provided. They do not understand why the instructor is less visible in the learning process, that the instructor may not lecture in the traditional sense, and that the instructor's role is one of facilitator rather than traditional teacher. They do not understand that the online learning process is less structured than a face-to-face classroom and requires significantly more from them to make it successful. All of these concepts must be conveyed to students before they embark on an online course. Many times difficulties emerge when teachers and students have differing expectations, and no attempt is made to clarify at the outset.

The transition to online learning brings to the fore some new issues for administrators as they field concerns and even complaints from the students enrolled. Students enter an online course with the expectation that the course will be more attuned to their needs as learners. This may mean that the course is more convenient for them because of distance or because of work and family demands. Or it may mean that they do not like large classes and prefer the increased instructor-student interaction that the online classroom has the potential to provide.

Many institutions are now creating online courses to teach students about online learning and mandating that students complete the online introduction before embarking on their first online classes. Others are incorporating mandatory face-to-face orientations in online programs and courses, although this adds a degree of inconvenience that participation in online learning seeks to eliminate. Regardless of the approach used, the idea is the same: we cannot assume that learners will automatically understand the new approach to teaching and learning that the online classroom exemplifies. In order to realize the educational potential that the online classroom holds and ensure that the learners are given the best chance of becoming empowered learners, we must pay attention to teaching our teachers how to teach and our learners how to learn when teaching and learning are virtual.

As with online faculty training, online student training allows students to experience this kind of learning before they take a course. But regardless of the means by which the training is conducted, the following topics should be included in a student orientation to online learning:

- The basics of logging into the course, accessing and navigating the course site, posting to the discussions, and submitting assignments
- What is required to become a successful online learner, including time requirements and time management
- The differences between face-to-face and online courses, including the role of the instructor and the roles of students, as well as expectations about how students will be evaluated
- How interaction between the instructor and student and between students occurs
- How to give feedback
- What is considered appropriate interaction and communication, including the rules of netiquette and appropriate means to deal with conflict or complaints
- How to get help when needed

Providing an online orientation course may not resolve all of the issues for students as they make the transition to the online classroom. But it certainly can help to give them a leg up and a clearer understanding of the differences in the type of educational experience they are about to undertake.

## Respecting Student Intellectual Property

In the previous chapter, we discussed intellectual property issues as they relate to instructors. Not only is it important to educate students about intellectual property, fair use, copyright, and plagiarism, as we discussed in chapter 4; it is also important to practice what we preach by respecting the intellectual property rights of students.

Increasingly instructors are researching and writing about the online classroom or using their experiences in teaching online as part of their own research. Our own work is a case in point since we incorporate and include snippets of student posts to illustrate the points we are addressing. We expressly ask students for their permission to have their work included in our writing; we remove any identifying information that might link our work to them and assign fictitious names. We have found our students to be very generous in allowing us to use their work as part of ours. Other instructors have not been so lucky in getting student consent to participate in their research in some fashion. In order to deal more effectively with this issue, some institutions are asking students for informed consent at their admission to an online course or program to archive courses with their contributions embedded within them but also so that the archived courses can be used in research after the course has ended. The type of potential research to be conducted is described and students have the ability to opt out. Although we consider this to be good practice, it may not fully protect the institution or its students. We recently consulted to an institution that has educated many students who later entered politics. Because of concerns that posts to an archived online course might be accessed later and essentially come back to haunt these former students who are now in the public eye, the institution has opted to make little use of discussion boards and does not archive its classes. Clearly, students' privacy and confidentiality need to be protected; asking for express consent to archive their material or participate in instructor or institutional research serves to protect their rights.

• • •

In this chapter, we have reviewed what we consider to be good practice in conducting learner-focused teaching online. Given the collaborative nature of this work, we now turn to the dynamics of online groups and suggest ways to work with them effectively.

---

### TIPS FOR SUCCESSFULLY WORKING WITH THE VIRTUAL STUDENT

- Do not assume that students will automatically know how to learn online. Do welcome them to this new learning experience, and create a warm, supportive environment in which they can learn.
- Provide some form of orientation to students as they embark on an online learning experience. If the institution does not offer an orientation course for students, an instructor can include some tips and guidelines for success on the course site.
- Construct a course that is varied and addresses different learning styles. This does not mean using complex forms of technology; instead it means designing assignments and approaches that require both action and reflection.
- Encourage and empower students to take charge of the learning process. Provide them with assignments that allow them to explore, research, and work collaboratively.
- Pay attention to changes in student participation levels, and address them promptly.
- Stay present, and be responsive to student needs and concerns. The instructor should engage in a balanced level of participation so students know that he or she is there.

---

CHAPTER EIGHT

# ONLINE CLASSROOM DYNAMICS

As we work with instructors in online teaching, we are frequently asked why some online classroom groups seem to flourish and others flounder. Despite instructors' best attempts at community development, the students never seem to achieve a rhythm with one another or with the instructor. The same, of course, might be said about face-to-face classrooms. The answer lies in the classroom dynamics, and more specifically, in the group dynamics. With increased knowledge of online group dynamics, instructors can more easily adjust their strategies for dealing with problems such as difficult students or waning participation. Luckily, this has become an area of increasing awareness and study (Becker, 2003; Bell & Kozlowski, 2002; Choon-Ling, Bernard, & Kwok-Kee, 2002; Holton, 2001; Potter & Balthazard, 2002).

Clearly a classroom, face-to-face or online, should not be viewed as a forum for group therapy. However, the need to develop a strong team, focused on learning collaboratively and completing collaborative assignments, promotes the need to understand team or group development. An instructor's knowledge of group dynamics might not be important when teaching a subject such as accounting in a face-to-face classroom unless collaborative small group work is being used as a learning technique. Online, however, where much of the work is collaborative, observation and knowledge of the dynamics of the group become more critical even in courses in accounting and the sciences. Becker's (2003) study of group work within an online class concluded that an understanding of group dynamics on the part of the instructor is not only important but also essential. This understanding allows the group to develop without unnecessary or potentially detrimental intervention on the part of the instructor.

In this chapter, we focus on the nature of groups online, examining theories of group formation and development and how they apply when the group is virtual. We consider formation issues, stages, and the process of group development, as well as leadership issues. In so doing, we review the importance of working with conflict when it arises. In addition, we explore why some virtual classroom groups work and others fail. We also discuss strategies for working with difficult students in the online environment.

## Group Dynamics and Online Classroom Dynamics

Until recently the literature on group development has focused on stage theory. The most accepted of the stage theories is the one proposed by Tuckman and Jensen (1977). Stage theory suggests that groups go through five distinct stages in a relatively linear fashion: forming, storming, norming, performing, and adjourning. We have seen all of our online groups go through the stages that Tuckman and Jensen describe, although not in that exact order. Frequently in the forming stage, online classroom groups discuss the guidelines for the class, especially if the instructor encourages them to do so. This may or may not lead to a storming stage, otherwise known as conflict. We find that conflict arises at varying points in the development of the group, and it is not uncommon for it to occur almost immediately. One of us had an experience with an online group that entered into a heated conflict in the second week of the class because two members felt that the expectations for course completion were unclear. In other classes, conflict has occurred later in the group's development, once members were feeling more comfortable with one another. All of our groups have performed to a lesser or greater extent throughout the course. The adjourning stage in online group development is also not distinct. We find that some classes end with no formal good-byes, and particularly if the group will be interacting with one another in other classes, either face-to-face or online, the group interaction continues, in essence "re-forming" to suit other circumstances.

Our experience, then, is more in line with work focused on the integration of systems theory into group development that has begun to question the linear nature of Tuckman and Jensen's model. McClure (2004) proposes a seven-stage model of group development: preforming, unity, disunity, conflict-confrontation, disharmony, harmony, and performing. He organizes these stages into a model of descent toward conflict and then ascent out of conflict with preforming, unity, and disunity as descending stages; conflict-confrontation as the apex of group development; and disharmony, harmony, and performing as ascending stages. "In small groups," McClure writes,

> individuals come together, create a purpose, and forge a collective identity. Initially in that process, individuality is constrained as a group identity forms. The descent represents the collective forging process. The vertex depicts the crucial conflict stage. This is the turning point in groups where responsibility is shifted from the leader to the members. Once a strong bond is established, responsibility assumed, and a group identity emerges, individuality can be reclaimed, asserted, and expressed. The ascent signifies that reclamation process. (p. 39)

McClure views group development as chaotic and self-organizing. Therefore, the movement between stages is not linear. In order to move from one stage to another, he proposes that the group must enter a chaotic phase that results in agreement—in verbal or nonverbal terms—by the majority to move to the next phase of development. He does not address the termination phase of the group because he believes that most groups rarely negotiate all of the ascent stages successfully. Instead, he proposes that groups move back and forth between harmony and disharmony, rarely achieving a true performing stage.

McClure also proposes that groups experience six issues of concern as they move through the phases of development: safety, affiliation, dependence, independence, intimacy, and risk taking. As with the stages, they may not experience the issues in order. Figure 8.1 illustrates the relationship of the stages and issues.

We have certainly seen all of the issues of concern emerge in online classroom groups and believe that they are influential in the development of a good learning community. They emerge in the following ways:

- In order to feel comfortable in participating in the online class, students need to feel safe. The instructor's responsibility is to create a safe container by providing guidelines and expectations that create a

## FIGURE 8.1 MCCLURE'S MODEL OF GROUP DEVELOPMENT

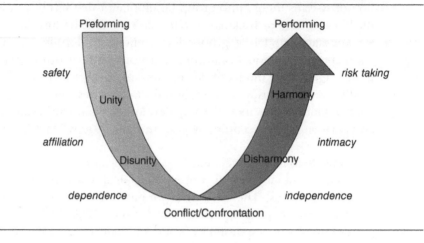

structure for the course and encouraging students to express themselves in whatever way seems appropriate to them within that structure. In addition, the fact that most online classes are password-protected offers a sense of privacy that encourages students to feel safe in the knowledge that their posts will not be read by anyone outside the class.

- Affiliation is a key to the development of a learning community. Students need to feel that they are a part of something greater than themselves: a group that is engaged in working together to achieve a goal.
- Dependence on one another is an important by-product of affiliation. In order to sustain the learning community, students need to feel that they can depend on the others to hold up their end of the bargain, so to speak. They need to know that they can count on their peers to provide feedback to them in a timely manner, contribute to online discussions, and do the work expected of them.
- Dependence on one another should not come at a price. Students in an online group need to feel that they can maintain their independence in the form of independent thought and feeling. Instructors should be on the lookout for groupthink—when students appear to feel pressured to express the same opinions as others—and intervene if this occurs to move the discussion back to a place where independent thinking is the norm.
- Many instructors have commented on the level of intimacy that online classroom groups can and do achieve. The relative anonymity involved with working online seems to free students to express thoughts they would likely not express face-to-face. Consequently, it is not unusual to

see members of online groups sharing details of their personal lives. In addition, students in online classes tend to form close bonds with one another that frequently extend beyond the online classroom. Another way in which closeness might be expressed is when students who are geographically dispersed get together with each other socially when visiting the area where another student lives. It is also not unusual to see conversations about meetings such as this occurring in the social area of the course site.

- Because of the sense of closeness that members of online groups feel with one another, members feel comfortable taking risks and expressing ideas that may be controversial or less than politically correct because they have a sense that they will not be rejected by the group for doing so. Steve's post about breast cancer research, which we presented in the previous chapter, is an example of the type of post an instructor might see when students are engaging in risk-taking behavior. Risk-taking behavior might also take the form of confronting a member who is not participating or who has flamed another member of the group. We tend to see risk-taking behavior increase as the class progresses.
- One of the downsides of the sense of relative anonymity is that students may feel free to say things that upset others with little awareness that this is so. Clearly this can lead to flaming and conflict and needs to be carefully monitored by the instructor and stopped before it gets out of hand.

Because McClure's model was developed in working with face-to-face groups, it raises some questions. How does a model like his apply to online groups? The preceding paragraphs described how McClure's six issues of concern might emerge. However, do all groups we work with in online classrooms experience the six issues of concern? When and where do these issues occur? How might the issues be addressed and encouraged? Figure 8.2 illustrates how these issues might be encouraged or emerge in an online class. To explore these questions and gain further understanding of McClure's model, we next look at the development of one online group.

## Applying What We Understand About Groups to Online Classes

This section describes one group of students in an online class. We view their development as a group using the stages proposed in McClure's model and provide examples to illustrate their movement through each stage.

## FIGURE 8.2  MCCLURE'S MODEL APPLIED TO ONLINE CLASSES

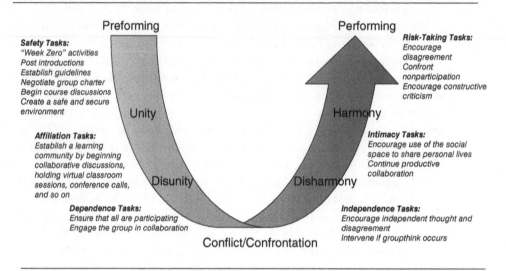

## Preforming

Many of the students entering this class had never met one another previously, and the instructor had not met any of the students face-to-face before the start of the class, which was delivered completely online. All students had taken at least one online class previously. The course, The Search for Soul and Spirit in the Workplace, was an elective. Students were drawn to the course by their interest in the subject matter. Coincidentally, the instructor was working with two of the students in another online class simultaneously.

The class began with the posting of introductions and learning objectives for the course, along with guidelines for communication. All of this was done to address the need for safety as well as to facilitate connections among students. The instructor responded to each introduction, welcoming the students to the class. Following the instructor's lead, students began to respond to one another, connecting with elements of the posted introductions. Here are some examples of the types of connection that began to occur early in the course that illustrate ways in which the preforming stage occurs:

Hi Sofia:

Thanks for your introduction. Sounds as though you are involved in some very creative and innovative projects. I am interested in reading your article regarding the common threads in all religions. The power of religious writings, I think, do come from the stories, examples and metaphors. Let me know when and where it will be available. It is interesting how each member of this group has expressed a delightful curiosity about spirit and soul. It should make for some great dialogue. And, hopefully it will help you in your search along your life path. Thanks for the intro . . .

Take care,
Karen

Hi Sofia:

Glad you looped back for the introduction! We have at least three things in common: the Midwest (Kansas, in my case), an interest in San Diego (you're there and I'd like to be) and a healthy suspicion of work environments that try to entice people to buy into the illusion that everything they need as an individual can come from the work experience. I'm looking forward to more conversation with you! Laurie

## Unity

As part of the course design, students were asked to take responsibility for facilitating one week of the discussion for the course based on their interest in either the topic for the week or some of the assigned reading. The group was able to complete this task with only minor difficulty.

Following the negotiations, lively and active discussion of course material began. Following are a couple of bits of discussion from the first week of the class, illustrating the group's attempts at coming together to achieve their learning objectives and affiliate with one another. The dialogue is supportive and professional, expressing slight disagreement but avoiding any areas of controversy. The avoidance of conflict or controversy is typical of a group in the unity phase of development:

> Thank you Peter for getting us started. I agree with what you have put out here for us to consider. I especially liked where you said "I think one way organizations could help their employees bring their soul and spirit into the workplace would be to start examining what's enough, and to relax some of the incessant pressure that seems to permeate today's workplace." I think this is a huge leap though . . . You are right on when you said "A more likely strategy would be for individual employees, you and I, to start asking that

question in our own personal lives. Once we've got enough, we're free to choose whether we'll work those extra hours or not. It really frees you up from your work; it provides the space required to restore a balance in your life—the space required to nurture your body, mind and spirit."—Sharon

Pete:

I think you have asked an important question, "why is it that everyone feels compelled to work so hard at their jobs?" Perhaps, this is the type of culture organizations have fostered and encouraged? Over a period of time it becomes an explicit or implicit expectation. People get caught on the treadmill and consider long hours normal behavior. Fortunately, there are people who are more reflective and mindful of the need for balance and harmony, both personally and professionally. People are truly searching for something more meaningful. I sense people have a lot more questions to these type of issues than they have answers. I am not sure the answers are as simple as taking more vacation time or more time off. Thanks for the conversation.—Karen

## Disunity

This group showed great interest in the topics discussed and actively engaged in conversation weekly, far exceeding the twice-weekly required number of posts. One member tended to hold divergent opinions from the rest but felt comfortable expressing them, and by two or three weeks into the course, she had no difficulty entering into disagreement with the other members. The risk-taking behavior and ability to disagree with the instructor and with each other, with no apparent repercussion, created an atmosphere of safety that allowed the group to move into the first of the conflict phases: disunity.

Sofia's contributions never went unacknowledged. At this phase of group development, whenever she posted a message, such as the one that follows, one member of the group would support her willingness to speak out without contradicting her opinions. This also illustrates the issue of dependence: in order to feel comfortable entering into disunity by expressing opinions that differed, students needed to feel some dependence on the others. The dependence took the form of expecting feedback and critique of posts. Without it, the group would not have been able to move forward in its exploration of the content:

*Sofia:* Sharon—. . . I love this interaction and these challenges to my thoughts. I have commented by each of yours below:

"How many times do we hear someone say 'I have the greatest job in the word because I get to do what I love most' and we think 'wow they sure are lucky'"? I never say this. I would never (never say never though) stay in a job that I did not thoroughly love. This life is precious to me, each moment counts. There is absolutely no reason to do anything short of what I love. But yes several other people do feel this way. I think this is an effect of not following their truth, or more often not knowing what their truth is. [truth is often used by me in the same frame as spirit—as I have here] What if "what they are" is not something that they can use to feed, clothe and house their families? If you do what you love, live your truth 100% the rest will follow. How many times have people finally stepped out of that comfort zone, said enough is enough and found that they are 500% better off than they were before. No one said it was easy—but it does work! . . . I attempt to live my truth, I love what I do, I wake up happier than the day before everyday and I would say I am doing pretty good in all aspects of my life so far . . . Combined with my experience with it—it works for me and that's all I can say.—Sofia

*Laurie:* Thanks for going out on a limb, Sofia . . . it's something I could have done more of throughout all of my courses. In response to your point that it isn't the organization's responsibility to bring spirit or soul into the workplace but it is their responsibility to allow it, I think I agree. I also think it is the organization's responsibility not to stifle it or destroy it. Maybe that means there is an omission and commission aspect to this. What do you think? I also agree with your idea that you either know that an organization lives its truth or doesn't, although I don't think you can see that as easily from the outside (and when you're inside it may be too late!). The way I think that the organization is dysfunctional because it is out of integrity with itself, much like your description.—Laurie

## Conflict-Confrontation

Unlike other groups we have worked with, this group never experienced a strong confrontational phase. They continued to disagree with one another and felt safe voicing that disagreement. Their disagreements continued to be professional and related to ideas rather than becoming personal. They continued to remain supportive of one another throughout. This may be because the group was enrolled in a graduate-level seminar. All were adult students who were working full time. Consequently, their level of maturity and professionalism as individuals was greater. They were able to create a safe atmosphere of healthy disagreement that did not result in confrontation. An unspoken norm of acceptance of all opinions was established by the group early on and maintained throughout the course.

This has not been true for all classes, however. In a class that was about team building, conflict emerged in one of the small groups within the class as they negotiated a team charter that was to guide their interactions as a small group. One member of the group did not log in until late in the first week of the class and then posted vehement disagreement with the direction the group was heading, pushing the group directly into conflict before it was ready to handle it effectively. The group had not completed the unity stage, which is where it was working, and had not established the necessary sense of safety or dependence on one another. Because of this, the conflict persisted throughout the term, forcing the instructor to hold several Skype sessions with the group in an attempt to work through the issues and get the group back on track.

## Disharmony

As the Soul and Spirit group moved toward the performing stages, participation remained strong for all but Sofia, whose participation became slightly spotty. Sofia, who tended to voice the most disagreement with the opinions of others in the group, dropped away for a short time, claiming first that she had a computer virus and then later a troubled friend who needed her attention. Other students expressed some concern about her absence and welcomed her when she rejoined the group. Although she described some personal issues in her life that had drawn her away, it is possible that she felt somewhat uncomfortable with being the group member to spark conflict and give voice to different and dissenting opinions and thus withdrew for a short time to allow the group to move beyond the conflict phases, expressing her own independence and also allowing each member of the group to assert their own. Even in face-to-face groups, this is not unusual. A vocal and more opinionated member of the group may not show up for a few sessions, leaving the other members to wonder about the reason. The shift in group functioning and norms causes a sense of unease or disharmony that frequently results in a reexamination of norms and expectations.

## Harmony

As we usually do when we create the course site for an online class, we included a social area—named The Café—on this one. About midway through the quarter, the group began making extensive use of The Café.

One student posted a work problem she was dealing with, and several students jumped into a discussion on virtual leadership that was unrelated to the course material. Another student experienced a health scare during the term. He posted this in The Café and received strong support from the others in the group.

This use of the social space also illustrates the growing sense of intimacy in the group. Simultaneously, the nature of participation in the course discussions became more harmonious. Sofia completely reengaged with the group and continued to feel safe expressing her opinions, demonstrating that risk-taking behavior in this group was acceptable and welcome. The following exchange is about her reentry into the group:

*Sofia:* I find this a hard question for some reason today. I have been grappling over these questions for hours, days it seems like. Had they been asked merely 6 months ago, last term for example, I could've popped up with a brilliant answer of my leadership gifts. I am left wondering if I can't find the answers today because I am in a transitionary period. Transitions seem to clear the slate for me. They remind me of what I do not know, of what I have not grasped yet. They are the moments when I first begin to step out of that comfort zone I have been hiding in . . . I think the biggest gift I offer people these days is power, personal power. I left my previous company because it misused power, stole power, misunderstood power and in the end lacked the power to achieve it's dream because of it. In my choice to leave, combined with the dive I took into the dark sea of myself, I found my own personal power. Through that I found the ability to lead others to their own.

*Karen:* I found your comments exceptionally powerful and thought provoking. What a wonderful gift of insight you have into your own behavior. It sounds as though you are really going through a wonderful and fascinating period of growth? And, the benefit is you have a better sense of yourself and what you want (at least for this moment in time) is that a correct assumption?

## Performing

As the term progressed, this became a high-performing group. Despite earlier disagreements, group members developed significant regard for each other, their ideas, and their work. They began to reflect on their learning experience and commented that it was unlike others they had experienced, either online or face-to-face. Participation levels throughout the term were extremely high. It was not uncommon for this group of seven students to generate somewhere between 110 and 150 postings per week. Despite personal issues that periodically interfered with the ability of a couple of students to participate at the same level as the others, overall participation was relatively evenly dispersed across the group. The instructor's learning objectives for the course were these: "This course will explore recent writings on the search for soul and spirit in the workplace, as well as how it affects the notions of meaningful work, leadership, and organizational change. We will also explore these concepts as they pertain to your personal search for meaning in the work you do."

Following is a student reflection on the achievement of learning outcomes in this course:

> As many have mentioned, this particular virtual environment has been an exceptionally open, engaging process. Jointly, we have raised thought provoking questions, responded to one another with care and respect and we have encouraged one another to reflect and think. I have routinely enjoyed logging on and reviewing the ongoing conversations and comments. Whatever the topic, some humorous, some serious, some soul-searching, I always felt we sincerely listened to each other. It seems as though we discovered a common ground for learning and we were willing to openly trust each other to honor our thoughts and our feelings. Perhaps for a brief moment in time we found a safe harbor, where it was acceptable to be vulnerable. I know I will reflect on our conversations as I continue to work through some of these issues of soul and spirit. It is an never ending process of discovery. I feel exceptionally blessed to have been surrounded by six talented and gifted learning partners in this journey. You hold a special place in my heart.—Karen

## Concluding Thoughts About the Soul and Spirit Group

The Soul and Spirit group did move through conflict on its way to the harmony and performing stages of group development. Early on, they worked hard to get to know one another and establish unspoken norms of open, accepting participation. Active participation also became a norm for this group: they far exceeded the mandatory guideline of two posts per week.

This may appear to be an ideal group experience, yet it is one that we have had often as we teach online classes. Allowing space for the group to move through its developmental phases contributes positively to the achievement of learning objectives. What would have happened if the instructor had stopped the emergence of conflict by silencing the dissenting voice? Most likely, this would have become what McClure describes as a regressive group, never able to move to the harmony and performing stages.

This example emphasizes how important it is for an instructor to look for signs that the group is moving through stages of development. It is not necessary to comment on this to the group, but it may become necessary to facilitate movement to the next stage if the group becomes stuck in the conflict phases, as was necessary with the group in the team-building class as well as others that we have facilitated. What's critical is for the instructor to maintain an atmosphere of safety, which allows space for the group to move and develop. Being aware of group dynamics and facilitating them skillfully has the benefit of supporting the development of the learning community and generating more effective collaboration.

## Other Ways of Looking at Online Groups

McGrath and Hollingshead's (1994) classic work on the study of online work groups sought to determine the impact of technology on team development. Rather than looking at online groups as moving through various stages, this model looked at the numerous factors that lead to successful or unsuccessful outcomes when online groups come together to perform various tasks.

The essential elements of McGrath and Hollingshead's model can be distilled down to three that have equal influence over each other: people, tasks, and technology. The authors further argue that there are three functions that online groups strive to achieve:

- Production, or the ability to complete a tangible task
- Well-being, or a sense of individual satisfaction and that individual needs are being met through the group
- Member support, or a sense that a safe space has been created through which members can support each other in achieving their collaborative task

Online groups attempt to achieve these functions through four modes of operation:

- Inception, or what McClure would likely call preforming, when group members begin to work together to understand their common task
- Problem solving, that is, the main reason that task-oriented groups come together online

- Conflict resolution, a critical factor in successfully completing tasks together
- Execution, or the completion of the task

McGrath and Hollingshead (1994) argued that rather than moving through the modes in linear fashion, online groups may move back and forth between each mode, with each function manifested in each mode. The example of our Soul and Spirit group illustrates all aspects of the McGrath and Hollingshead model. Certainly the group completed their task together, felt good about what they were able to accomplish in the process, and supported one another throughout. They were able to discuss and solve problems together, resolve conflict easily, and perform well as a group.

Pratt (1996) adds to our understanding of the individual level with his description and discussion of what he terms the *electronic personality*. He proposes that when individuals enter the online environment, they allow parts of their personalities that are not seen face-to-face to emerge. Introverts tend to flourish online because of the absence of the social cues and body language that are somewhat inhibiting to them in face-to-face situations. They therefore tend to become more extroverted in their participation in online groups. Extroverts, in contrast, have more difficulty establishing a presence online. Because they tend to be more verbal in face-to-face situations, they can easily make social connections and let others know who they are. This is more difficult for them to do in a flat, text-based medium. The ability to free up parts of ourselves online helps level the playing field in online groups, allowing more even participation from all members regardless of their introversion or extroversion. It also allows people to try out new roles and behaviors.

Another issue with online groups is that the pacing of responses creates time gaps, which can be both positive and negative in terms of group development. The time gaps can promote reflection but can also create discomfort for members who feel that the group is not addressing their needs and concerns. Some researchers, however, support our own experience that it is possible to develop greater group cohesion in a shorter period of time in technology-based groups (Mennecke, Hoffer, & Wynne, 1992). The ability to engage in informal discussion unrelated to the task that brings the group together assists with this process. In other words, groups need to be given a space in which they can connect with each other on a social level and begin to know each other as people apart from the task that brings them together. In face-to-face teams or groups, informal connections happen outside the classroom and may be encouraged by the instructor or facilitator. The same opportunity needs to be provided for online groups in order to allow group cohesion and more satisfactory task completion. The Soul and Spirit group made good use of the social area created for their course. They supported one another through life and health crises, discussed work issues, and also discussed issues related to their personal lives as a group.

Finally, the environmental realm is clearly made up of the technology that is used. The technology should be a vehicle that ensures clear, unrestricted communication in order to support good group development. In addition, group members need access to technical support should anything occur that interferes with their ability to communicate with the group.

Figure 8.3 summarizes the theories of group development as they relate to online groups. It shows the connections between the individuals, the group, the facilitator, and the technology as these elements relate to the completion of a common task. The list in the center of the diagram describes the activities through which online groups become unique and illustrates how all the elements overlap.

## FIGURE 8.3 CHARACTERISTICS OF EFFECTIVE ONLINE GROUPS

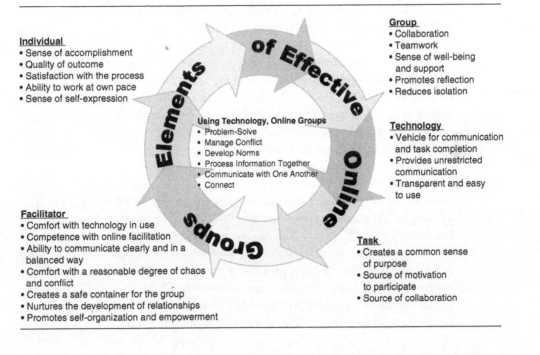

**Individual**
- Sense of accomplishment
- Quality of outcome
- Satisfaction with the process
- Ability to work at own pace
- Sense of self-expression

**Group**
- Collaboration
- Teamwork
- Sense of well-being and support
- Promotes reflection
- Reduces isolation

**Using Technology, Online Groups**
- Problem-Solve
- Manage Conflict
- Develop Norms
- Process Information Together
- Communicate with One Another
- Connect

**Technology**
- Vehicle for communication and task completion
- Provides unrestricted communication
- Transparent and easy to use

**Facilitator**
- Comfort with technology in use
- Competence with online facilitation
- Ability to communicate clearly and in a balanced way
- Comfort with a reasonable degree of chaos and conflict
- Creates a safe container for the group
- Nurtures the development of relationships
- Promotes self-organization and empowerment

**Task**
- Creates a common sense of purpose
- Source of motivation to participate
- Source of collaboration

*Elements of Effective Online Groups*

If we further examine the elements of effective online groups, we can begin to see the roles of the individual student, group, instructor/ facilitator, task, and technology as they relate to online classes.

## The Student

Students enter online classes with a concern about the task to be accomplished. In other words, they hope to complete the course in which they have registered with a minimum of difficulty and to feel good about the outcome. What attracts individual students to online classes is the ability to work at their own pace using asynchronous communication and other means. They are often surprised at their ability to engage with the material and the instructor in a different way than they would in face-to-face classes. They are also sometimes surprised by the more facilitative role of the instructor, the directive to function both more independently and collaboratively at the same time, and the need to become good managers of their own time given the demands of online classes.

## The Group

The role of the group is critical to the success of online classes. A well-designed online class intentionally builds a learning community by providing opportunities for teamwork, the completion of collaborative assignments, and the ability to reflect on the process and the learning. Working with an online group can serve to reduce the sense of isolation that some students have described in taking online classes that lacked interaction. Encouraging students to become part of a whole by joining an online classroom group increases the likelihood that they will stay involved and motivated, because successful completion of the task (in other words, completion of the course) is a collaborative effort.

Another reason that a learning community is important is that it provides social connections that allow students to get to know one another as people. This too increases the likelihood that students will want to stay involved. They will be reluctant to let down their friends by not participating in discussions or other activities. They come to see their contributions as important to the learning process of the whole group and not just to the achievement of their own learning objectives. The focus, then, becomes the learning process and involvement in a learning community, and not simply completing the course or earning a passing grade.

## The Instructor/Facilitator

We have already discussed some of the critical characteristics of a successful online instructor, including flexibility, responsiveness to students, a willingness to learn and a self-perception as a lifelong learner, an ability to balance the amount of participation in the group, and, most important, comfort with and the ability to facilitate the development of an online learning community. Instructors who are flexible, open, and willing to go with the flow of an online class are likely to have a successful experience. They must, however, be prepared to deal with the conflict that will inevitably emerge in an online group and develop a means by which to work with it successfully so that the group can move on to achieve its task together.

## The Task

Clearly the task that brings students together is to complete the course. In that regard, the task creates the sense of purpose for both the students and the instructor. A well-developed course should motivate students. If the material presented is relevant and the task is structured to empower students to take charge of the learning process, they will be more likely to stay with it through successful completion. Multiple opportunities for teamwork and collaboration will reinforce the sense of common purpose and provide opportunities for students to take charge of their learning.

## The Technology

The course technology is only a vehicle for its delivery and should be transparent and easy to use with minimal instruction. The technology allows for the creation of a meeting place online where students can connect with one another for both social and task-oriented reasons. The technology therefore is not the reason a course is offered; rather, it is an important supportive factor in its success. In addition, supportive technologies that assist the group in working together (virtual classroom technology, wikis, blogs, and chat, for example) should be used.

# Conflict Revisited

McClure (2004) states that conflict is a central feature of all groups, a theory that is widely shared by those who study group dynamics. It is not a feature that should be feared but instead welcomed, because the presence of conflict indicates that the group is developing successfully. McGrath and Hollingshead (1994) also noted that in online groups, the ability to resolve conflict is one of the central tasks to be accomplished in order for the goals to be achieved and the tasks completed.

Frequently the word *conflict* brings to mind an all-out struggle, complete with anger, hurt feelings, flaming, and a win-lose outcome. In online groups, however, conflict may simply take the form of disagreement with the instructor or between students. At times it may become heated and be perceived as an attack. When this happens, the instructor should step in to resolve it. However, in many cases, students can resolve these disagreements for themselves. Sometimes resolution may take the form of agreeing to disagree.

Asking students to reflect on the conflict and its resolution can add an element to the learning experience that can be extremely useful to them in their overall reflections about online learning and how it differs from the face-to-face classroom. The following example of conflict and confrontation over the spotty participation of a group member demonstrates growing understanding on the part of students about the need for everyone to be involved if learning online is to be successful. Although the tone is somewhat harsh, it reflects these students' strong feelings about their dependence on one another in order for their learning objectives to be achieved:

*Larry:* You [Phillip] have mentioned on 3 or 4 occasions, how busy you have been, sleepless nights, coming into this process late, an outcast, x number of consulting proposals . . . Focus on the participation, learning and the contribution. Let this other stuff go. We are all extremely busy and quite frankly not interested in being reminded how overwhelmed we all are. The boat we are in is the same. The waters are equally turbulent, only our perspectives differ . . . You are always selling! Seek to understand first.

*Phillip:* I want to "jump" in here and offer some observations on things that I have seen. I agree Larry, that asking questions is paramount to understanding. I can see that you are striving to "read between the lines" and understand all that is being said. I appreciate this endeavor very much. However, I also agree with Allison's statement: "Not EVERYthing can be answered with another question.—I'm really worried that this is coming out whiny or out of line, but I wanted to state an observation of mine . . . a personal opinion (I don't think that was whiny at all, by the way). In my opinion Larry, I also agree with her that you seem to be a little defensive . . . and I will even add . . . sometimes it comes across with a little bit of an "attacking" feeling to me. Perhaps this is simply your pure desire to understand.

I know that this is what you are constantly seeking to teach me . . . "Seek first to understand." I appreciate this very much and will strive to do so. I also am reminded of a proverb, which basically says, "people often teach what they most need to learn." Just food for thought. Asking the kinds of questions you tend to ask are extremely important and I am thankful for your insight and attempts to clarify and hope to be able to ask such penetrating questions myself. However, there seems to be something missing in your responses and I think that there is not very much sharing of something deeper . . . no collaboration. You mainly just respond by asking for further clarification or with a reason for your previous response. It's a real cognitive approach. I wonder how do you "feeeeeel." That is what I want to know, instead of always being asked another question. So I will ask you now, how do you feel about me, what are you so angry with me about?

What might be interpreted by some as petty bickering actually signals the presence of conflict. In fact, this exchange opened the door for others in the group to begin discussing what they saw as appropriate participation. Although Larry and Phillip settled their difference easily once the conflict surfaced, the issue of levels of participation continued well into the course and resurfaced involving other students. They soon began to realize that their expectations of one another and their need to rely on one another for their learning was the issue. Beginning with this exchange, the group overall learned something important about the process of an online class.

A good rule of thumb is for students to wait twenty-four hours before responding to a post they feel is negative to allow a cooling-off period and time to reflect. A student who returns to a post that he or she initially saw as offensive may find, on second reading, that it is not so bad. This time-out also gives students a chance to respond from a place of reason rather than anger, thus helping to reduce the possibility that the conflict will escalate.

In the previous series of exchanges, Larry is asking Phillip to do just that—wait and reflect rather than react. He is asking Larry to look at the way in which he approaches not only him but also the rest of the group. These students are demonstrating the ability to manage their own conflict situation. The instructor intervened only to ask the students to reflect overall on the process and waited until the conflict had abated before doing so:

*Rena:*  Just thought I'd stick my nose in for a second—several of you have been commenting about the need for Phillip to get involved with this process and fearing that he would not. He did—in a big way, in my humble opinion—in his last post by opening himself up to the group in a rather courageous way, I thought, and contributing his thoughts on the task and process. The response was nothing, nada, zilch! I thought it was interesting to note, and thought it was important for all of you to reflect on it a bit.

*Mia:*   Rena, you are right, Phillip did jump in and no one commented. I thought that it was great that Phillip is back in the game. But, as Stasi said, wasn't going to applaud until I see results over time. It is sort of like making friends. It is not difficult to be nice, witty, thoughtful, etc. for one day . . . I am looking for a commitment to the group. That commitment means more than popping in once a week on the weekends.

*Rena:*   I really think, gang, that you need to take a look at the role that Phillip is playing in this group and your responses (or lack thereof) to him. I also need to say that if it weren't Phillip, it would be someone else. I just noticed something that clearly the others of you didn't based on your confusion in response to my post—you've been asking him to jump in and some have expressed concern that he wouldn't. When he did, you just kept on rolling like nothing had happened . . . Again, I'm not blaming, shaming, defending, or anything else like that—just asking you to reflect on your own process and dynamics . . . I have noticed, and there's no judgment intended with this comment—again neutral observation—that everyone is fine with the level with which Chad is able to participate (which is low compared to others) and yet when Phillip participates at actually a higher level, it's his participation that gets questioned. I'd like you, once again, to simply reflect on this. Maybe no comment is even necessary—just notice and reflect.

The response to the instructor's observations in this case was a series of "aha" moments for the group's members. They began to recognize what conflict looks like. They also began to understand the roles that various group members were playing and their responses to their own expectations about other members. The following posts reflect the changes that occurred as a result and indicate that the group was beginning to move out of conflict:

*Mia:*   I am feeling particularly disappointed and frustrated. I would say that my experience with teams, in general, has not been totally gratifying. There are probably several reasons for that, partly due to what may be unrealistic expectations on my part and partly due, in my opinion, to others not fulfilling their obligation to the group or the agreed upon norms or rules. I guess that I am trying to understand where Phillip and Chad are coming from and I am frustrated because I can't seem to engage Chad in dialogue and Phillip doesn't seem to get what people are saying. I take participation and leadership on a team very seriously. In regard to my participation, I have had to work very hard to meet the norm of reading once a day and posting every other day. And, I have tried to provide something in the posts that would add or expand the group's work, help move the group forward, and/ or encourage and recognize group members. Maybe this is the norm I have established for myself and it is unrealistic to expect it from others . . .

*Larry:* I have read your comments pointed to Chad and Phillip as well as the other Cohort member's comments and have decided not to play in this arena, until now. I am clear that norms have been established and I am also excited with the participation from the group. I look positively at the direction we have taken, the progress that we have made and value everyone's input. My focus remains on what we are accomplishing collectively as well as what I am learning through this process. I am delighted with the results. There is so much stuff that goes on in other people's lives that I try (not always successful) to give them the full benefit of the doubt. I am still learning to hold everyone legitimate and sometimes it is not easy for me. Rena's posting with regard to the group's lack of response to Phillip's posting helped me advance my understanding in this regard even more. This group has dealt with a lot. I have learned so much in such a short time and I am grateful. There will never be a group where there is "equal participation" in everyone's eyes and the value of the individual contribution is the real jewel.

It is best, then, for instructors to take a position of noninvolvement and observation when conflict first surfaces. Often students are very capable of working through the issues and achieving successful resolution. However, if the conflict escalates, interferes with progress of the class, or turns into personal attacks or flaming, then the instructor must intervene. Things often begin to quiet down after a post by the instructor setting a limit or asking students to take the conflict off-line, or after the instructor has individual conversations with the students involved. If these actions do not work or the conflict is perpetuated by a difficult student, it may become necessary to take additional steps.

## Working with Difficult Students

Just as in the face-to-face classroom, difficult students appear in the online classroom. The difficulty can take many forms: being unable to adjust to the technology; dominating the conversation; refusing to participate at an adequate level; blaming the instructor, other students, or the program for their lack of satisfactory progress; and bullying other students or the instructor through flaming. In the face-to-face classroom, an instructor may become quickly aware of the presence of a difficult student. But in the online classroom, difficulties may not show up as quickly or may be unrecognizable at first. For example, it is common for students new to online learning to experience some problems with the technology. Some may require the assistance of the instructor or other technical support staff to resolve their technical difficulties. When difficulties go on for several weeks, however, red flags may start to go up for the instructor and the other students: Is this someone who truly is having difficulty, or is this a smokescreen for refusal to participate at the level required?

When instructors diagnose a difficult student, it is important to take steps that they would also take in a face-to-face situation. For example, scheduling an individual conversation with a student who is causing problems such as dominating classroom conversation or being argumentative is useful. The conversation might take place by e-mail, or the instructor may choose to have a telephone conversation, Skype session, or face-to-face meeting with the student.

Not all conversations need to happen on the course site. Sometimes taking the problem off-line can be more helpful than trying to confront or deal with the student publicly. Regardless of how and where the conversation occurs, it is important for the instructor to provide concrete examples of the behavior in question. The beauty of the online classroom is that asynchronous discussion is archived on the course site, and synchronous sessions can be recorded. Therefore, it is relatively easy for the instructor to point out where and how the problem occurred and give specific suggestions for improvement.

If a problem student is unresponsive to instructor intervention, then best practices should prevail. Perhaps the student's access to the course should be suspended until the problem is resolved. The instructor may need to request help from department or program administration if an administrative solution, such as permanently removing the student from the class, becomes necessary.

As we've noted many times, successful achievement of learning outcomes is dependent on the creation of a learning community. Students depend on good participation from one another to build that community. Consequently, an instructor cannot afford to take a passive stance or wait too long when problems crop up. Decisive action must be taken and limits set when behavior is unacceptable in order to salvage the learning experience for the majority.

## When It Simply Isn't Working

There are times when, despite our best efforts, we are unable to facilitate successful formation of an online learning community or create a sense of group among the learners. It is easy for an instructor to blame himself or herself when this occurs, saying, "Surely there is something else I could have done." However, when we have experienced this situation, there is usually a student who offers a voice of reason by giving us some feedback that offers clues to what went wrong. The following story of such an experience includes excerpts from an online conversation between one student and the instructor after the class ended during an attempt to discern what transpired in an unsuccessful online learning experience. Interestingly, the class in question was another section of The Search for Soul and Spirit in the Workplace offered at a graduate level.

The class began in fairly typical fashion with the instructor asking that introductions be posted online. This was not the first online class this group of students had taken, and the students had met one another at a face-to-face session to kick off other classes they had taken before this one. However, the instructor was not present at that session. Because of this, the instructor faced an immediate challenge of establishing a relationship with and presence in the group. What became apparent to the instructor rather quickly was that there were two subgroups in the class based on the grouping of the students when they met face-to-face. In addition, there were other concerns about the nature of the group, as one of the students, Beth, points out here:

> As you know, I was so inspired by the course topic and drawn to the class, I had high hopes for rich dialogue and learning. The class size was small, and all female. I remember making an early comment on that and asking if people thought it was significant that we were all women. The answers that came back were just more questions. I do wonder if the balance in the class would have been different if we had some male participants.

Although this was a problem for the group, the concern about group composition was put aside when students began complaining about a lack of clarity in the course design and an inability to determine what was expected of them. This proved confusing to the instructor, who had used the same course design very successfully several times previously. Beth continues:

Unfortunately, we had some early disconnects in the class—in the first week. People were unclear about the assignments (which is normal and has occurred in every class. We simply then post for clarification). One participant was particularly harsh and caustic in the tone of her writing. She was upset that you [the instructor] needed to travel for two or three days in the first week of the class and that you had some trouble connecting online. A second participant joined in the disappointment. What I remember most was the tone of the exchange. It was accusatory and very judgmental, non-forgiving. I think we never fully recovered from this exchange that occurred so early in the class.

Once the instructor was able to rejoin the class after only two days of absence, she was surprised to find the level of confusion and upset present in the group. Quickly this group had entered a phase of disunity and conflict from which it was difficult to recover. The conflict was directed not only toward the instructor but also occurred between the two subgroups within this small group of six students. The instructor expressed her concern and confusion over the level of hostility in the group. But any attempts she made to intervene in the conflict and reduce it were met with resistance and anger. Beth observed:

I would bristle whenever I read what the "toxic" participant would write. It was harder to log on and less rewarding than other classes I have been in where the exchange and discussion is so rich and supportive. I would come downstairs after doing schoolwork and debrief some of the things this one participant said and how she said it with my husband. I thought they missed a big point of the learning.

Because participation continued to be poor and interchanges between the two students and the instructor and a few of the students with one another often bordered on flaming, the instructor attempted to have individual contacts with all of the students in the group, by both e-mail and phone. One student refused all contact with the instructor, whereas others responded fairly favorably to these exchanges. The instructor also enlisted the aid of the program chair who, when she attempted to intervene, also met with resistance and challenge. The difficult student withdrew from the class for a period of time and eventually made a decision to withdraw from the program, returning only to complete the class, much to the dismay of the instructor who had no control over this decision. Overall, students never fully participated in this class or achieved their learning objectives due to the early problems in the group. Beth reflected on the outcome:

> I . . . observed how hard it was for you to try to mitigate all this online. It was helpful when you all would report that you had a conversation. If I recall, we had some improvement after that, but never a full recovery . . . My approach was to stay focused on the reasons I was in the class, continue to respond to everyone and try to foster dialogue, and to rise above what I saw as pettiness and lack of maturity . . . It was interesting and puzzling how individuals drawn to the topic of soul and spirit in the workplace spent so much time and thought on the dark side of spirit. Maybe they showed us the dark sides of their own spirits. Maybe they felt they had permission to do so, given the topic. I don't know. At the end of the class, I remember thinking, for a class on soul and spirit, we didn't have very much soul or spirit in our learning community. How sad.

What are the lessons learned from working with a group such as this one? What can an instructor do when, despite all efforts at intervention, a learning community fails to form? These are the key issues as they relate to these questions:

- The group in question contained not one but two difficult students, and the instructor was not clear about the programmatic guidelines in dealing with a student who is inappropriate in the online classroom.
- Decisive action was not taken with the difficult members, thus giving them "permission" to continue to act as they had. In hindsight, both the instructor and the program administrator agreed that had decisive action been taken early on, such as setting clear limits on acceptable behavior in the class, the learning experience might have been saved. In addition, the decision to allow the student back into the class at the end was deemed a mistake by the program chair, further disempowering the instructor and adding to the disillusionment and lack of safety the other students felt.
- The makeup of the group was a problem from the beginning—small numbers, all female, all with the same level of online experience. McClure (2004) notes issues that emerge when a group is all female with a female leader and describes them as follows: "early stages of group development are further complicated by member reactions to the female leader. These reactions range from ambivalence to confusion and rebellion" (p. 100). He attributes this to what he terms

"status incongruence"—groups often attribute more status to male leaders than to female leaders. Thus, this is rarely seen in groups that are all male. When debriefing this experience with administrative staff, it was noted that this fact should have been caught during registration and an attempt made to balance the group's gender composition if at all possible.

- The group was what McClure (2004) would refer to as "regressive." In other words, it resisted movement out of conflict into harmony and performance. Some group members were intent on "killing the leader," in McClure's terms. When other group members refused to join them in their stance, the dynamics spiraled downward.

The important lesson from a group that fails to establish itself successfully as a learning community is that often more than one factor contributes to the problems. It is rarely just the instructor and his or her facilitation techniques; we have seen good outcomes with inexperienced instructors who are just finding their way in online instruction. What is most important is for the instructor to try everything: openly discuss concerns about poor participation on the course site; contact students individually; if possible, have meetings with students; and when necessary, contact department or program administration to take decisive action with difficult students and consult with peers or colleagues for advice. Instructors must never allow students to flounder; they must act. Once the experience has ended, it is essential to review it, preferably with supportive colleagues or a willing student participant, in order to glean the important lessons that will assist in avoiding the same situation in the future.

● ● ●

In this chapter and chapter 7, we have discussed the critical importance of looking at and working with student issues in the development and delivery of an online course. Although we have repeatedly described this form of education as learner centered, we have been as guilty as our colleagues in forgetting that students are and should be the central focus of all online programs and courses. Focusing on the students and avoiding assumptions about what they know about online learning, how they might work through the process of the course, and why they may or may not be successful online has been a crucial piece of our own learning as online instructors. With this in mind, in our final chapter, we summarize the lessons we have learned in working in the virtual classroom and take a look ahead not only at new developments in online learning but also at the impact of online learning on education as a whole. We apply this learning to instructors and those who are responsible for training instructors, instructional designers, and administrators.

## TIPS FOR WORKING WITH ONLINE CLASSROOM DYNAMICS

- Be clear about the instructor role as a facilitator. Making this explicit at the beginning of an online class can prevent confusion and create agreement between the instructor and students about expectations.
- Be clear about group tasks and expectations. The clearer the instructor is about what is to be accomplished in the course, the less likely that students will become confused and flounder.
- Expect students to move through phases as they develop their working group. Asking questions about group development, such as, "How comfortable are you feeling with one another as a group?" as well as about their comfort level, with the process can help.
- Facilitate the process. Although we strongly support the empowerment of students to take on their own learning process, instructor guidance and intervention is necessary to keep things moving and on track. Chaos can ensue when students lack appropriate instructor participation.
- Always assume good intent. If a student flames another student or the instructor, assume that it is inadvertent and came out of good intentions, and respond accordingly.
- Wait twenty-four hours before responding to what you may consider to be a personal attack; advise students to do the same. The intensity of the message always seems to wane with time.
- Always address flaming. A skilled online facilitator put it well: "One voice can be much louder online than off-line . . . As a facilitator one must decide if they will protect the right of anyone to say anything, or to draw a line or embrace a certain set of norms which, at some point, pulls that one voice back out of the spotlight to allow others back in. For me, this balance between control and emergence is the most difficult, artful, and when it happens, glorious moment for an online group facilitator when they can hold a space for both" (White, 2000.)

- Expect conflict. Instead of viewing it as unhealthy, welcome it as a sign that the group is developing. Facilitate movement through conflict so that students can create norms for working with one another and successfully complete their tasks.
- Don't mistake confusion for conflict. Sometimes students do become confused about course expectations, guidelines, and assignments, and a simple explanation on the part of the instructor is all that is needed to move the process forward.
- Ask for support and help when necessary, especially when dealing with difficult students. We have no problem doing that when teaching face-to-face, and the same should be true online. Having individual meetings, by phone or in person, is appropriate when dealing with a difficult student. It is important also for instructors to know that they have the support of the administration to remove a difficult student from their online classes should that become necessary.
- Use sidebar or off-line conversations carefully with students to avoid having all communication move through you. Encourage students to use sidebars only for personal exchanges unrelated to the course. Concerns and comments about the course should be made on the course site, and whenever possible, conflict resolution with difficult students should occur there as well.

CHAPTER NINE

# LESSONS LEARNED IN THE VIRTUAL CLASSROOM

What key lessons have we learned in our exploration of all the myriad issues and concerns involved with the design, development, and delivery of online courses and programs? We end this book with a review of the most important lessons from the virtual classroom: we take another look back, an additional look at the present, and then a look ahead into the near future of online education. Changes are occurring rapidly, making it almost impossible to see very far into the future of distance learning. However, some predictions are being made based on current developments that are encouraging yet also indicate a need for caution and measured action. We organize the lessons as those for faculty; support staff who support faculty, such as instructional designers and faculty developers; and administrators responsible for online courses and programs.

## A Look Back

It's hard to believe that online learning hasn't been part of the academic landscape for very long. We began our own work online in 1992, using a primitive dial-up electronic bulletin board with little to no security and the ability to post only text messages that were not linked to one another in the form of discussions as we know them today. The precursors to this form of learning were correspondence courses, broadcast television courses generally delivered over public television, interactive TV, and computer-based training. The World Wide Web as we know it now was not available to the public until 1994, and online searches for the beginning of online education cite the dot-com boom, which occurred between 1999 and 2001, as the point at which online learning was born.

We now see the introduction of new technologies, such as mobile technologies, as having a significant impact on the ways in which teaching and learning happen online. Bandwidth has increased, as has access to computer technology and the Internet. Collaboration and networking are now the norms. Despite this, we cannot forget that there are still students who have to dial up to access their online courses and may not have the most up-to-date technologies. The digital divide still exists, although it may have narrowed a bit. And questions about the quality of online courses still persist. With this as a backdrop, we can explore the lessons learned and take yet again another look ahead.

The sections that follow present the lessons that may be taken from the virtual classroom. First, we explore some myths that continue to surround online learning and that have an impact on the lessons learned.

## The Myths

Despite the ubiquity of online learning today, these myths persist:

- *Classroom instruction offers a higher quality of education as compared to distance learning.* As the recent Allen et al. (2012) study indicates, instructors continue to hold this belief, which leads to skepticism of and resistance to teaching online.
- *Online students lose interaction with instructors and other students.* As we have discussed, a well-designed online class should be highly interactive and should promote collaboration and a sense of community. Many students comment that they feel closer to their student colleagues and professors in online courses that are interactive and well facilitated.
- *Employers value degrees earned from classroom instruction more than those earned from an online school.* Although this was true in the past, the increasing acceptance of online learning has helped to reduce this practice. Brain Track (n.d.), a website that assists prospective students

in finding courses and programs, interviewed job recruiters who noted that for the most part, employers seek qualified graduates of accredited universities and are not concerned about whether the degree was earned online.

- *The role of the professor is less important in online learning programs.* We contend that the role of the professor online is extremely important. As we have discussed and others have also noted, if the instructor is not present in the course, participation wanes. Some have pointed to the emergence of MOOCs (massively open online courses), which we discuss later in this chapter, as evidence that an instructor is not needed. Even MOOCs, however, when done well are constructed to facilitate networking and the development of a sense of community.

- *An online degree is easier to earn than a degree from a traditional school.* As we have been stressing, online learning is not the softer, easier way to earn a degree. Participating in an online course requires more time and effort on the part of both instructors and their students. Students may enter an online course with this myth in mind but quickly find the opposite to be true. Communicating this to students as part of an orientation to online learning is extremely important.

## Lessons for Faculty

### Instructors Need Not Fear Online Learning

A 2012 survey of faculty views of online education (Allen, Seaman, Lederman, & Jaschik, 2012) indicates that instructors both fear and avoid online learning because of concerns about quality. A response to the survey by a professor who participated in it notes, "Learning how to teach online probably would be one of the best steps a professor could take to assure viability in the 21st century. The most dysfunctional response by a professor today would be to dismiss or ignore both the technology and the social consequences online learning has" (Thelin, 2012, para. 2). The survey itself states that those who teach online hold online learning in higher esteem than those who have never done so.

A look at the history of online education shows that some form of teaching at a distance has been in existence in education throughout its history. Thelin (2012) indicates that online education is a part of higher education's heritage and that new formats and media for the delivery of education have always been attractive to what he terms "outstanding scholars." He suggests that online education can and should coexist with the more traditional methods of teaching, such as lectures, seminars, and fieldwork, with the ability to support and cross-fertilize one another rather than eliminating one another. Instead of fearing the quality of online learning, instructors need to work together to address these concerns to create online courses that are robust and rigorous.

## Course Development Needs to Focus on Interactivity, Not Content

The key to success in an online class rests not with the content that is being presented but with the method by which the course is delivered. To reiterate a point we made earlier, the most beautifully designed course—complete with audio, video, and other graphic and multimedia tools—can fail dismally if the instructor is not a skilled online facilitator working to build a learning community among the learners. A well-delivered course provides multiple means by which students and the instructor can interact, including e-mail, discussion boards, and careful use of synchronous discussion. The effective use of the means by which interactivity is fostered deepens the learning experience and creates a more satisfying outcome for everyone. Content can be creatively delivered through facilitation of effective discussions, collaborative assignments that promote teamwork and interaction, Internet research, and links to interesting websites outside the course site. Content that is delivered in multiple ways also addresses different student learning styles and creates a more interesting course overall. But it is the interaction and connections made in the course that students will remember as the keys to learning in an online course. Pedagogy, not technology, is what is critical to the success of an online course.

## Instructor and Student Roles Need to Change

In order for a high degree of interactivity to occur in an online course, the roles of instructors and students need to change: instructors need to be willing to give up a degree of control and allow the learners to take the lead in learning activities. Although this sounds easy, both instructors and students bring previous educational experience and expectations to the online classroom. Students expect to be "taught," and instructors expect to "teach." Consequently, students need to be oriented to their new role and the ways in which learning occurs online. A formal training program can assist in this process. However, when a training program is not available, instructors can get students started by posting material to the course site in the form of an initial discussion item, static information that students can access at any time, an audio or video presentation orienting them to the course and their expectations, or a frequently asked questions file about the online learning process.

What is most important is to encourage instructors to move away from the lecture mode of teaching and toward the use of more active learning approaches. Instructors should be encouraged to take stock of their peda-gogical approach and ask themselves: How do I see myself as a teacher? How do my students respond to my teaching style? What types of learning activities do I currently incorporate into my classes? What changes in those activities do I need to make to move into the online environment? Many instructors—ourselves included—have found that the changes required to deliver an online class successfully also work well in the face-to-face class-room. Our own face-to-face teaching has changed as the result of our expe-riences online. The use of the collaborative, interactive, active learning techniques we have described can thus enhance the learning experience of students in the traditional classroom. Once again, learner-centered ped-agogy is everything when it comes to teaching online or face-to-face.

# Lessons for Instructional Designers and Faculty Developers

## Both Faculty and Students Need Training

In order to understand the key lessons of the need for interactivity and the changes in faculty and student roles, both faculty and students need training. Rather than focusing on technology, however, training needs to address what it takes to teach and learn online successfully. Other fac-ulty development concerns include the importance of customizing an online course developed by another entity or faculty member, dealing with students and student problems in the online classroom, working with online classroom dynamics, and matching the ways to use technology and approaches to teaching in order to address student learning styles. Both faculty and students certainly need training in the technology they will be using in online classes, but this should not be the primary concern.

Training should not be a one-size-fits-all proposition. In *The Excellent Online Instructor* (2011), we proposed a model of training that meets fac-ulty where they are in terms of their expertise and experience with online teaching. Novice instructors need very different training from those who are considered master instructors and have taught online for many years.

Creating training that matches experience levels helps to engage all instructors and meet a variety of training needs. Master instructors can be recruited as trainers and mentors for those just entering online teaching. Their experiences are invaluable and will assist novice instructors in avoiding time-consuming and frustrating mistakes.

### Faculty Who Teach Online Need to Feel Supported

Instructors who teach online need to feel supported in addressing course and student issues. An instructor trying to deal with a difficult student needs to know the parameters within which he or she can operate in order to respond to the situation with minimal disruption to the rest of the group. Faculty orientation to the online environment in a given institution should offer policies or at least some discussion of resources that can be used if a difficult situation is encountered. Instructors teaching online can feel isolated from the institution. If the instructor's ties to the institution are strengthened in any way, it will result in an overall online program that appears cohesive and well planned. Furthermore, in order to build a learning community, instructors need to be able to create a safe container within which the learning community can flourish. To do that, they need to feel supported by the institution, meaning that the institution must deal swiftly and fairly with the student problems they encounter. When student problems are not adequately addressed, a sense of safety may not prevail.

Based on our own experience, we can say that when an instructor does not feel a sense of institutional support for the action he or she needs to take in the online classroom, the results can be almost disastrous: students may leave the course or program; they may become very vocal in expressing their dissatisfaction with the way a situation was handled; and, most important, learning outcomes for the entire group may not be achieved. Our students are our customers. Providing them with a successful learning experience takes more than putting a course online, training an instructor to deliver it, and hoping for the best.

## Lessons for Administrators

### Support Online Faculty Through Fair Compensation

Instructors are more likely to engage in online course design and teaching if they have reasonable compensation for the work. This means that online teaching should be included in the faculty workload and not be viewed as additional work, putting instructors into an overload situation. They also need compensation for course development in the form of pay or release time. If master online instructors are used to support the development of novice instructors, they should also be compensated for this work.

## Institutions Should Develop a Strategic Plan

Institutions need a strategic plan focused on technology as well as policies related to course and program development, ownership, and governance. Rather than muddling through in order to get courses online and compete with other institutions that are doing the same, institutions are better served to use a strategic planning process. The process should include discussion and development of policies related to course and program development, course ownership, and governance issues including decisions about which courses and programs should be taught online, faculty compensation, faculty teaching loads, and enrollments.

Furthermore, preparation for the development of such a plan requires a realistic market assessment. Too often assumptions are made about the students who are likely to enroll in online programs without any research to validate those assumptions. Often administrators assume that online courses will dramatically extend the reach of the institution. Aslanian and Clinefelter (2012), however, found that 69 percent of online students live within fifty miles of the campus of the institution in which they are enrolled and 80 percent live within one hundred miles. If online courses and programs are offered, then, which students will the institution likely attract? Would such offerings serve on-campus students in addition to extending the institution's reach off-campus?

Answering these questions should help to determine which courses to offer and which programs to develop in response to student needs. Including faculty in this process is critical in order to move these decisions through the institution's regular governance process. In addition, an inclusive process can help to alleviate disagreements over course ownership and intellectual property issues. The key to success in this area is reaching agreement on issues of governance, ownership, and faculty compensation before embarking on the development of courses and programs.

## Institutions Should Develop an Infrastructure First

Faculty and students need administrative and technical support in order to teach and learn online effectively. When institutions decide to put a course or two online, they often do so without first creating an adequate structure for faculty and student technical support. Significant problems may result:

- How will students register for online courses?
- How will faculty receive enrollment information?
- Will faculty be expected to enter student information into their courses, or will that be done by someone in registration or instructional technology?
- Who responds when students or faculty encounter technical difficulty?
- What happens when and if the server crashes and both faculty and students are unable to access the course site?
- What happens when the technology used for online courses becomes outdated?
- How do decisions about technology purchases and upgrades get made?

These are but some of the questions that need to be adequately answered in order for online courses and programs to be delivered smoothly and professionally.

Once again, we have learned from experience that institutions that do not address these questions will eventually face these issues whether they want to or not. We were hired to conduct an online faculty training for a department in an institution that intended to offer online courses with or without institutional support, as the institution had not responded to their requests for help to develop online programs. One participant decided to experiment with the student information tool embedded in the course management system and practice entering students into a course she had created as a part of the training. Although she had been given information about the correct way of doing so, she chose to create a softer, easier way. It crashed the server that housed the system and took three days for the one instructional technologist hired by the institution to clean up the damage. And it took less than a week for the institution to engage in discussion to create policies for entering student information into courses, including who does so and how to do it. The result was the removal of the student information tool from the course management system. Information is now generated by the registrar's office, which also is responsible for course enrollment.

## Technology Should Be Chosen by an Inclusive Committee

Administrators often ask us, "How can we sell faculty on the idea of teaching online? This is the greatest obstacle we face." Our answer is that inclusion in the decision-making process around the adoption and use of technology can greatly assist faculty in buying into the development and delivery of online courses and programs. They will feel more comfortable with the process if their voices are heard and the focus remains on teaching and learning rather than maximizing profits. Furthermore, when faculty are involved in the process, they can help to identify their training and support needs. If they are included in the planning process and there is a realistic assessment of student learning needs, that can help to avoid myriad problems and lead to the development of a responsible and responsive online program.

Faculty resistance also stems from fears that they will be overloaded in online course development and teaching responsibilities, especially in an area that may not contribute to promotion and tenure decisions. As we have noted, this is less of an issue than it was ten years ago, but still needs attention in some institutions. Developing clear policies in this area that recognize this work as scholarship and providing stipends or release time can help. Faculty fears and resistance can also be minimized with good training that focuses on pedagogy and support for the delivery of courses. When instructors realize that it is the process of good teaching—a process they know about—that leads to success in the online classroom, and not the technology itself, their anxiety level decreases.

### Pay Attention to the New Regulatory Environment

Government oversight of online courses and programs is increasing and is likely to continue to do so due to concerns about the level of student loan debt that exists and continuing concerns about the quality of online courses and programs. Interestingly, the highest level of concern is directed toward the for-profit institutions that are offering fully online degrees. However, Aslanian and Clinefelter (2012) found that 65 percent of those enrolling in online courses and programs are doing so at nonprofit colleges and universities; only 35 percent enroll at for-profit institutions. Although concerns about quality and adherence to regulations need to occur in all sectors, it appears that the focus on for-profit institutions may be somewhat misplaced. Regardless, courses and programs need to be designed with an eye toward career development as well as efficiency of delivery without sacrificing learning and academic quality.

## A Look into the Near Future

As we look at the lessons from the virtual classroom that we have learned thus far—some of them painful, others positive—we continue to think about what the future holds for online education. What can institutions, instructors, and their students expect to see over the next few years as online learning becomes an even greater part of not only the academy but the K–12 world as well? Although there continue to be no certain answers to these questions, we suspect that we will see more changes in the following areas: technology, course, and program quality and development; professional development; the ways in which faculty and students interact; and increased research into online education.

As we explore each of these, we begin to fit together the pieces of the mosaic that is the future of online education and higher education as a whole.

## Technology

With the move to mobile technology, which has become increasingly affordable, access to online courses is improving, and the ability to use chat, audio, and video will continue to become more accessible and therefore more usable in an online class. At the same time, commercially developed and owned course management systems have become increasingly expensive, allowing open source course management systems to flourish. Both commercial and open source systems have become more responsive to user demands and needs, incorporating social networking tools, wikis, and blogs into the systems and generally becoming more robust, allowing inclusion of multimedia tools.

It has been predicted, however, that course management systems may become a thing of the past as personalized learning spaces become the norm. Students may be given spaces on a server individually or in groups, or they may establish their own space online using applications such as Google Apps, where they can collect learning objects, interact with others, and collaborate on projects to pursue their own learning goals. McLoughlin and Lee (2009) note that with the advent of Web 2.0 and social networking tools, learner control over the learning process needs to be encouraged. They state, "Digital-age students want an active learning experience that is social, participatory, and supported by social media" (p. 639). Personalized learning spaces allow students to create learning experiences by accessing and engaging in learning communities across the globe and piecing together learning that is meaningful to them. Personalization allows students to determine what they learn as well as when and how. In personalized learning, learners are guided by a teacher who helps to co-create and co-design the learning experience. Hargreaves and Shirley (2009) note that this is an important means by which to create more flexibility in learning experiences, but they also warn that this should not simply be used as a means by which to incorporate more multimedia into learning. They express the concern that personalized learning could be mistaken for something deeper than what it is. The debate about personalized learning spaces is likely to occur for quite some time as more traditional academics wrestle with the concept and more learners gravitate toward it.

As the demand for online education continues to grow, we are likely to see additional means by which this form of education can be delivered. Simultaneously, as universities become more informed consumers of technology, increasing demand for responsiveness and quality is likely.

## Course and Program Quality and Design

There is little agreement at present as to what constitutes a quality online course or program. Furthermore, the accrediting of Jones International University by the North Central Association of Schools and Colleges in 1999 raised significant concerns on the part of faculty and traditional institutions about how the accreditation of completely online programs might be accomplished. Questions included these: "Can accreditors truly evaluate a university based solely on distance learning—with classrooms, libraries, and faculty members located somewhere in cyberspace—in the same way that they evaluate a traditional institution? Can we really call those institutions 'colleges' or 'universities' if they lack both a critical core of full-time faculty members and a system of governance by which the faculty is responsible for developing curricula and academic policy? Can accreditors actually determine that new, on-line institutions meet the same basic criteria for quality—or at least equivalent criteria—that traditional accredited institutions must meet?" (Perley & Tanguay, 1999, p. B4).

These questions, first posed more than a decade ago, are still being asked, begging the need to develop quality standards that are accepted across institutions. The Quality Matters Program (QM) has been one response, and the QM rubric has become increasingly recognized as a good measure of quality in an online course. A course that bears the QM stamp of approval is generally recognized as a good one. QM, however, deals with design only, not the facilitation of the course, although these standards are now in development. In order to truly assess course quality, both must be taken into account. Thus, continued work needs to occur on what is considered best practice in online facilitation. The International Association for K–12 Online Learning standards developed for K–12 online teaching are a good example and could guide higher education as well.

Despite this, we hope that standards will be created with an eye toward academic freedom. There is wide variation occurring in current course development, yielding a need for discussions of quality in online program development. The ideal outcome of those discussion should be a range within which faculty and institutions can comfortably work.

## Professional Development

What does it really mean to be a "guide on the side" or a "learning facilitator" rather than an instructor? How does an instructor successfully make the transition required to teach an online course so that students become empowered learners and take charge of the learning process? Is it possible to develop every instructor into a good online instructor? How can institutions tell the difference between someone who will do well online and someone who will not, be they faculty or student?

The questions are designed to help stimulate thinking about what might be needed in a good training and development program for faculty. However, they also point out that we need to think carefully about who should be encouraged to teach online. Earlier in this book, we made the point that not all faculty are suited to the online environment, just as not all students should consider taking online courses. We even put forth the fairly controversial idea that faculty who are highly entertaining face-to-face may not make the best online instructors. Not all faculty, even after participating in online teacher training, will do well in that environment. And although some authors predict that the face-to-face, traditional classroom will go the way of the Model T (Barone & Luker, 2000), we believe it is more likely that most colleges and universities will deliver at least a portion of their course offerings online, a trend that is already emerging (Allen et al., 2012). Consequently there will be room for those who choose to teach in the classroom along with those who choose to teach online.

Greater attention should be paid to what instructors need to be able to teach online successfully. Rather than focusing on the technology itself, training and faculty development should focus on increasing interactivity in online classes, building a learning community among the learners, delivering course content in new and creative ways, incorporating collaboration into the learning process, empowering learners, and evaluating learners and learning outcomes in ways that make sense in the online arena. As faculty become veteran facilitators online and as the online learning environment itself evolves, training and development needs will change. Consequently, faculty development to prepare faculty to teach successfully online should be fluid and responsive to the changes that are sure to come.

## How Faculty and Students Interact

One of the changes already occurring that has been noted is the ways in which faculty and students interact. Today's student is less likely to be an eighteen to twenty-one year old seeking a one-time educational experience. Instead, today's online student is likely to be a member of a range of students, from those in K–12 classrooms, to those considered to be traditional undergraduates, to adults returning to school to obtain knowledge and skills needed to compete and advance in the workplace. Adult students are more likely to be lifelong learners embarking on the beginning of what may be a learning process that results in the pursuit of multiple degrees, courses, or certifications. However, even traditional undergraduates are seeking learning experiences that will lead to employment, and colleges and universities are being asked by governmental entities to demonstrate that their course and program offerings will do so. Although previously schooled to engage with instructors in traditional ways—expecting the instructor to be the expert with knowledge and wisdom to impart—lifelong learners are looking to enter a partnership that results in the achievement of their learning objectives (Bates, 2000; McLoughlin & Lee, 2009).

The partnership students seek is with an academic institution that understands their needs and is capable of meeting them. Thus, a shift is occurring in the academic world; academic institutions are recognizing that like other types of organizations, they must be responsive to those they serve. The result is a shift from the traditional faculty-centered institution to a learner focus. Consequently, the relationship between faculty and student has to change as well.

Add technology and online teaching to the mix, and other changes begin to occur. Because the most effective way to achieve learning outcomes in the online classroom is by using active learning techniques, students are encouraged to become empowered learners. Today's technologies promote the ability of learners to significantly contribute to and co-create their learning experiences. More fully engaged, active learners are likely to bring new demands to the learning situation and will not be able to return to business as usual in subsequent learning situations, face-to-face or online. We noted that the changed relationship between faculty and student in the online classroom is spilling over into the face-to-face classroom as faculty discover that active learning techniques work well there. Similarly, faculty who have historically made good use of active learning techniques face-to-face are finding that their transition to online learning is eased through the use of those techniques. Bates (2000) notes, "Modern learning theory sees learning as an individual quest for meaning and relevance. Once learning moves beyond the recall of facts, principles, or correct procedures and into the area of creativity, problem solving, analysis, or evaluation (the very skills needed in the workplace in a knowledge-based economy, not to mention in life in general), learners need the opportunity to communicate with one another as well as with their teachers. This of course includes the opportunity to question, challenge, and discuss issues" (pp. 13–14).

The emergence of MOOCs is an interesting development that is calling into question not only the ways in which instructors and students interact but also delivery models of higher education. According to Stewart (2012), the originators of the concept, Stephen Downs, George Siemens, and Dave Cormier, were looking to devise an alternative environment for learning and were not necessarily intending to disrupt higher education as we know it. Using a lecture-based model that mimics the flipped classroom, MOOCs offer snippets of lectures that are twelve to fifteen minutes long, with quizzes and other assignments to be completed in between lectures. MOOCs are currently not credit-bearing courses and are not the same as the type of online course we have been discussing, but pathways to college credit are being forged at the time of this writing, and it will be interesting to see the impact this has on the direction of online learning in the future.

Currently, MOOCs are being offered by many elite universities as well as for-profit entities that are partnering with universities to offer MOOCs. They are free and capable of enrolling tens of thousands of students. Although predominantly lecture based, some involve the ability to network with other participants. Kim (2012) comments on the differences between what are now termed traditional online courses and MOOCs by stating, "A well constructed traditional online course is not a vessel to deliver content from the brains of the professor to the brains of the students, but rather an opportunity for faculty to guide, shape, reinforce, and support student learning . . . This work requires that the faculty have the opportunity to interact with the students" (para, 9). Are MOOCs a threat, or will they help us to reexamine the ways we currently offer courses and teach?

Rather than feeling threatened by this shift in relationship and course design, faculty should feel challenged by it. Faculty too are lifelong learners. The changing relationship with their students serves to expand the network through which they can learn. When we enter a new online course, we always believe that we have as much to learn from our students as they do from us. We find this to be an exciting element of our online work and one that we welcome.

## Research into Online Education

When we wrote our first book in 1999, we found a paucity of research on online learning. However, we noted that interest in the area was growing and that the research would follow. That prediction has become increasingly true as online learning has established a stronghold in higher education. Individual instructors are writing and publishing articles about their experiences online. Studies are being conducted that compare face-to-face and online delivery of the same class for outcome effectiveness. The Institute for Higher Education Policy published a report (Phipps & Merisotis, 1999) reviewing contemporary research on the effectiveness of distance learning. Since that time, many studies have been published looking at the characteristics of effective online courses and the critical elements practice that supports their development.

Because this is a growing area in academia with exciting new developments emerging daily, research efforts are likely to increase and continue. Those of us teaching online welcome the opportunity to contribute to this body of literature. The educational experiences that are the result of teaching online are so different from those that we have had in the traditional classroom that we want to share them with our colleagues so that they might understand the power of online teaching in delivering education in today's knowledge society.

James Duderstadt (1999) noted:

> Today's technology is rapidly breaking the constraints of space and time. It has become clear that most people, in most areas, can learn—and learn well—using asynchronous learning (that is "anytime, anyplace, anywhere" education) . . . Lifetime education is becoming a reality, making learning available for anyone who wants to learn, at the time and place of their choice, without great personal effort or cost . . . Rather than an "age of knowledge," could we instead aspire to a "culture of learning," in which people are continually surrounded by, immersed in, and absorbed in learning experiences? . . . This may become not only the great challenge but the compelling vision facing higher education as it enters the next millennium. (pp. 24–25)

This prophetic statement has proven true. Research that documents the effectiveness of our efforts in creating the culture of learning to which Duderstadt refers has occurred and continues to emerge. Sharing our experiences and lessons learned, whether positive or negative, as we explore the territory of online learning is equally important.

We closed our first book, *Building Learning Communities in Cyberspace,* by commenting on our own experience of online teaching: "Not only are we helping to shape the creation of empowered, lifelong learners, our participation as equal members of a group of learners supports us in our quest for lifelong learning. For us, this is the power of online distance learning" (Palloff & Pratt, 1999, p. 168). Stansbury (2011) supports this statement and what we have been discussing in this book by providing five characteristics of the effective educator today: anticipates the future, is a lifelong learner, fosters peer relationships, can teach and assess all levels of learners, and is able to discern effective versus ineffective technology. Today this not only remains true for us but increases with every online class we teach, every book we write, and every faculty group we train. We never cease to learn. We also never cease to wonder about and seek out what might be next. We have only begun to explore the virtual classroom and its important and powerful role in the future of education.

---

## TIPS FOR CREATING SUCCESSFUL COURSES AND PROGRAMS

- Always strive to make online courses as interactive as possible.
- Use multiple means to deliver content and evaluate student progress.
- Give faculty a voice in the selection of technology and in policy-making around course ownership, governance, compensation, course loads and class size, and intellectual property.
- Provide training for both faculty and students in the new roles required to create online learning communities and complete courses successfully.
- Provide adequate administrative and technical support to faculty who are developing and delivering courses and to students who are enrolled in courses.
- Include issues such as course development, purchase of technology, faculty compensation for course development and delivery, and, training in the institution's strategic plan, and budget for a strong infrastructure to support online courses and programs.

# SAMPLE TRAINING FOR FACULTY

There are two sample trainings presented in this appendix. The first is a basic training syllabus that we have used for online delivery of new faculty training and that we initially presented in *The Excellent Online Instructor* (2011). We have modified it to include concepts discussed in this book, and it can be further modified in terms of length of time required for training. Topics can also be added or deleted. As presented, this represents a four-week training. Immediately following is a more intensive training focusing on community building in online courses. Appendix B lists resources and websites that can be used to supplement a faculty training course.

## Introduction to and Best Practices in Online Teaching

*Instructors*

Rena M. Palloff, PhD

E-mail: rpalloff@mindspring.com

Keith Pratt, PhD

E-mail: drkpratt@mindspring.com

This course is designed as a four-week online orientation to online teaching. It will focus on developing a shared vocabulary of technical language and will discuss the pedagogical concerns in delivery of quality online education. In addition, focus will be on creating online courses that lead to desired learning outcomes by effectively blending course content with appropriate use of technological tools.

*Required Reading*

> Palloff, R., and Pratt, K. (2013). *Lessons from the Virtual Classroom: The Realities of Online Teaching.* San Francisco: Jossey-Bass.
>
> Palloff, R., and Pratt, K. (2005). *Collaborating Online: Learning Together in Community.* San Francisco: Jossey-Bass.

*Recommended Reading*

> Palloff, R., and Pratt, K. (2007). *Building Online Learning Communities: Effective Strategies for the Virtual Classroom.* San Francisco: Jossey-Bass.

*Prerequisites*

- No prior course work in online teaching and learning is required.
- Basic computer and word processing skills, such as copy and paste.
- Basic understanding of the use of e-mail and the ability to access the course site and other sites on the Internet.

*Recommended*

- Access to a smart phone or tablet computer
- Review of course texts recommended prior to beginning the course

*Learning Outcomes*

- Experience an online course from the perspective of the learner.
- Explore and integrate various online teaching and learning strategies.
- Explore and integrate the concept of learning communities in online teaching.
- Explore and integrate mobile learning into a course.
- Begin planning for the development of your own online course.
- Apply the concepts of good course development to a course that can be immediately implemented and delivered.

- Be able to critique the positive elements in courses developed by others as well as make appropriate suggestions for improvement.
- Integrate good assessment techniques into an online course.

## LEARNING UNITS

## Week 1

### Unit 1: Intros, Learning Objectives, Guidelines (3 Days)

*Unit Overview*

This unit is designed to help us get to know one another and to discuss how we will work together online. It will help you become more familiar with your course management system as we navigate it together, post introductions, review learning objectives for the course, and discuss guidelines for participation. The following are a few guidelines for participation in this course:

- Given the short duration of the course (four weeks), you are expected to log on almost daily.
- You are expected to post to the discussion at least once per unit and in response to one of your colleagues at least once.
- All assignments should be completed on time so as not to hold up progress in the course.
- All communication will be professional and will observe the rules of netiquette. For more information about netiquette, visit www.albion .com/netiquette.

*Unit Objectives*

- Meet one another.
- Develop a contract for learning during this course.

*Assignments*

- Post an introduction to the discussion board in the appropriate discussion forum. Include not only information about your background but also your experience with online teaching and learning. Reflect on the following questions in your introduction: What drew you to teach online? How do you see yourself as an instructor? What are your hopes and fears about beginning your online teaching experience? Feel free to record a brief video introduction using your phone, tablet, or computer and upload it to the course site. You can also visit Glogster (www.glogster .com) and create an online poster as your introduction. If you choose to do this, provide us the link to your poster so that we can view it.

- Respond to at least one other person's introduction.
- Post a message to the discussion board indicating your willingness to work within the guidelines listed in the overview for this unit. Are there any guidelines that should be added? Any guidelines you might have difficulty meeting?

### Unit 2: Syllabus Development in Online Learning (3 Days)
*Unit Overview*

The syllabus forms the backbone of any course and, in the online course, is critically important, as it is the main way that students gain understanding of what is expected of them in the online classroom. Consequently, very little can be left to assumption in the syllabus for the online course. As online instructors develop syllabi, there is a need to leave behind what has been done in the face-to-face classroom and to rethink the course for online delivery. There are several questions to ask in order to do so:

- Who are my students?
- What do I want to accomplish through this course? What do I want my students to know, feel, or do as a result of this course? What course content will support these objectives?
- What guidelines, rules, roles, and rituals need to be established for this course?
- How do I plan to deliver course material?
- How comfortable do I feel including collaborative activity, personal interaction, promoting knowledge acquisition by learners, and releasing control of the learning process?
- How do I want to organize my course site?
- How will I assess student performance?
- How will I address attendance requirements?
- What do I want to see students walk away with when they conclude this class?

In addition to answering these questions, online instructors need to consider new and different activities to access course content. Read-and-discuss online courses are not engaging and may lead to poor participation down the line. Consequently, thinking creatively is strongly encouraged!

*Unit Objectives*

- Develop a stronger understanding of the nature of online learning.
- Consider and experiment with new ways to deliver course material.

*Assignment*

- Review the textbooks for this course and then post answers to the following discussion questions in the appropriate forum on the discussion board: What ideas do you have for presenting course material? What activities might you try? What concerns do you have about the questions to consider listed in the unit overview and how might you address them?

## Week 2

### Unit 3: Choosing Appropriate Learning Activities (3 Days)

*Unit Overview*

Now that you are more familiar with your course management system, the purpose of this unit is to help you choose and more fully develop activities for your class. Chapters 2 and 7 in *Lessons from the Virtual Classroom* (Palloff & Pratt, 2013) discuss best practices in online learning, including understanding who your students are and how they learn, as well as what they need to support them in their learning. *Collaborating Online* (Palloff & Pratt, 2005) offers a number of suggestions for engaging online learners in collaborative activities. In addition, visit YouTube and view a video or two on the use of Web 2.0 technologies, such as wikis and blogs, to promote collaboration. With these as a guide, revisit your prospective learning activities and more fully develop them for implementation in your own course.

*Unit Objectives*

- More fully develop a set of learning activities for implementation in an online course.
- Explore the concept of engagement and how to integrate that into a course.

*Assignments*

- Review chapters 2 and 7 in *Lessons from the Virtual Classroom* and the entire book, *Collaborating Online*. Given these materials as a backdrop, how can you more fully develop the activities you suggested in unit 2?

What makes these activities effective, and how will they tie into your learning objectives for your course? Which tools will you use to deliver these activities and why?

- You will be paired with a partner to provide feedback to one another on your activities. Post your answers to these questions in the appropriate discussion forum on the discussion board and then provide feedback to your partner.
- How do you view the concept of engagement? How will you ensure that your students are fully engaged in your course? Please post your answers to the appropriate discussion forum and respond to at least one other colleague.

### Unit 4: Promoting Participation (3 Days)

*Unit Overview*

Effective delivery of an online course demands high participation on the part of students and instructors. You have been developing ideas for your course, but if you cannot get students to participate, your efforts have been for naught. The following suggestions will help maximize participation (Palloff & Pratt, 2007):

- Be clear about how much time the course will require of students and faculty in order to eliminate potential misunderstandings about course demands. Include this information in your syllabus.
- Teach students about online learning. Include a "frequently asked questions" area of your course, as well as a place where students can ask you questions as they arise.
- As the instructor, be a good model of participation by logging on frequently and contributing to discussions. Plan to participate as often as you ask your students to participate.
- Be willing to step in and set limits if participation wanes or if the conversation is headed in the wrong direction.
- Remember that there are people attached to the words on the screen. Be willing to contact students who are not participating and invite them in.
- Create a warm and inviting atmosphere that promotes the development of a sense of community among the participants.

Keeping these points in mind can help to maximize participation and create a satisfactory learning experience for both students and faculty.

*Unit Objectives*

- Develop strategies to effectively engage students in an online course.
- Establish and implement practices that maximize student participation online.

*Assignments*

- Review the sample participation guidelines presented in exhibit 5.3 in *Lessons from the Virtual Classroom*. Present the guidelines you intend to use in your online course in the appropriate forum on the discussion board and provide feedback to at least one other colleague on his or her set of guidelines.
- After completing your guidelines, write a welcome letter to your students and post it on the discussion board. Provide feedback to at least one other colleague on his or her letter.

## Week 3

### *Unit 5: Collaboration and Reflection (3 Days)*
*Unit Overview*

In the online environment, collaboration is the cornerstone of the educational experience. It forms the foundation of a learning community while bringing students together to support learning and promoting creativity and critical thinking. In addition, collaboration creates an environment of reflection: as students engage in collaborative work, they are required to reflect on the process as well as the content being explored. The result is a transformative learning experience: the student no longer views the content in the same way. Social interaction, rather than individual exploration, expands students' views of the topic and what they thought they knew. It allows them to question previously held beliefs and explore new ones. In addition, the use of collaborative activity in a class helps to address issues of learning style and culture, allowing students to work from their areas of strength. Collaboration helps students to become more than just students: they become reflective practitioners. It is important to remember, however, that collaboration does not just happen. The instructor plays a critical role in preparing students for collaborative work. The stages for collaboration are as follows:

- Set the stage.
- Create the environment.

- Model the process.
- Evaluate the process.

Think about the collaborative activity you may be planning for your online course with these phases in mind. How might you facilitate the collaborative process?

*Unit Objectives*

- Plan for collaborative work in an online course.
- Create activities that promote reflection and transformative learning.

*Assignments*

- Review once more the activities that you are proposing for your online course, and answer the following question in the appropriate forum on the discussion board: What might you do to incorporate collaborative work in your online course? If you have already planned a collaborative activity, how do you plan to get students ready for it? How might you need to prepare them? Post your plan, and provide feedback to at least one other plan.
- Answer the following question on the discussion board: How will you promote reflection in your course? Will this be a graded activity?

### Unit 6: Incorporating Evaluation (3 Days)
*Unit Overview*

Assessment of student performance is a critical component of any class, face-to-face or online. As we learned from our reading, good assessment aligns with teaching activities and is not seen as an added burden by either the student or the instructor. Angelo and Cross (1993) note that good assessment has these characteristics:

- Learner centered
- Teacher directed
- Mutually beneficial
- Formative
- Context specific
- Ongoing

In this unit, we will spend more time thinking about critical assessment and evaluation activities in your online course.

*Unit Objectives*

- Develop appropriate assessment activities for the online course.
- Prepare and present a grading rubric for assessments.

*Assignments*

- Review the assessment activities presented in *Collaborating Online*. Post the following to the appropriate forum on the discussion board: What assessment activities are you preparing for your online course? Discuss how they align with course objectives and learning activities. Give at least one colleague feedback on his or her proposed assessments.
- Prepare and post to the discussion board at least one draft grading rubric for one of the learning activities in your course. Provide feedback to at least one colleague on his or her rubric.

## Week 4

### Unit 7: Prepare a Lesson (4 Days)

*Unit Overview*

You are now ready to begin creating your course. During the next few days, you will be expected to pull one learning unit together in draft form and present it for review.

*Unit Objectives*

- Complete a draft of one learning unit of your course, including all learning and assessment activities.
- Give and receive critical feedback for lesson improvement.

*Assignment*

- Present the draft lesson with activities and assessments and/or rubrics to the partner you worked with in unit 3. Provide a critique of the lesson your colleague posted, and respond to the critique your partner provides about your lesson.

### Unit 8: Final Reflections on the Learning Experience (2 Days)

*Unit Overview*

Congratulations! You made it through this very intensive training experience! Now that you have, it's time to take a deep breath and reflect a bit on what you've learned over the last four weeks. Think about how you will approach your online course and your students and what you might yet need to help you with your development as an online instructor.

*Unit Objectives*

- Critically reflect on the training experience.
- Define areas that need further work and final questions.

*Assignment*

- Respond to the following questions in the appropriate forum on the discussion board: What new learning have I gained from participating in this training? How might I do things differently in my online class than I might have without the training? What unanswered questions do I still have?

## Intensive Training Focused on Collaboration and Building Online Learning Communities

This syllabus is for intensive training focused on creating collaboration and building learning communities. It can be used with instructors of any experience level from novice to master faculty and can be delivered in a time frame as short as one week, although ideally, two weeks would work well for this training.

• • •

Hello and welcome to your Building Online Learning Communities course!

Here are a few guidelines to help you get going in this brief, intensive experience. First, although we're studying online learning communities this week, please don't expect that you will form a solid community in such a short time. We've certainly seen the start of good communities in a week, but it's just the beginning of a much longer process. You will be engaged in a collaborative activity with your small group to facilitate this process. Because of this, you need to make a commitment to participate over the next five days. Please don't let your emerging community down! Make sure to set aside adequate time daily to work on this course. We hope that through your networking with one another, community can flourish as you move forward beyond this course!

The group is divided into smaller working groups. Your task within each group is to participate in a collaborative project that results in some form of a group paper or presentation that explores or demonstrates ways to build community in an online class. You can choose to submit your project in the form of a wiki, a paper that has been completed jigsaw style (meaning that each member of the group contributes a piece), a Prezi (www.prezi.com) or PowerPoint presentation, or a Glogster (www.glogster.com) poster (Glogster is a graphic blogging application). Each group will negotiate roles for the completion of the activity. We want you to share these roles:

- *Daily observer:* Each of you should take a turn in sharing your observations. There should be at least five of you in the group, and you can choose the day to observe that is most convenient for you. Your observations of each day's work will be posted in the Report Out area of the discussion board.
- *Project leader:* Appoint one person whose job will be to coordinate the group's work on the final project.
- *Seeker:* More than one person can fill this role. Seekers find material for the group to use as you all work on the project.
- *Weaver:* There can be more than one weaver, but we suggest no more than two people filling this role. The weaver(s) will edit and smooth out the final work to ensure that it is well presented and coherent.

Although we will be observing your daily discussions and project work, we will not be participating in the small groups unless you invite us in for some reason, for example, if you have specific questions from your small group or there are participation issues. The daily observer should be the person who contacts us and asks us to participate. Instead of participating in your groups, we have an area on the discussion board entitled Questions for Drs P&P. Please interact with us in that area and ask questions about our ideas, the book, issues emerging from your own discussions, and so forth. Please go beyond asking us questions about what's due when. This is our area to interact with you around the ideas presented, and we welcome that discussion!

To begin, log in and post an introduction in the Introduce Yourself area so you can begin to know one another. To be successful, please plan to log in daily and participate actively in the daily discussions and project work. Here are the additional requirements you need to fulfill in order to get credit for the course:

- Write a final reflective paper about the process and the project for the week. There is no required length or format. Just give us your reflections as they relate to the reading, discussion, and collaborative work! ☺

- One week after the course ends, e-mail your paper to Rena and Keith at rpalloff@mindspring.com and drkpratt@gmail.com.

Please ask questions as you go. We look forward to working with you all!

Warmly,
Rena and Keith

## Day 1: Defining and Recontextualizing Community

Welcome to our online course on Building Online Learning Communities! We look forward to working with you this week as we explore the importance of interactivity and community building in online classes. This course involves reading chapters from our book, *Building Online Learning Communities*, listening to brief audio pieces related to the topic of the day if you so choose, discussing the concepts and issues in the discussion area of the course, and, most important, working on a collaborative activity throughout the week to help you form your own learning community. For more description of the project, please refer to our welcome message sent to you in this course. We have also included a social and networking area, which you can feel free to use to get to know one another apart from the course content. We hope that this week together will give you an overview that will allow you to begin applying concepts to your own online teaching. Enjoy!

On our first day, we'll look at how we define or recontextualize community, particularly as it applies to an online class. In addition, we'll talk about how we can effectively facilitate community development online. You will experience this through the development of a group charter to assist you in doing your collaborative work. We've posted a bit of material to help you do that and some questions you'll probably want to consider as you think about how you'll work together this week.

*Assignments for Day 1*

- Read chapters 1 and 2 in *Building Online Learning Communities*.
- Listen to the audio clip for day 1.
- In order to make group work successful, all group members must agree to abide by norms established by the group. As your group is forming, please reach consensus on the following items and post your group's charter to the discussion board in your group area:

o   How will your group identify itself? (Your group may choose a name under which to function.)

o   How will the group communicate (for example, through the discussion board, e-mail, virtual classroom, phone, or a combination of methods)?

o   What time during the day will the discussion begin, taking into account time zone differences and busy schedules?

o   How quickly should group members be expected to respond to e-mails or discussion board postings (for example, within two hours, within one day, or something else).

o   What role or duties will each person in the group perform? Among the possible roles are initiator, secretary, liaison to the instructor, motivator, organizer, and the roles assigned by Rena and Keith.

o   Who is responsible for posting group responses to the main discussion board?

o   How will the group handle a member who is not participating?

- Discuss any other topics that are unique to your group.
- Respond to the following question in the discussion area: Do you see community building as an important element of an online course?
- Ask any questions you might have in the Questions for Drs P&P forum in the discussion area.

## Day 2: Human and Practical Considerations in Online Learning

On to day 2! Today we'll look at the elements that both help to facilitate the development of an online community as well as some of the elements that might interfere with that development. Some of these elements are fairly obvious—such as group size to facilitate community building and our need to connect and be part of something. Other elements are not so obvious, such as the rituals and connectedness that contribute to the spirituality of online community. We hope that you will have some of your own "aha's" about these and other elements involved in online community as you participate in today's discussion and negotiate your own project.

*Assignments for Day 2*

- Read chapters 3 and 4 in *Building Online Learning Communities.*
- Listen to the audio clip for day 2.
- Negotiate in your small group what your final project will look like. Will you build a wiki, do a paper in jigsaw fashion, create a Glogster, a

PowerPoint, or a Prezi presentation? Given the short time you have to complete the work, you really need to figure this out TODAY!

- Respond to the following question in the discussion area: How would you as an online instructor work with the elements of online community as they appear?
- Ask any questions you might have in the Questions for Drs P&P forum in the discussion area.

## Day 3: Moving Teaching and Learning Online

We're about halfway through an intense and productive week! Welcome to day 3! Today we'll be looking at how instructors can effectively make the transition from the face-to-face classroom to the online classroom. How does our role as instructor change when we teach online? How can we be effective online facilitators? What role does the learner play in all of this? And finally, how can we construct a course to ensure that all of this happens? Through our reading and discussion today, you will gain more understanding of how you can effectively make this transition and begin to implement community-building techniques in your online classes.

*Assignments for Day 3*

- Read chapter 6 in *Building Online Learning Communities.*
- Listen to the audio clip for day 3.
- Continue the work on your collaborative project.
- Discuss the following question in the discussion area: What changes will you need to make in your teaching practice in order to be successful online?
- Ask any questions you might have in the Questions for Drs P&P forum in the discussion area.

## Day 4: Promoting Collaborative Learning

You're all doing a great job! We're heading into the home stretch, but as we do, we'll be tackling some topics that are of particular importance in working successfully online. Today's topic will be all about collaboration. The online classroom provides a wonderful environment in which collaboration can occur, and the numerous Web 2.0 applications that have emerged in the past few years are helping to facilitate that process. Today we clarify what we mean by collaboration and discuss ways in which effective collaboration can happen.

*Assignments for Day 4*

- Read chapter 8 in *Building Online Learning Communities.*
- Listen to the audio clip for day 4.
- Go to the following Prezi site and watch the presentation: http://prezi .com/obqzirjhtf-q/web-20-in-the-classroom/.
- Continue the work on your collaborative project.
- Discuss the following question in the discussion area: What kinds of collaborative assignments would you feel comfortable incorporating into an online class?
- Ask any questions you might have in the Questions for Drs P&P forum in the discussion area.

## Day 5: Transformative Learning

You made it! Welcome to the final day of the course! Don't leave us yet because today we'll be talking about an extremely important topic: transformative learning and reflection. Just as you've found from being in this brief and intensive course, this medium encourages us to reflect on questions, material, and the contributions of everyone involved. As a result of all of this reflection, our thinking and learning processes are transformed. In fact, many learners report that after they take a well-designed online course, they feel transformed as a learner.

Today we will complete our course with a discussion of reflection and transformative learning and discuss ways in which to build reflection into the online learning process. You'll also post your project or a link to your project. As you reflect, also reflect on this project and what it was like to work on it with your small group.

We hope that this course has met all of your expectations! In the spirit of reflection, we'd love to hear from you about your experience with this course so that we can improve it for those that follow you. Good luck in implementing all of what we've discussed and with all of your online teaching!

*Assignments for Day 5*

- Read chapter 9 in *Building Online Learning Communities.*
- Listen to the audio clip for day 5.

- Post your final project or a link to that project in the discussion area.
- Discuss the following questions in the discussion area: Reflect on your own learning this week. What have you learned? How have you experienced online learning? What recommendations would you make to learners who come after you regarding participation in this online learning experience?
- What final questions do you have this week? Post them in the Questions for Drs P&P forum in the discussion area.

## APPENDIX B

# ADDITIONAL RESOURCES

This appendix contains resources for faculty and those who support them to assist with the development of their online courses. Included are links to and suggestions for these areas:

- Communities of practice
- Mobile technologies and Web 2.0 technologies
- Certificate programs in online teaching
- Online conferences
- Online journals
- Professional organizations
- Course evaluation rubrics

## Communities of Practice

These are just a few of the communities of practice devoted to online teaching:

- Learning Times, a host for online communities, training, and conferences on topics in online and distance learning. http://www .learningtimes.net

- Merlot (Multimedia Educational Resource for Learning and Online Teaching), a repository of learning objects; also produces an online journal and hosts discipline-specific communities of practice. http://www.merlot.org
- Tapped In, a community of practice primarily geared toward K–12 teaching that has been expanding its focus to include higher education faculty. http://tappedin.org/tappedin/

## Mobile Applications and Web 2.0 Applications

Mobile applications are too numerous to list. However, there are sites where applications are aggregated, and we include a few that we have used in teaching both face-to-face and online courses:

- Google Mobile, http://www.googlemobile.com
- iTunes and the Apple App Store, http://www.apple.com
- Fresno State University, a site that reviews and features mobile applications that support teaching and learning. Each month a new application is featured; previously reviewed and featured applications are housed on the site. http://www.fresnostate.edu/academics/tilt/toolsforteaching/apps/index.html

Other useful applications follow:

- Polleverywhere, used for polling opinions or answers on any topic and can be used as a substitute for clickers
- Wiffiti, which allows instructors to receive text messages and display them in one place; useful for polling, answering quiz questions, and the like.
- Posterous, for creating private spaces on the Web where students and instructors can post material of any kind
- Google Docs, for document sharing and collaborative editing
- Broadcastr, which turns a smart phone into a multimedia guide by streaming photos and audio based on the location where the user is
- SCVNGR, which builds real-world scavenger hunts

Among the useful Web 2.0 applications are these:

- Glogster, which creates graphic blogs that can include audio and video
- Prezi, an alternative to PowerPoint that allows presentations to pan and zoom
- HootCourse, which provides virtual classroom space using Facebook and Twitter

## Certificate Programs in Online Teaching

Numerous certificate programs exist in the area of online teaching. In this sampling of the best known, some offer graduate-level credit along with certification:

- Fielding Graduate University: Interactive Learning Online; Emerging Technologies in the K–12 Classroom; Social Media in Education. This university offers three academic certificate programs that go beyond use of the technological tools to delve into the pedagogy of online teaching and learning and building learning communities. Each program is delivered completely online, and credits can articulate into Fielding's doctoral program in educational leadership and change. The program director and faculty is Rena Palloff, along with other well-known names in online learning. http://www.fielding.edu/programs/elc/
- University of Wisconsin-Stout: E-Learning and Online Teaching Graduate Certificate. Designed to meet professional development goals to be certified as highly qualified in the area of e-learning instruction and online training. Students can take one or two courses per term. The program is five semesters if one course is taken or nine months if two courses are taken per term. Courses can count toward elective credit in three master's degree programs in education. http://www.uwstout.edu/soe/profdev/elearningcertificate.html
- LERN (Learning Resources Network): Certified Online Instructor (COI) Program. The Certified Online Instructor designation has been created to serve faculty in higher education and others teaching online who want to gain recognition for their knowledge and skills. The COI program involves taking three core one-week intensive courses, teaching two courses online, having a course critiqued, gathering student evaluations of the online courses taught, and taking an exam. http://www.teachingonthenet.org/courses/certified_online _instructor/index.cfm

- University of Wisconsin-Madison Extension Division: Professional Certificate in Online Teaching. Flexible, self-paced certificate program that focuses on helping new online instructors get up to speed quickly or reinforces and advances skills of experienced online instructors. The program provides knowledge and skills, examples, and best practices in online teaching through opportunity to practice and demonstrate what has been learned in a course planning project that uses the instructor's own course materials. http://www.uwex .edu/disted/depd/cert_benefits.cfm
- Illinois Online Network: Master Online Teacher Certificate. The Master Online Teacher certificate is a comprehensive faculty development program based on the MVCR (Making the Virtual Classroom a Reality) series of online faculty development courses. This program recognizes and certifies faculty, staff, and administrators who achieve a measurable level of knowledge related to online course design, online instruction, and other issues related to online teaching and learning. In order to earn the certificate, a student must successfully complete four core courses, one elective course, and the online teaching practicum. http://www.ion.uillinois.edu/courses/students /mot.asp

## Online Conferences

Online conferences are growing more popular due to economic constraints associated with travel costs and registration fees and the convenience of participating from home or the office. Some extend over two or three days, while others are brief seminars. The additional benefit of online conferences is their low cost:

- Wiley Learning Institute, http://www.jbfacdev.com
- International Online Conference, http://www.internationalonline conference.org/
- Smithsonian Conference on Problem Solving, http://www.smithsonian conference.org/expert/
- TCC (Technology, Colleges, and Community) Online Conference, http://tcc.kcc.hawaii.edu/2010/tcc/welcome.html
- Academic Impressions, http://www.academicimpressions.com/
- Magna Online Seminars, http://www.magnapubs.com/calendar /index-cat-type.html

## Online Journals About Online Teaching

Numerous journals are now online. This list identifies some that are devoted to the topic of online teaching:

*Journal of Online Learning and Teaching* (JOLT), http://jolt.merlot.org/
*Online Journal of Distance Learning Administration,* http://www.westga .edu/~ distance/ojdla/

*T.H.E. Journal* (Transforming Education Through Technology), http:// thejournal.com/articles/2004/09/01/faculty-training-for-online-teaching.aspx

*EDUCAUSE Review,* http://thejournal.com/articles/2004/09/01 /faculty-training-for-online-teaching.aspx

*Innovate: Journal of Online Education,* http://innovateonline.info/

*Journal of Asynchronous Learning Networks* (JALN), http://www .sloanconsortium.org/publications/jaln_main

*Journal of Interactive Online Learning,* http://www.ncolr.org/

*International Review of Research in Open and Distance Learning,* http://www .irrodl.org/index.php/irrodl/index

*International Journal of Instructional Technology & Distance Learning,* http:// www.itdl.org/index.htm

*The Technology Source Archives,* http://www.technologysource.org/

*Distance Education Journal,* http://www.odlaa.org

## Professional Organizations

Following is a partial list of professional organizations of interest to faculty teaching online and to faculty developers:

- International Society for Technology in Education (ISTE): Dedicated to supporting the use of technology in the teaching and learning of K–12 teachers and students.
- Association for the Advancement of Computing in Education (AACE): To advance information technology in education and e-learning research, as well as its development and practical application.

- U.S. Distance Learning Association (USDLA): Promotes the development and application of distance learning for education and training at all levels.
- League for Innovation in the Community College: Supports the work and publications focusing on the integration of technology in teaching.
- American Association of Community Colleges (AACC): Provides resources and research for and about community colleges, although it is not directly focused on the use of technology in education.
- Professional Organizational Development Network (POD Network): Provides resources and support for faculty developers.
- North American Council for Staff, Program, and Organizational Development (NCSPOD): Provides resources and support for faculty developers.
- American Association for Adult and Continuing Education (AAACE): Provides leadership in the field of adult and continuing education through advocacy and research.

## Course Evaluation Rubrics

Several institutions and organizations have created rubrics for evaluating quality in an online course. They can be downloaded and used to evaluate one's own course or can be used as part of a course evaluation effort at the department or institutional level. These are the best known:

- Quality Matters, http://www.qualitymatters.org/
- California State University-Chico Rubric for Online Instruction, http://www.csuchico.edu/celt/roi/
- Illinois Online Network, Quality Online Course Initiative Rubric, http://www.ion.uillinois.edu/initiatives/qoci/rubric.asp

# REFERENCES

Akridge, J., DeMay, L., Braunlich, L., Collura, M., & Sheahan, M. (2002). Retaining adult learners in a high-stress distance education learning environment: The Purdue University executive MBA in agribusiness. *Motivating and Retaining Adult Learners Online: A Journal of Research Articles and Practitioner's Tips*, 62–71.

Albrecht, B. (2006). *Enriching student experience through hybrid learning* (Research Bulletin, 2006, no. 12). Washington, DC: Educause Center for Applied Research.

Allen, I. E., & Seaman, J. (2004). *Entering the mainstream: The quality and extent of online education in the United States, 2003 and 2004*. Wellesley, MA: Sloan Consortium.

Allen, I. E., & Seaman, J. (2005). *Growing by degrees: Online education in the United States*. Wellesley, MA: Sloan Consortium.

Allen, I. E., & Seaman, J. (2007). *Online nation: Five years of growth in online learning*. Wellesley, MA: Sloan Consortium.

Allen, I. E., & Seaman, J. (2011). *Going the distance: Online education in the United States, 2011*. Wellesley, MA: Sloan Consortium and Babson Research Group.

Allen, I. E., Seaman, J., Lederman, D., & Jaschik, S. (2012). *Conflicted: Faculty and online education, 2012*. Babson Survey Research Group and Quahog Research Group.

American Association of University Professors. (1999, May-June). Distance education and intellectual property. *Academe*, 41–45.

Anderson, K. M., & Avery, M. D. (2008). Faculty teaching time: A comparison of Web-based and face-to-face graduate nursing courses. *International Journal of Nursing Education Scholarship*, 5(1), 1–12.

Angwin, J. (2009, March 7–8). How to twitter. *Wall Street Journal*.

Aslanian, C. B., & Clinefelter, D. L. (2012). *Online college students 2012: Comprehensive data on demands and preferences*. Louisville, KY: Learning House.

Baron, A., Hogarty, K., Holkfelt, T., Loggie, K., Schullo, S., Gulitz, E., . . . & Sweeney, P. (2005, June 27–30). *Intellectual property and online courses: Policies at major research universities.* Paper presented at the National Educational Computing Conference, Philadelphia.

Barone, C., & Luker, M. (2000). The role of advanced networks in the education of the future. In M. Luker (Ed.), *Preparing your campus for a networked future.* San Francisco: Jossey-Bass.

Barsch, J. (1980). *Barsch learning style inventory.* Retrieved from http://hcc.hawaii.edu /intranet.vCom/guidebook/teachtip/lernstyl.htm

Bates, A. W. (2000). *Managing technological change.* San Francisco: Jossey-Bass.

Bates, A. W., & Sangrà, A. (2011). *Managing technology in higher education: Strategies for transforming teaching and learning.* San Francisco: Jossey-Bass.

Becker, K. L. (2003). Just tell me what to do: Group dynamics in a virtual environment. In *Proceedings of the Women in Research Conference,* Rockhampton, Australia.

Beddall-Hill, N., & Raper, J. (2010). Mobile devices as "boundary objects" on field trips. *Journal of the Research Center for Educational Technology,* 6(1), 28–46.

Bell, B. S., & Kozlowski, S.W.J. (2002). A typology of virtual teams: Implications for effective leadership. *Group and Organization Management,* 27(1), 14–50.

Blackboard. (n.d.). *Educational benefits of online learning.* Retrieved from www.black board.com

Boettcher, J. (1999, September). What does knowledge look like and how can we help it grow? *Syllabus,* 64–66.

Boettcher, J. V., & Conrad, R. (1999). *Faculty guide for moving teaching and learning to the Web.* Mission Viejo, CA: League for Innovation in the Community College.

Boettcher, J. V., & Conrad, R. (2010). *The online teaching survival guide: Simple and practical pedagogical tips.* San Francisco: Jossey-Bass.

Bonk, C. J., & Graham, C. R. (Eds.). (2006). *Handbook of blended learning: Global perspective, local designs.* San Francisco: Jossey-Bass/Pfeiffer.

Bourne, K., & Seaman, J. (2005). *Sloan-C special survey report: A look at blended learning.* Needham, MA: Sloan Consortium.

Bower, B. (2001). Distance education: Facing the challenge. *Online Journal of Distance Learning Administration,* 4(2). Retrieved from www.westga.edu/~distance/ojdla /summer42/bower42.html

Brain Track. (N.d.). *Are online degrees helpful or harmful for getting hired? Recruiters are saying* . . . Retrieved from http://www.braintrack.com/online-colleges/articles /recruiters-opinions-of-online-degrees

Brookfield, S. (1995). *Becoming a critically reflective teacher.* San Francisco: Jossey-Bass.

Brookfield, S. (2006). *The skillful teacher: On technique, trust, and responsiveness in the classroom.* San Francisco: Jossey-Bass.

Brooks, J., & Brooks, M. (2000). *In search of understanding: The case for constructivist classrooms* (2nd ed.). New York: Pearson.

Cartwright, G. P. (1996, July-August). Planning for academic computing: Important trends and issues. *Change.* Retrieved from http://contract.kent.edu/change /articles/julaug96.html

Choon-Ling, S., Bernard, C., & Kwok-Kee, W. (2002). Group polarization and computer-mediated communication: Effects of communication cues, social presence, and anonymity. *Information Systems Research,* 13(1), 70–92.

Clough, G., Jones, A. C., McAndrew, P., & Scanlon, E. (2008). Informal learning with PDAs and smartphones. *Journal of Computer Assisted Learning*, 24(5), 359–371.

Conceição, S., & Lehman, R. (2011). *Managing online instructor workload: Strategies for finding balance and success.* San Francisco: Jossey-Bass.

Coombs, N. (2010). *Making online teaching accessible: Inclusive course design for students with disabilities.* San Francisco: Jossey-Bass.

Dabbagh, N. (2007). The online learner: Characteristics and pedagogical implications. *Contemporary Issues in Technology and Teacher Education*, 7, 217–226.

Dabbagh, N., & Bannan-Ritland, B. (2005). *Online learning: Concepts, strategies, and application.* Upper Saddle River, NJ: Prentice Hall.

Dahl, B. (2012). *Interregional accreditation guidelines for online programs.* Retrieved from http://barrydahl.com/2012/02/10/interregional-accreditation-guidelines-for -online-programs/

Deubel, P. (2008, January 10). K–12 online teaching endorsements: Are they needed? *T.H.E. Journal.* Retrieved from http://thejournal.com/articles/2008/01/10/k12 -online-teaching-endorsements-are-they-needed.aspx

Dickinson, G., Agnew, D., & Gorman, R. (1999). Are teacher training and compensation keeping up with institutional demands for distance learning? *Cause/Effect Journal*, 22(3). Retrieved from http://www.educause.edu/ir/library/html/cem9939.html

Duderstadt, J. (1999). Can colleges and universities survive in the information age? In R. Katz & Associates (Eds.), *Dancing with the devil.* San Francisco: Jossey-Bass.

El-Hussein, M. O., & Cronje, J. C. (2010). Defining mobile learning in the higher education landscape. *Journal of Educational Technology and Society*, 13(3), 12–21.

Engel, G., & Green, T. (2011). Cell phones in the classroom: Are we dialing up disaster? *Tech Trends*, 55(2), 39–45.

Feenberg, A. (1999, September-October). No frills in the virtual classroom. *Academe*, 26–31.

Finkelstein, J. (2006). *Learning in real time: Synchronous teaching and learning online.* San Francisco: Jossey-Bass.

Foshee, D. (1999). Instructional technologies—part one: Leveraging the technology menu—a practical primer for new learning environments. In M. Boaz, B. Elliott, D. Foshee, D. Hardy, C. Jarmon, & D. Olcott (Eds.), *Teaching at a distance: A handbook for instructors.* Mission Viejo, CA: League for Innovation in the Community College and Archipelago.

Frohberg, D. (2006). *Mobile learning is coming of age: What we have and what we still miss.* Paper presented at the DELFI 2006, Darmstadt, Germany. Retrieved from http://www.ifi.uzh.ch/pax/uploads/pdf/publication/71/2006_DELFI_Darmstadt _MLearn_Framework.pdf

Garrison, D. R. (2011). *Elearning in the twenty-first century* (2nd ed.). New York: Routledge Falmer.

Garrison, D. R., & Vaughn, N. D. (2008). *Blended learning in higher education: Framework, principles, and guidelines.* San Francisco: Jossey-Bass.

Garrison, R., Anderson, T., & Archer, W. (2001). Critical thinking, cognitive presence, and computer conferencing in distance education. *American Journal of Distance Education*, 15(1), 87–105.

Grandzol, C. J., & Grandzol, J. R. (2010). Interaction in online courses: More is NOT always better, *Online Journal of Distance Learning Administration*, 13(2). Retrieved from

http://www.westga.edu/~distance/ojdla/summer132/Grandzol_Grandzol132
.html

Green, T., Alejandro, J., & Brown, A. H. (2009). The retention of experienced faculty
in online distance education programs: Understanding the factors that impact their
involvement. *International Review of Research in Open and Distance Learning,* 10(3), 1–15.

Hanson, D., Maushak, N., Schlosser, C., Anderson, M., Sorenson, C., & Simonson,
M. (1997). *Distance education: A review of the literature* (2nd ed.). Washington, DC:
Association for Educational Telecommunications and Technology Research, Insti-
tute for Studies in Education.

Harasim, L., Hiltz, S. R., Teles, L., & Turoff, M. (1996). *Learning networks.* Cambridge,
MA: MIT Press.

Hargreaves, A., & Shirley, D. (2009). *The far side of educational reform.* Ottawa: Canadian
Teachers' Federation. Retrieved from www.ctf-fce.ca/.../Briefs/Report_Education
-Reform2012_EN_web.pdf

Hawke, C. S. (2000). *Computer and Internet use on campus: A legal guide to issues of intellectual property, free speech, and privacy.* San Francisco: Jossey-Bass.

Hebert, M. (2006). Staying the course: A study in online student satisfaction and retention. *Online Journal of Distance Learning Administration,* 9(4).

Holton, J. A. (2001). Building trust and collaboration in a virtual team. *Team Performance Management,* 7(3/4), 36–48.

Huberman, B. A., Romero, D. M., & Wu, F. (2009). Social networks that matter: Twitter
under the microscope. *FirstMind,* 14(I-5). Retrieved from http://firstmonday.org
/htbin/cgiwrap/bin/ojs/index.php

Illinois Online Network. (2007). *Pedagogy and learning: What makes a successful online
facilitator?* Retrieved from http://www.ion.uillinois.edu/resources/tutorials
/pedagogy/instructorProfile.asp

Illinois Online Network. (2010). *What makes a successful online student?* Retrieved from
http://www.ion.uillinois.edu/resources/tutorials/pedagogy/StudentProfile.asp

Internet World Stats. (2012). *Facebook users in the world.* Retrieved from http://www
.internetworldstats.com/facebook.htm

Jonassen, D., Davidson, M., Collins, M., Campbell, J., & Haag, B. B. (1995). Constructiv-
ism and computer-mediated communication in distance education. *American Journal of Distance Education,* 9(2), 7–26.

Kapus, J. (2010, June 25). Five quick tips for using streaming media in your blended
or online courses. *Faculty Focus.* Retrieved from http://www.facultyfocus.com/arti
cles/asynchronous-learning-and-trends/five-quick-tips-for-using-streaming
-audio-or-video-in-your-blended-or-online-courses/

Kearsley, G. (N.d.). *Tips for training online instructors.* Retrieved from http://home
.sprynet.com/~gkearsley/OItips.htm

Keegan, D. (2002). *The future of learning: From elearning to mlearning.* FernUniversitat-
Hagen. Retrieved from http://www.fernuni-hagen.d/ZIFF/mlearn.htm

Kim, J. (2012 July 18). Parsing the NYTimes coverage of the growth of MOOCs.
*Inside Higher Ed.* Retrieved from http://www.insidehighered.com/print/blogs
/technology_and_learning

Kim, K., & Bonk, C. (2006). The future of online teaching and learning in higher education: The survey says . . . *Educause Quarterly,* no. 4. Retrieved from net.educause
.edu/ir/library/pdf/eqm0644.pdf

Kircher, J. (2001, July 18). *What are the essential characteristics of the successful online teacher and learner?* Issue-oriented dialogue white paper, Virtual Pedagogy Conference, University of Wisconsin, Oshkosh. Retrieved from http://uwsa.edu/ttt/kircher.htm

Knowles, M. (1992). *The adult learner: A neglected species.* Houston, TX: Gulf.

Kolb, D. (1984). *Learning style inventory.* Boston: McBerr.

Koole, M., McQuilkin, J. L., & Ally, M. (2010). Mobile learning in distance education: Utility or futility? *Journal of Distance Education, 24*(2), 59–82.

Kromrey, J., Barron, A., Hogarty, K., Hohlfeld, T., Loggie, K., Schullo, S., . . . Sweeney, P. (2005). Property and online courses: Policies at major research universities. In *Proceedings of the National Educational Computing Conference.* Retrieved from htmlscript.auburn.edu/. . ./Intellectual_Property_and_Online_Courses

Lefoe, G. E., Olney, I. W., Wright, R., & Herrington, A. (2009). Faculty development for new technologies: Putting mobile learning in the hands of the teachers. In J. Herrington, A. Jerrington, J. Mantei, I. Olney, & R. Ferry (Eds.), *New technologies, new pedagogies: Mobile learning in higher education* (pp. 15–27). Wollongong: University of Wollongong. Retrieved from http://ro.uow.edu.au/

Litzinger, M., & Osif, B. (1993). Accommodating diverse learning styles: Designing instruction for electronic information sources. In L. Shirato (Ed.), *What is good instruction now? Library instruction for the 90s.* Ann Arbor, MI: Pierian Press.

Lorenzo, G. (2011). *Job outlook for teachers.* Williamsville, NY: Lorenzo Associates. Retrieved from http://www.edpath.com/guidetool/job%20outlook%20teachers.html

Lukin, R., Akass, J., Cook, J., Day, P., Ecclesfield, N., Garnett, F., Gould, M., Hamilton, T., . . . Whitworth, A. (2007). Learner-generated contexts: Sustainable learning pathways through open content. *OpenLearn07.* Retrieved from http://kn.open.ac.k/public/getfile.cfm?documentfileid=12188

Lunsford, J. (2010). Using handheld technologies for student support: A model. *Journal of the Research Center for Educational Technology, 6*(1), 55–69.

Magennis, S., & Farrell, A. (2005). Teaching and learning activities: Expanding the repertoire to support student learning. In G. O'Neill, S. Moore, & B. McMullin (Eds.), *Emerging issues in the practice of university learning and teaching.* Dublin: AISHE.

Major, H., & Taylor, D. (2003). Teaching for learning: Design and delivery of community college courses. *Community College Enterprise, 9*(2), 63–75.

Maloney, W. (1999, September-October). Brick-and-mortar campuses go online. *Academe,* 18–25.

Manning, S., & Johnson, K. M. (2011). *The technology toolbelt for teaching.* San Francisco: Jossey-Bass.

Marquis, C. (2004). *WebCT survey discovers a blend of online learning and classroom-based teaching is the most effective form of learning today.* Retrieved from http://www.webct.com/service/ViewContent?contentID=19295938

Martin, W. A. (1999, September-October). Being there is what matters. *Academe,* 32–36.

McClure, B. (2004). *Putting a new spin on groups* (2nd ed.). Hillsdale, NJ: Erlbaum.

McGivney, V. (2004). Understanding persistence in adult learning. *Open Learning, 19*(1), 33–46.

McGrath, J., & Hollingshead, A. (1994). *Groups interacting with technology.* Thousand Oaks, CA: Sage.

McLoughlin, C., & Lee, M.J.W. (2009). Personalised learning spaces and self-regulated learning: Global examples of effective pedagogy. In *Same places, different spaces. Proceedings Ascilite Auckland 2009.* Retrieved from http://wwwascilite.org.au/conferences/auckland09/procs/mcloughlin.pdf

McNett, M. (2002, May-June). *Curbing academic dishonesty in online courses, Pointers and clickers: ION's technology tip of the month.* Retrieved from http://Illinois.online.uillinois.edu/Pointers/2002_05/default.asp

Menges, J. (1996, October). Feeling between the lines. *CMC Magazine.* Retrieved from http://www.december.com/cmc/mag/

Mennecke, B. E., Hoffer, J. A., & Wynne, B. E. (1992). The implication of group development and history for group support systems theory and practice. *Small Group Research,* 23, 524–572.

Merisotis, J. (1999, September–October). The "what's the difference?" debate."*Academe,* 47–51.

Merisotis, J. (2000, March). *Quality on the line.* Washington, DC: National Education Association and Blackboard.

Middle States Commission on Higher Education. (2011). *Distance education programs: Interregional guidelines for the evaluation of distance education (online learning).* Philadelphia: Middle States Commission on Higher Education. Retrieved from http://www.msche.org

Moore, J. C., & Fetzner, M. J. (2009). The road to retention: A closer look at institutions that achieve high course completion rates. *Journal of Asynchronous Learning Networks,* 44(3), 3–22.

Naismith, L., Lonsdale, P., Vavoula, G., & Sharples, M. (2005). *Report 11: Literature review in mobile technologies and learning.* Bristol, UK: NESTA Futerlab Series.

National Education Association (N.d.). *Guide to teaching online courses.* Retrieved from http://www.nea.org

Nesson, R. (2007, May 17). Teaching in second life: One instructor's perspective. *Terra Nova: A Weblog About Virtual Worlds.* Retrieved from http://terranova.blogs.com/terra_nova/2007/05/teaching_in_sec.html

Nielsen, J. (2010, December 15). College students on the Web. *Alertbox.* Retrieved from http://www.useit.com/alertbox/students.html

Nipper, S. (1989). Third generation distance learning and computer conferencing. *Mindweave.* Retrieved from http://www-icdl.open.ac.uk/mindweave/chap5.html

North American Council for Online Learning. (2007). *National standards for quality online teaching.* Retrieved from http://www.nacol.org

Olcott, D. (1999). Instructional technologies—part two: Strategies for instructor success—selecting and using distance education technologies. In M. Boaz, B. Elliott, D. Foshee, D. Hardy, C. Jarmon, & D. Olcott (Eds.), *Teaching at a distance: A handbook for instructors.* Mission Viejo, CA: League for Innovation in the Community College and Archipelago.

Palloff, R. M., & Pratt, K. (1999). *Building learning communities in cyberspace: Effective strategies for the online classroom.* San Francisco: Jossey-Bass.

Palloff, R. M., & Pratt, K. (2004). *Collaborating online: Learning together in community.* San Francisco: Jossey-Bass.

Palloff, R. M., & Pratt, K. (2007). *Building online learning communities: Effective strategies for the virtual classroom.* San Francisco: Jossey-Bass.

Palloff, R. M., & Pratt, K. (2009). *Assessing the online learner: Resources and strategies for faculty.* San Francisco: Jossey-Bass.

Palloff, R. M., & Pratt, K. (2011). *The excellent online instructor: Strategies for professional development.* San Francisco: Jossey-Bass.

Park, J., & Hee, J. C. (2009). Factors influencing adult learners' decision to drop out or persist in online learning. *Journal of Educational Technology and Society,* 12, 207–217.

Patten, B., Anredillo Sánchez, I., & Tangney, B. (2006). Designing collaborative, constructionist and contextual applications for handheld devices. *Computers and Education,* 46, 294–308. doi:10.1016/j.compedu.2005.11.011

Perez, E. (2009, April 26). Professors experiment with Twitter as a teaching tool. *JSOnline*9. Retrieved from http://jsonline.com/news/education/43747152.html

Perley, J., & Tanguay, M. (1999, October 29). Accrediting on-line institutions diminishes higher education. *Chronicle of Higher Education,* B4–6.

Phipps, R., & Merisotis, J. (1999, April). *What's the difference?* Washington, DC: Institute for Higher Education Policy.

Pomales, C., & Liu, Y. (2006). Web-based distance learning technology: The impacts of Web module length and format. *American Journal of Distance Education,* 20, 163–179.

Potter, R. E., & Balthazard, P. A. (2002). Understanding human interaction and performance in the virtual team. *Journal of Information Technology Theory and Application,* 4(1), 1–23.

Pratt, K. (1996). *The electronic personality.* Unpublished doctoral dissertation, Fielding Graduate University.

Rice, M. (2001). Faculty involvement in planning for the use and integration of instructional and administrative technologies. *Journal of Research on Computing in Education,* 33, 328–336.

Rice, K., & Dawley, L. (2007). *Going virtual! The status of professional development for K–12 online teachers.* Research report presented at the Virtual School Symposium, Louisville, KY. Retrieved from http://edtech.boisestate.edu/goingvirtual /goingvirtual1.pdf

Rocco, S. (2007). Online assessment and evaluation. *New Directions for Adult and Continuing Education,* 113, 75–86.

Rockwell, S. K., Schauer, J., Fritz, S., & Marx, D. (1999). Incentives and obstacles influencing higher education faculty and administrators to teach via distance. *Online Journal of Distance Learning Administration,* 2(4). Retrieved from http://westga .edu/~distance/rockwell24.html

Rowe, N. C. (2004). Cheating in online student assessment: Beyond plagiarism. *Online Journal of Distance Learning Administration,* 7(2). Retrieved from http://www.westga .edu/%7Edistance/ojdla/summer72/rowe72.html

Rovai, A., & Barnum, K. (2003). On-line course effectiveness: An analysis of student interactions and perceptions of learning. *Journal of Distance Education,* 18(1), 57–73.

Russell, T. (1999). *The no significant difference phenomenon.* Chapel Hill: Office of Instructional Telecommunications, North Carolina State University.

Savery, J. (2005). Be vocal: Characteristics of successful online instructors, *Journal of interactive online learning,* 4(2), 141–152. Retrieved from http://ncolr.org/jiol

Schaffhauser, D. (2012, March 12). Social media as a teaching tool. *Campus Technology.* Retrieved from http://campustechnology.com/articles/2012/03/12 /social-media-as-a-teaching-tool.aspx

Schutte, J. (1996). *Virtual teaching in higher education.* Retrieved from http://www.csun.edu/sociology/virexp.htm

Seaman, J. (2009). *Online learning as a strategic asset, Vol. 2: The paradox of faculty voices: Views and experiences with online learning.* Washington, DC: Association of Public and Land-Grant Universities.

Sloan Consortium. (2012). *The 5 pillars: Sloan-C quality framework.* Retrieved from http://sloanconsortium.org/5pillars

Smith, A. (2010). *Mobile access 2010.* Retrieved from http://pewinternet.org/Reports/2010/Mobile-Access-2010.aspx

Smith, A., & Brenner, J. (2012). *Twitter use 2012.* Retrieved from http://pewinternet.org/Reports/2012/Twitter-Use-2012.aspx

Smith, R. (2008). *Conquering the content: A step-by-step guide to online course design.* San Francisco: Jossey-Bass.

Social Compare. (2012). *Facebook vs Myspace vs Twitter vs Google Buzz.* Retrieved from http://socialcompare.com/en/comparison/facebook-vs-myspace-vs-twitter-vs-google-buzz-68b8cl5

Stansbury, M. (2011, September 9). Five characteristics of an effective 21st century educator. *eSchool News.* Retrieved from http://www.eschoolnews.com/2011/09/09/five-characteristics-of-an-effective-21st-century-educator/

Stewart, B. (2012, July 10). Slouching toward Bethlehem: Unpacking the MOOC as buzzword. *Inside Higher Ed.* Retrieved from http://www.insidehighered.com/blogs/university-venus/slouching-towards-bethlehem-unpacking-mooc-buzzword

Strasburg, J. (2000, March 26). Pushing for Net access. *San Francisco Chronicle,* B1–B3.

Strayer, J. (2011). Flipped classroom infographic. *Knewton.* Retrieved from http://www.knewton.com/flipped-classroom/

Thelin, J. (2012, July 10). Professors shouldn't be afraid of online learning. *Inside Higher Ed.* Retrieved from http://www.insidehighered.com/views/2012/07/10/professors-shouldnt-be-afraid-online-learning-essay

Tomei, L. (1999, September). The technology facade. *Syllabus,* 32–34.

Traxler, J. (2010). Will student devices deliver innovation, inclusion, and transformation? *Journal of the Research Center for Educational Technology, 6*(1), 3–15. Retrieved from http://www.rcetj.org/index.php/rcetj/article/view/56

Truman-Davis, B., Futch, L., Thompson, K., & Yonekura, F. (2000). Support for online teaching and learning. *Educause Quarterly, 2,* 44–51.

Tuckman, B., & Jensen, M. (1977). Stages of small group development revisited. *Group and Organizational Studies, 2*(4), 419–427.

Van Dusen, C. (2009, November-December). Beyond virtual schools. *eSchool News, Special Report.* Retrieved from eSNNoveDec09SpRptVeyondVirtualSchools.pdf

Varvel, V. (2005). Honesty in online education. *Pointers and Clickers, 6*(1). Retrieved from http://www.ion.uillinois.edu/resources/pointersclickers/2005_01/index.asp

Watson, J. F., & Kalmon, S. (2006). *Keeping pace with K–12 online learning: A review of state level policy and practice.* Naperville, IL: North Central Regional Educational Laboratory.

White, N. (2000, January 8). *Rena's case study.* Posting to Online Facilitation listserv.

Yeonjeong, P. (2011). A pedagogical framework for mobile learning: Categorizing educational applications of mobile technologies into four types. *International Review of Research in Open and Distance Learning*, 12(2), 78–102.

Young, R. C., & Chamberlain, M. A. (2006). Ready to teach online? A continuum approach. In *Proceedings of the 22nd Annual Conference on Distance Teaching and Learning*. Retrieved from http://www.uwex.edu/disted/conference

# INDEX

Page references followed by *fig* indicate an illustrated figure; followed by *t* indicate a table; followed by *e* indicate an exhibit.